THE TRADITION VIA HEIDEGGER

THE TRADITION VIA HEIDEGGER

AN ESSAY ON THE MEANING OF BEING
IN THE PHILOSOPHY OF MARTIN HEIDEGGER

by

JOHN N. DEELY

MARTINUS NIJHOFF / THE HAGUE / 1971

PRINTED IN THE NETHERLANDS

TO
RALPH AUSTIN POWELL,
FIRST OF ALL,
AND TO
JACQUES AND RAÏSSA MARITAIN,
FROM A DISTANCE,
THIS ESSAY
IS
DEDICATED

ACKNOWLEDGEMENTS

Some attempt must be made to acknowledge those debts of the spirit which, because they are of the spirit, bind us to our fellows in ties that last as long as we ourselves and in truth make us who we are.

The writer wishes to express his lasting debt to Benedict Ashley, former President, and to the entire faculty of the Aquinas Institute, by whose teaching and example my studies were initially oriented toward the great themes of philosophical inquiry; and in particular, to my friend Dr. Ralph Powell of the Graduate Faculty, whose philosophical insight communicates itself with a ceaselessly astonishing compass and richness of detail in such a way as to make it impossible for those who have worked under him to be finally satisfied with any effort which, while claiming to be philosophical, contents itself with categories of language, culture, or even history, let alone the partisan doctrines of any "school", ancient or modern.

Special thanks must be given too to Dr. William J. Richardson, of Fordham University, who most graciously provided an incisive and authoritative critique of an early draft of this study, as is explained in the "Postcript" at the end of this book.

On a more "practical" plane, finally, I want to thank Eva Leo, Léon Pearson, Simone Deely and Joseph Novak, for their generous assistance in proof-reading the final text.

PREFACE

This book is not addressed to beginning students in philosophy so much as it is addressed to those who, though fairly well-versed in the philosophical tradition, find themselves frankly baffled and brought up short by the writings of Martin Heidegger, and who—while recognizing the novelty of the Heideggerean enterprise – may sometimes find themselves wondering if this "thinking of Being" is after all rich enough to deserve still further effort on their part.

That at least was my own state of mind after a couple of years spent in studying Heidegger. Then one day, in preparing for a seminar, I suddenly saw, not indeed all of what Heidegger is about, but at least where he stands in terms of previous philosophers, and what is the ground of his thinking. After that, it became possible to assess certain strengths and weaknesses of his thought in terms of his own methodology vis-a-vis those earlier thinkers who, without having dreamed of anything quite like a *Daseinsanalyse*, had yet recognized in explicit terms the feature of experience on which the identification of *Sein* (and consequently the *Daseinsanalyse*) depends for its possibility.

This book does not pretend, therefore, to be in any way a comprehensive survey of the rich growth or future import of Heideggerean thought. I may even say that this book is concerned almost exclusively with the seed and roots of Heidegger's work, and with the soil in which that work germinates; the leaves and branches of his thought, so far as they are not purely formal, i.e., methodologically determined articulations, are not part of this study.

There are, in short, many other aspects to Heidegger besides the one I have focussed on; but I believe that I have brought into view an altogether fundamental feature of his thought, and the one that renders his notion of Being (*das Sein*) unmistakably identifiable in terms of previous philosophy.

In this connection, I would say now that there are basically two facts which, considered together, suffice to explain why it is that Heidegger's guiding concern is so hard to identify in any straightforward traditional sense. First, there is the simple fact that Heidegger has got hold in an original way of an insight that did not clearly appear in philosophy until somewhere around the twelfth century, first probably in the writings of Averroes (1126-1198), only to disappear again from the philosophical mainstream around the seventeenth century. The second fact is that Heidegger himself shows no awareness of the formulations of this insight which both antedate and supplement his own.

The combined effect of these two facts is to lend the *Denken des Seins* an air of discontinuity and novelty (in the mind of Heidegger and his reader alike) not only on the side of the *Daseinsanalyse*, which really is a new departure in philosophy, but also on the side of *Sein* itself, which was not unknown to previous philosophy, however fitfully it has been grasped.

And it has indeed been grasped but fitfully. Most of what offers itself today as "philosophy of knowledge," for example, would more accurately be designated a study of the conditions under which affirmations and negations are justified or verified. Yet if it is true, both logically and ontologically, that the conditioned as such is always other than (though not necessarily separable from) its necessary and sufficient genetic conditions, no statement, however thorough, of the conditions for this or that kind of knowledge ever adds up to a statement of what knowledge itself generically is. When it comes to the question of what *is* knowledge considered in itself and not just in its conditions, however, modern and contemporary philosophers are strangely silent. Some have quite forgotten about the analytical and existential irreducibility of the conditioned effect to its conditions, and so have gone on to mistakenly identify the study of conditions of knowing with the study of knowledge itself. Yet the "philosophy of knowledge," unequivocally conceived, is something quite other than the analysis of, say, the nervous mechanisms thanks to which and the environmental circumstances under which we know. In these terms, the great Kantian *Critiques* have this much in common with the scientific vogue for neurophysiological studies: they afford us no direct understanding of what knowledge, taken as such and in terms of itself, is.

If I may hazard in a sentence a formulation of my own, I would say that the insight which alone makes possible a philosophical understanding of what knowledge in itself is, and which in modern times is directly seized upon and recognized (with the probable exception of Hegel) apart from the guiding influence of Arabic and Latin Aristotelianism only by Heidegger, is the realization that there is an order of being (Heidegger calls this unique and elusive order *Sein*) which is neither substantial nor accidental in what is proper to it, and therefore neither "subjective" nor "objective" (*nicht*

Seiende, as Heidegger says) in the Cartesian and modern senses of these words.

The demonstration of this unwitting confluence, no more and no less: such is the contention and interest of this book.

A NOTE ON REFERENCE STYLE

I have devised four more or less idiosyncratic techniques for economy of reference in writing this book.

Firstly, the works which are frequently cited have been coded by using only key letters from their titles – e.g., Heidegger's *Einführung in die Metaphysik* is referred to as EM, followed by the appropriate page references. All such coded references have been gathered in the "List of Symbols Used," which is indicated in the Table of Contents.

Secondly, of all the works extensively quoted, I tried to take account for the reader's convenience of English translations available at the period when the substance of this book was written. A number of translations of Heidegger's writings have since appeared, some for the first time, others as sorely needed alternatives to earlier translations; but for any number of technical reasons, it has not been possible to incorporate these later translations into the page references supplied in the present work. Translations which have been included, however, are noted according to the following convention: after giving the page numbers for reference to the original work, I added a slash and the corresponding page numbers of an available English rendering. Thus a footnote referring to "EM, p. 91/104," would indicate that the citation in question should be found on p. 91 of Heidegger's *Einführung in die Metaphysik*, and on p. 104 of the English translation of the *Einführung, An Introduction to Metaphysics*. Where no translation of a cited work was available (at least to my knowledge), of course, only the original is noted.

Thirdly, in the case of Heidegger's two works, *Zur Seinsfrage* and *Was ist das – die Philosophie?*, the available English text happened also to be a bilingual edition. Hence, in referring to these works, I dispensed with original editions entirely, making only the single reference to the German page where a facing English rendering is available. In the case of *Sein und Zeit*, an opposite procedure was called for. Since the Macquarrie-Robinson translation includes the German page numbering in its margins, I have cited only the original German pages in referring to this work.

Fourthly and finally, in constructing the bibliography (which is by and large limited to works expressly mentioned in footnotes), I proceeded alphabetically by authors and titles in the usual way, except to insert immediately after a given work the available English translation, regardless of alphabetical considerations. For example, in the bibliography under "Heidegger, Martin," the *Einführung in die Metaphysik* occurs in the proper alphabetical order, but it is immediately followed by the entry of *An Introduction to Metaphysics*. Such insertions ore obviously inappropriate on alphabetical grounds, but appropriate enough as an indication that an English translation of the *Einführung* is available and was consulted in the preparation of this study.

I hope that these brief remarks may serve to obviate some needless inconveniences for the reader. I add the hope that the text and references as here published are free of all errors – but this no one, I think, can safely promise.

LIST OF SYMBOLS USED

CI   Maritain, *Creative Intuition in Art and Poetry*
DS   Maritain, *Les degrés du savoir*
EM   *Einführung in die Metaphysik*
G   *Gelassenheit*
HB   *Brief über den "Humanismus"*
H:TPT   Richardson, *Heidegger: Through Phenomenology to Thought*
HW   *Holzwege*
ID   *Identität und Differenz*
KM   *Kant und das Problem der Metaphysik*
SF   *Zur Seinsfrage*
SG   *Der Satz vom Grund*
SZ   *Sein und Zeit*
VA   *Vorträge und Aufsätze*
WG   *Vom Wesen des Grundes*
WM   *Was ist Metaphysik?*
WM:Ep   *Was ist Metaphysik?* Nachwort
WM:In   *Was ist Metaphysik?* Einleitung
WW   *Vom Wesen der Wahrheit*

CONTENTS

ANALYTIC TABLE OF CONTENTS

Chapter IV.   FROM MAN AND THE "COGITO SUM" TO DASEIN

Chapter VI.   INTENTIONALITÄT AND INTENTIONALE: TWO DISTINCT

NOTIONS   78-87

INTRODUCTION

"Die Aufgabe der bisherigen Betrachtungen war, das *ursprüngliche Ganze* des faktischen Daseins . . . existen-zial-ontologisch *aus seinem Grunde* zu interpretieren. . . . aber gleichwohl . . . das *Ziel* ist die Ausarbeitung der Seinsfrage überhaupt. Die *thematische* Analytik der Existenz bedarf ihrerseits erst des Lichtes aus der zuvor geklärten Idee des Seins überhaupt. Das gilt zumal dann, wenn der in der Einleitung ausgesprochene Satz als Richt-mass jeglicher philosophischen Untersuchung festgehal-ten wird: Philosophie ist universale phänomenologische Ontologie, ausgehend von der Hermeneutik des Daseins, die als Analytik der *Existenz* das Ende des Leitfadens alles philosophischen Fragens dort festgemacht hat, woraus es *entspringt* und wohin es *zurückschlägt*. Freilich darf auch die These nicht als Dogma gelten, sondern als Formulierung des noch 'eingehüllten' grundsätzlichen Problems: lässt sich die Ontologie *ontologisch* begründen oder bedarf sie auch hierzu eines *ontischen* Fundamentes, und *welches* Seiende muss die Funktion der Fundierung übernehmen?
Martin Heidegger, *Sein und Zeit*, p. 436.

This book looks closely at the highly structured problematic of the early Heidegger in order to see if what made that structuring possible can be discerned and isolated. By the "early Heidegger", "we understand the Heidegger of *Being and Time* and of those earlier works prior to 1930, which share the same perspectives."[1]

I entirely agree with the best Heideggerean scholarship (corroborated by Heidegger's own explicit testimony) "that the question that preoccupies the later Heidegger is no different from the question of Heidegger I: What is the meaning of Being? The difference between the two is simply this: in the early years Heidegger approaches the question through an analysis of *Dasein*; in

[1] William J. Richardson, "Heidegger and the Quest of Freedom," *Theological Studies*, 28 (June, 1967), p. 288.

the later years he tries to think Being for itself and from itself."[2] But I intend
to make it unmistakably clear that this "simple difference" between the early
Heidegger's approach to the question of the meaning of Being through an
analysis of Dasein, and the later Heidegger's attempt to think Being for itself and from itself, is the measure of the limits of phenomenological philosophy integrally conceived. Baldly stated, I intend to show that the original
possibilities of the problematic of *Sein und Zeit* depend on a metaphysical
presupposition.

To accomplish this, it will be necessary and sufficient to indicate the precise
sense of Heidegger's ontic/ontological distinction as giving rise to the
existentiell/existential analytical couplet, making it clear how these terms
are to be adequately correlated with the scholastic *entitativum/intentionale*
distinction which I say can (once freed from the arbitrary restrictions imposed
on its sense by Brentano and Husserl) translate the early Heidegger's vocabulary and meaning.

In making it clear that the essential thought of Heidegger is concerned
principally with what scholasticism has referred to in passing (so to speak) as
the order of *esse intentionale* strictly understood, however, I intend to make
it equally clear that with Martin Heidegger *philosophy itself* has achieved a
measure of progress. For if the area of *esse intentionale* has been clearly
delimited by the great scholastics, it has been almost entirely neglected or
misunderstood by the majority of philosophers; and even in those rare
writings, such as the works of John of St. Thomas, where its fundamental
structure is rightly characterized, its proper actuality is never rendered fully
thematic. Even as the ancients knew full well that the earth was a globe, yet
knew nothing of the actual topography of the other side, so is the notion of
esse intentionale the *"antipodes"* or unexplored region in their metaphysical
topography concerned, as it was, principally with tracing the nature of
change and the substance/accident dimension of act-potency compositions,
i.e., with *esse entitativum*, rather than with the dimension of intersubjectivity
and the then little realized problem of intersubjectivity *par excellence*, the
nature of the domination of man's existence by a total view of reality
(culture, *Weltanschauung*, etc.) not known to reduce to fact, or of *Historicity*.

It is no secret that in the matter of the exegesis of history, which a reflective
examination of human nature shaped by traditions can scarcely do without,
scholasticism, outside of Hegel, has had little to say. "History," Gilson
frankly remarks, has up to now been "not exactly the forte of scholasticism.

---

[2] *Ibid.*, p. 300. Cf. Heidegger's "Vorwort" to Fr. Richardson's masterful *Heidegger:
Through Phenomenology to Thought* (The Hague: M. Nijhoff, 1963), pp. VIII-XXIII.

Deep within themselves, scholastics rather despise and mistrust history."[3]

It is no secret either that this silence, more embarrassed than eloquent, lies behind the charge of irrelevance flung at Thomistic thought, today, like a gauntlet, from nearly every quarter. Precisely because the thought of Martin Heidegger has thematized principally (and, in the end, preclusively) the level or order of *esse intentionale*, an assimilation of his thought enables Thomism at last to take up that gauntlet.

From this point of view, the entire study to follow is no more than a concrete exemplification and particular justification of Maritain's remark concerning the necessarily progressive and inventive character of the philosopical enterprise:

We have not only to defend the value and necessity of a philosophic tradition against the prejudices of minds revolutionary on principle. We must also take due account of the constant novelty characteristic of philosophic wisdom, and defend the necessity of renovation and growth inherent in its nature, in this case against the prejudices of minds conservative on principle.[4]

For the philosophy of Martin Heidegger, in my estimation, affords an extraordinary opportunity to illustrate at once and in a striking way both these features of philosophy's historical reality – namely, its organic continuity sustained by novelties of growth.

I do not by any means promise the reader an easy game; but I do hope to be able to show anyone who will take the trouble to understand the pages I have written something of the bounds of the questioning in *Sein und Zeit*, or, what amounts to the same thing, the limits in principle of phenomenological philosophy. Surely that is a claim worth the trouble of investigating!

Yet however complex and subtle accuracy compels its detailed analyses to be, this book has a simple ground plan. It develops through eight stages, covered by ten chapters:

1. Stage one does no more than place our considerations in the context of contemporary currents of thought, pointing out the difficulty and utility of arriving at a consistent understanding of the direction of Heidegger's thought (Chapters I and II).
2. Stage two consists in a direct consideration of Heidegger's original philosophical experience as providing an approach to the meaning of "Being" in terms of the presence of beings in awareness and social life rather than simply in themselves (Chapter III).
3. Stage three delineates the difficulty of formalizing this experience of intersubjectivity in a definite question serving to guide further inquiry, of translating the

[3] Etienne Gilson, *The Philosopher and Theology*, trans. by Cécile Gilson (New York: Random House, 1962), p. 97.
[4] Jacques Maritain, *A Preface to Metaphysics* (New York: Mentor, 1962), p. 19.

mystery of Being into a structured problematic accessible to properly philosophical research (Chapter IV).

4. In stage four are brought out the double set of considerations necessary to analytically adequate the structured unity of Dasein as disclosed by virtue of the fact that Dasein's uttermost (*äusserst*) possibility is at the same time its ownmost (*eigenst*) and *non-relational* (*unbezügliche*) (Chapters V and VI).

5. The fifth stage makes clear that the contribution of Heideggerean thought to the progress of philosophy stems principally from rendering the intersubjective dimension of human reality thematic, from thematizing that dimension of Dasein according to which it enjoys its "objectively scientific priority," as Heidegger puts it, for phenomenological research (Chapter VII).

6. Stage six makes clear the functional interdependence which obtains between the ontic-ontological structure of Dasein's temporal unity and the priority in philosophy of the phenomenological over the metaphysical sense of the Being-question (Chapter VIII).

7. Stage seven examines the identity of Heidegger's conception of the phenomenological attitude and research-mode with his thought of Being (*Denken des Seins*) (Chapter IX).

8. The final stage traces the passage from the early to the later Heidegger as necessitated from within by the suppression of the act-potency structures which gave determinateness and direction to the analyses of *Sein und Zeit*, showing that in these terms the celebrated turning in Heidegger's way of thought provides the justification and completes the demonstration of each sequential stage in our Retrieve.

The net result of this eightfold analysis is the contention that the Heideggerean problematic does free philosophy from subjectivity at a single stroke, opening up the historical dimension of humanity in its proper ontological ground, but cannot authentically be said to surpass Metaphysics. For the high degree of structure characteristic of the early Heidegger (*Sein und Zeit*) was possible in the first place, I shall show, only because (and to the extent that) the intrinsically a-phenomenological idea of natural being or the so-called entitative order was allowed to provide the context giving setting and structure for the investigations of *Sein und Zeit*, in that *das Sein* was understood by way of counterdistinction to *das Seiende*.

Pöggeler points out that the concern of Heidegger from the first was to bring together transcendental truth and history.[5] Now it is plain that history belongs primarily to the order of *esse intentionale* and only secondarily to the order of *esse entitativum*, first of all from the peculiar manner in which the past subsists and insinuates itself into the very fabric of present "reality" long after the physical events which define it as past have disintegrated; and in the second place, from the very nature of historicity as the temporal context of the human reality ultimately irreducible to "fact", i.e., to physical

---

[5] See Otto Pöggeler, *Der Denkweg Martin Heideggers* (Pfüllingen: Neske, 1963).

data. Heidegger then was on the right track in turning his inquiry away from the so-called natural world and seeking the place of truth and historicity, *das Sein des Seienden*, in "nothing", that is, "No-thing", *das Nicht-seiende.* "No thing," he tells us in his *Einführung in die Metaphysik*, "corresponds to the word and the meaning 'Being'."

But the difficulty which in the end caused a great philosophy to collapse into virtual incoherence was one of method. Taking over from Husserl the phenomenological research-mode and its guiding principle, "*zu den Sachen selbst,*" Heidegger came to realize that the "things themselves" referred in this case neither to "objects" independent of the mind (something which Husserl also realized) nor to images and internal representations constituted within subjectivity (something which Husserl did not come to realize), but rather to a way of existing only which supervenes upon beings in order that they may appear or manifest themselves, which existence itself is neither the proper form or "being" of the subject known (object) nor of the knowing subject, but between them both (*das Zwischen*) as that which makes an encounter from the outset possible.

Yet to take our orientation from this "between" would still be misleading. For with such an orientation we would also be covertly assuming the beings between which this "between", as such, "is", and we would be doing so in a way which is ontologically vague. The "between" is already conceived as the result of the *con-venientia* of two things that are present-at-hand. But to assume these beforehand always *splits* the phenomenon asunder, and there is no prospect of putting it together again from the fragments. Not only do we lack the "cement"; even the "schema" in accordance with which this joining-together is to be accomplished, has been split asunder, or never as yet unveiled. What is decisive for ontology is to prevent the splitting of the phenomenon – in other words, to hold its positive phenomenal content secure. To say that for this we need far-reaching and detailed study, is simply to express the fact that something which was ontically self-evident in the traditional way of treating the "problem of knowledge" has often been ontologically disguised to the point where it has been lost sight of altogether.[6]

---

[6] "Irreführend bliebe die Orientierung an dem 'Zwischen' trotzdem. Sie macht unbesehen den ontologisch unbestimmten Ansatz des Seienden mit, wozwischen dieses Zwischen als solches 'ist'. Das Zwischen ist schon als Resultat der convenientia zweier Vorhandenen begriffen. Der vorgängige Ansatz dieser aber *sprengt* immer schon das Phänomen, und es ist aussichtslos, dieses je wieder aus den Sprengstücken zusammenzusetzen. Nicht nur der 'Kitt' fehlt, sondern das 'Schema' ist gesprengt, bzw. nie zuvor enthüllt, gemäss dem die Zusammenfügung sich vollziehen soll. Das ontologisch Entscheidende liegt darin, die Sprengung des Phänomens vorgängig zu verhüten, das heisst seinen positiven phänomenalen Bestand zu sichern. Dass es hierzu weitgehender Umständlichkeit bedarf, ist nur der Ausdruck davon, dass etwas ontisch Selbstverständliches in der überlieferten Behandlungsart des 'Erkenntnisproblems' ontologisch vielfältig bis zur Unsichtbarkeit verstellt wurde." M. Heidegger, *Sein und Zeit* (8th ed.; Tübingen: Max Niemeyer Verlag, 1963), p. 132.

This already explains why the idea of an entitative order, though acknow-ledged in *Sein und Zeit*, is acknowledged as an altogether negative clue to the sense of *Sein*, formally recalcitrant to the phenomenological research-mode – i.e., as an intrinsically a-phenomenological notion, a concept spilling over the reservoir of pure *noein* into straightforward *judicium*; and this passage already suggests too why the idea of the entitative order disappears even as a negative clue from the later writings: they are simply an unqualified expres-sion, as *Sein und Zeit* was not (contextually, I mean), of the phenomenologic-al attitude. Formally taken, of course, the problematic of the early no less than the later Heidegger was strictly phenomenological: it takes its orienta-tion accordingly neither from consciousness (*Bewusstsein*) nor still less from the things of which we are conscious (*das Seiende*), but rather from the Being of both elements or poles of awareness, the common denominator of encounter as presence – namely, *das Sein*. Thus the Being of beings, says Heidegger, *das Sein des Seienden*, is the Being of our consciousness of things and of our self-consciousness alike – a conception which comes across with drama from the very structure of the German words which give it expression: *das SEIN des Seienden ist das SEIN des BewusstSEINs und Selbstbewusst-SEINs*; while from the standpoint of the proper actuality of a given entity, that is, with respect to *das Seiende als solche* or with respect to *der Mensch insofern Seiende*, *das Sein* is *das Nichts*, i.e., it is the proper actuality neither of any substance nor of its accidents.

Now this phenomenological perspective on the human reality gives rise to the notion of Dasein in this way. We are never conscious of everything at once, not even of everything that is part of our "biography", nor could we be so conscious even if we wanted to. And yet, our awareness, even though limited as regards its explicit elements, always maintains itself within a transcendent unity, a horizon of possible encounter. Such a horizon is ob-viously not explained on the basis of any substantial, entitative unity, since such unity is what isolates and locates us as a being among other beings *in rerum natura*, in everyday time and space. Therefore it is maintained in a non-entitative way, within "Nothing", by the Being of consciousness and awareness-possibility generally. If we designate the substantial, biological-individual unity of man by the traditional term *suppositum*, then we shall have to forge another term to designate the unified dimension of (possible) encounter or World-horizon, which, as "nothing", makes the manifestation or "presence" of any given facet of the World, any given thing, in the first place possible. Heidegger chooses the term *Dasein*.

Moreover, just as substantial unity is biological-individual, so the unity of *Dasein* is social-personal. It is the dimension in which our self-identity as persons maintains itself, although the Dasein itself is not "personal" except in a terminative way, is a "we" in ways more fundamental than it is a "me" – though it is in every case "mine." Neither can Dasein be subjected in what is proper to it to governance by logical rules or forms. Since it is as intentional intersubjective ("the Dasein is the Being of the Between"[7]), it cuts across the confines of subjectivity, making one to be other things in a manner which is other than his natural being (therefore neither an "accident" nor *anima* as *forma substantialis*) or the natural being of the things which he becomes. The intentional life of man, in short, the existence of man as Dasein counter-distinguished from the life of man as organism, does not require in and of itself individuation nor infallibility (certitude), and consequently in its integral conscious-unconscious-preconscious elements (see Chapter VII below) accounts for historicity as the domination of human life by a total view of reality not known to reduce to fact. That is why Dasein is historical, culture-bearing man, a *seinsgeschichtliches Wesen* – "an essence freighted with Being" – the *humanitas* of *homo humanus* rather than the *ratio* of *homo sapiens*.

Thus the great insight of Heidegger lies with the notion of man as Dasein. It is as Dasein that man bears a tradition and lives a historical existence. It is as Dasein that man stands outside of his subjectivity as that being whose *Wesen* is to-be-in-a-World *au sens phénoménologique*. Yet this ecstatic ontological or intentional dimension of man in his Dasein demands in final accounting to be understood along with the ontic or entitative dimension considered according to what is proper and primary and formal to *it*, for both are integrally constitutive of and equiprimordial to the human reality. For if the intentional order does not formally touch the entitative order in the particular kind of act/potency relation known as substance/accident composition, yet it does permeate it through other modes of act/potency composition – which is but to say that act/potency analysis as such cannot be reduced to substance/accident ontology, and that it is the former, not the latter, which provides the genuine categories of first philosophy, that is, of Metaphysics.

[7] "In welche Richtung gilt es zu sehen für die phänomenale Charakteristik des In-Seins als solchen? Wir erhalten Antwort durch die Erinnerung daran, was bei der Anzeige des Phänomens dem phänomenologisch behaltenden Blick anvertraut wurde: das In-Sein im Unterschied von der vorhandenen Inwendigkeit eines Vorhandenen 'in' einem anderen; das In-Sein nicht als eine durch das Vorhandensein von 'Welt' bewirkte oder auch nur ausgelöste Beschaffenheit eines vorhandenen Subjekts; das In-Sein vielmehr als wesenhafte Seinsart dieses Seienden selbst. Was anderes stellt sich aber dann mit diesem Phänomen dar als das vorhandene commercium *zwischen* einem vorhandenen Subjekt und einem vorhandenen Objekt? Diese Auslegung käme dem phänomenalen Bestand schon näher, wenn sie sagte: das *Dasein ist das Sein* dieses 'Zwischen'." *Sein und Zeit*, p. 132. These are in fact the opening lines of the passage cited above in footnote 6.

For the rest, for the detailed demonstration and clarification of all these issues, I must refer the reader to the body of this study. As regards the translations which appear in its pages, I must of course assume full responsibility for them. The reader who wishes to take exception to a provided translation is welcome to have recourse to the original German, French, or Latin (as the case may be) reproduced in the footnotes.

With this much said, let us turn our energies to the task at hand, the philosopher's task of passing beyond contention over conclusions in order to investigate presuppositions and clarify the order of primary intuitions; of uncovering relationships and discerning fundamental structures in order that to each insight might be accorded its proper value for knowledge and truth within a given problematic.

CHAPTER I

THE SITUATION OF HEIDEGGER IN THE TRADITION OF CHRISTIAN PHILOSOPHY

> "On peut voir s'entrecroiser dans ces spéculations une foule d'influences diverses, parmi lesquelles les chrétiennes ne sont pas les moindres. . . . Sa philososphie de la vérité est en gros celle des scolastiques. Il se meut dans un plan avant tout moral. . . . Tout schéma relationnel lui paraît déficient pour exprimer le rapport de l'objet et du sujet dans la vie et la connaissance. La conscience ne peut pas se séparer des choses pour se mettre *ensuite* en relation avec elles. . . . On doit affirmer "la dépendance de l'être par rapport à la compréhension de l'être par l'existence," c'est-à-dire par l'homme. . . . Pour M. Heidegger, ce qui doit retenir l'attention, c'est l'existence en tant qu'existence, "l'être de l'existence," comme il dit. . . . Le point de départ le plus sûr est l'existence qui nous est conjointe, l'existence humaine, dont le caractère propre est que son essence coïncide avec son existence, ce qui n'est pas le fait des êtres inférieurs, dont l'existence ne s'achève que dans la nôtre."
> A.-D. Sertillanges, *Le Christianisme et les Philosophies*, pp. 541, 536, and 537, *passim*.

The thought of Martin Heidegger is strange not only in its language, but in its effect upon philosophers of the most diverse orientations. As is well known, he has caused reactions ranging from virulence to adulation. But within scholastic circles both philosophical and theological, as well as among Protestant intellectuals, his writings seem more than anything else to have created a ferment and stirring of ideas that have already borne rich fruit through influences felt in the writings, among others, of Rahner, Bultmann, and a number of fine scholars of Louvain. This sphere of influence within scholasticism particularly, already provides some important clues as to the nature of Heidegger's *Denken des Seins*. Dondeyne, Rahner, De Waelhens, and the centers of thought they represent – all were profoundly influenced by the scholasticism of Joseph Maréchal in its overriding concern with the history and theory of the problem of knowledge.[1] In these currents of Maréchalian scholasticism Heidegger's notion of Being has remained, as elsewhere, disconcertingly enigmatic, but with this difference: the notion has somehow, as though by a secret affinity, seemed to match the mood and share the spirit of that thought which first brought scholasticism into confrontation with the full complexity and radical concerns of the epistemological problematic. It is by no means incidental to note that the deepest influence of Heidegger has been in this circle of scholasticism.

For there is another quite distinct and highly influential circle of scholasticism, that of Gilson and Maritain, which has primarily affected the intellectual clime in America (even as Maréchal's strongest influence has been toward Germany), and where the Heideggerean Thought of Being has, up to the present, found little resonance or deep sympathy. This scholastic circle was stirred in its depths and centered originally not by Kantian critical philosophy, as was the case for Maréchal's research, but by, I shall not say Bergsonism so much as by Bergson himself: "What Bañes considered the correct interpretation of the Thomistic notion of Being has been spontaneously rediscovered by some of our own contemporaries, and it is worthy of note that among these there is hardly one who, at one time or another, has not been under the influence of Bergson."[2] What is important for us to remark has already been suggested, namely, the difference in primary concern separating these men from the Maréchalian circle. It is precisely the domain of conscious awareness taken precisely as such: primary in Maréchalian thought, it definitely plays a secondary role in the thought of, say, Maritain.

True enough, a major work of Maritain is titled precisely *Distinguer pour unir ou Les degrés du savoir*, and even states at one point that " 'philosophy of being' is at once, and *par excellence*, 'philosophy of mind'."[3] But this affirmation must be seen in context, as an affirmation, that is to say, of the organic place of noetic within the larger and more fundamental concerns of

[1] According to Joseph Donceel, the "school" of Maréchalians "has begun to call itself the Thomasian system of philosophy or transcendental Thomism." "Philosophy in the Catholic University," *America*, 115 (24 September 1966), 331. Bernard Lonergan prefers to more simply say that "what has come from Fr. Maréchal is, not a set of fixed opinions, but a movement." "Metaphysics as Horizon," *Cross Currents* (Fall, 1966), 494.

[2] Etienne Gilson, *The Philosopher and Theology*, trans. by Cecile Gilson (New York: Random House, 1962), pp. 157-8.

[3] "... la philosophie de l'être est en même temps, par excellence, une 'philosophie de l'esprit'." Jacques Maritain, *Les degrés du savoir* (7th ed., revue et augmentée; Paris: Desclée de Brouwer, 1963), p. viii. Cf. Jacques Maritain, *The Degrees of Knowledge*, trans. from the 4th French ed. under the supervision of Gerald B. Phelan (New York: Charles Scribner's Sons, 1959), p. ix. Hereafter this work will be referred to as DS. Page references to the seventh French edition will be given first, followed by a / and the corresponding pages in Phelan's translation.

Metaphysics: "Critique of knowledge or epistemology does not exist as a discipline distinct from metaphysics."[4] Moreover, "the task of critique is purely and exclusively reflexive and secondary (not only in the order of time but by its very nature as well)."[5] The vocabulary of Metaphysics in its direct and primary intent "has to do with the operations and means of knowledge taken in their relation to extramental being."[6] What would happen if a methodology were founded which precisely circumscribed and in that sense isolated the full noetic problematic from, or better, within, Metaphysics? "To give it a separate existence is to set a third term between realism and idealism, between yes and no."[7] We shall return to this.

The Thomistic scholasticism of Joseph Maréchal faces the problematic of human awareness more directly and radically than that of Jacques Maritain. On the other hand, Maritain is more careful to locate and sketch the exact perspective which that problematic presents within the larger framework, or better, the spiritual organism,[8] of Thomistic thought. With the help of Maritain's careful sketch, I shall show why it is that Heidegger's way of philosophizing thrives best in the scholastic atmosphere of a Maréchal; but I shall do this by locating that area of philosophical reflection where Thomas' analyses and the thought of Heidegger literally share a common concern. That is what I mean by the situation of Heidegger in the tradition of Christian philosophy.

The core of the analysis I undertake here was first developed in a seminar paper under the less ambitious title, "Heidegger: Phenomenological Thought of Being." There, my sole concern was to touch on the primal intuition or 'experience' at the origin of Heidegger's thought – indeed, it was Heidegger who verified for me in a dramatic way the truth of Bergson's reflections on the philosophical mind gathered under the title "Philosophical Intuition":

You recall how the demon of Socrates proceeded: it checked the philosopher's will at a given moment and prevented him from acting rather than prescribing what he should do. It seems to me that intuition often behaves in speculative matters

---

[4] "La critique de la connaissance ou l'épistémologie n'existe pas en tant que discipline distincte de la métaphysique." (DS, p. 154/80).

[5] "... le travail de la critique est purement et exclusivement réflexif, second (non seulement dans l'ordre du temps, mais en nature)..." (DS, p. 145/75).

[6] "... le vocabulaire de la métaphysique (... se rapporte aux opérations et aux moyens de conaissance pris dans leur relation à l'être extramental)..." (DS, p. 792/398).

[7] "Lui donner une existence à part, c'est poser un troisième terme entre le réalisme et l'idéalisme, entre le oui et le non, ce qui est toute la prétention des modernes avec leur impensable notion de pur 'phénomène', qui vide de l'être le concept même de l'être, le plus général de tous nos concepts." (DS, pp. 154-5/80). Latent in this observation is the entire problematic of integral Phenomenology: see chapters IX and X below.

[8] DS, p. xv/xiii.

like the demon of Socrates in practical life; it is at least in this form that it begins, in this form also that it continues to give the most clear-cut manifestations: it forbids. . . . Is it not obvious that the first step the philosopher takes, when his thought is still faltering and there is nothing definite in his doctrine, is to reject certain things definitively? Later he will be able to make changes in what he affirms; he will vary only slightly in what he denies. [9]

Bergson's observations are certainly verified in Heidegger. Heidegger's initial and continuous experience of the Being-question (*Seinsfrage*) precisely forbid him to accept its formulation in (and since) Aristotle. In terms of Heidegger's original flash of intuitivity, Aristotle's question concerning the ultimate nature of Reality overlooked and bypassed the phenomenon of Being, literally forgot Being (*Seinsvergessenheit*). For many, this profound opposition of thought still remains more or less concealed in the language superficially common to the two lines of thinking.

Because I was concerned in my original essay with bringing out both *that* and *how* the question of Being as Heidegger experiences it is different from that framed by Aristotle and subsequently Aquinas (even granting the advance of the latter over the former), I was likewise concerned with the radically anti-philosophical opinion (whether it be acknowledged as such is another issue) which still enjoys some currency that Heidegger's fundamental orientation to the Being-question cannot be achieved outside the cultural angle built into the German philosophical language as he appropriates it. I was of course familiar with the fact that *Dasein* is an everyday word in Germany. I knew too that it had been in use in German philosophy for many, many decades before Heidegger. But I had acquired in the course of my researches the strongest conviction that Heidegger's employment of the term stands apart from both of these usages in an altogether proper appropriation. [10]

For the Heidegger of *Sein und Zeit*, the idea of Dasein (therefore of Being as well) and the idea of Phenomenology stand in a reciprocal, or perhaps I should simply say a correlated, relationship. The former can only be understood in terms of the latter, as a hat must be understood in terms of a head. It seemed to me accurate that Dasein as Heidegger fashioned the notion should be characterized as a new point of departure for a new way of thought, much more concrete in the sense of prior to because more fun-

[9] Henri Bergson, *The Creative Mind*, trans. from the French by Mabelle L. Andison (New York: The Philosophical Library, 1946), pp. 109-10.
[10] Cf. Martin Heidegger, "Einleitung" to *Was ist Metaphysik* (Franfurt: Klostermann, 1965), p. 14. English translation by Walter Kaufmann, "The Way Back into the Ground of Metaphysics," in *Existentialism from Dostoevsky to Sartre*, Walter Kaufmann, ed. (New York: Meridian Books, 1956), p. 213. Hereafter this text will be referred to as WM: In; German page references will be followed by a / and the corresponding page numbers in Kaufmann's translation.

damental than the initial concerns of both Idealism and Realism (but for that very same reason incapable of housing the ground-question of Thomistic Metaphysics or occupying a share of its *direct and primary* concern).

All this seemed to me important and worth bringing out, all the more so in view of the fact that these several key points seemed to be nowhere taken together or consistently understood by scholastic thinkers of either the existentialist – in the sense of *esse* – orientation (Maritain) or the cognitional, "transcendental," orientation (Maréchal). Let me provide some justification for this allegation.

Gilson achieved a decisive insight when he wrote that "the phenomenology of Dasein is without a counterpart [in any genuinely thematic sense] in the doctrine of Saint Thomas." But he in a certain sense betrays this same insight when he writes in the very next sentence: "Concerning the notion of Being itself, and that of metaphysics which is bound up with the notion of Being, the comparison is on the contrary possible and the Heideggerean language is perfect." Basing his remarks on the text of Heidegger, *Was ist Metaphysik*, Gilson considers that "the terminology of the new Metaphysic is comparable to that of tradition. Heidegger distinguishes in effect between *existence or 'to be'* (*Sein*) and *being* (*das Seiende*). This is the Thomistic distinction between *esse* and *ens* . . ."[11]

Parallelling this false lead of Gilson, Lotz, in a fascinating and provocative analysis, attempts to show that latent in Thomas' use of *ens* is the *Sein* of Heidegger – and Lotz of course (in one kind of accustomed Thomistic form) proceeds to bring out this virtuality.[12] Having done this, Lotz is able to reach some remarkable conclusions. The relation between Being and beings in Heidegger's "ontological difference" is revealed as "the force behind all the proofs for God's existence, including the 'quinque viae' of Aquinas."[13] Moreover, "in this process" whereby Being "offers itself to the view of the mind," says Lotz, "reflection is first. . ."[14] Being (*Sein, ens*) in fact "does not stand over against consciousness as other, but is basically one with it."[15] And

[11] ". . . la phénoménologie du *Dasein*, est sans contrepartie que je puisse discerner dans la doctrine de Saint Thomas. Sur la notion d'être elle-même, et sur celle de la métaphysique qui s'y trouve liée, la comparaison est au contraire possible et la langage heideggerien est parfait. . . . la terminologie de la nouvelle métaphysique est comparable avec celle de l'ancienne. Heidegger distingue en effet entre *être (Sein) et étant (das Seiende)*. C'est la distinction thomiste entre *esse* et *ens* . . ." Etienne Gilson, *L'Etre et l'essence* (deuxieme ed.; Paris: Vrin, 1962), pp. 366-7.
[12] Johannes B. Lotz, "Being and Existence in Scholasticism and in Existence-Philosophy," trans. by Robert E. Wood, *Philosophy Today*, X (Spring, 1964), 16-17, 34 fn. 1, 38 fn. 54, esp. 39 fn. 67, 41 fn. 68, esp. 41 fn. 69.
[13] *Ibid.*, p. 43 fn. 81; cf. 43-4 fn. 85.
[14] *Ibid.*, p. 23.
[15] *Ibid.*, p. 20.

of course, Aquinas stands out from the history of Western ontology as the sole thinker not guilty of the forgetfulness of Being, not to be considered therefore under the Heideggerean indictment covering the metaphysics of subjectivity.[16]

Apart from the fact that Lotz' reading of Heidegger's ontological difference in Thomas can in nowise account for Heidegger's identification of Being (*Sein*) with Non-being (*das Nichts*),[17] one might have expected Lotz' exculpation of Aquinas from the forgetfulness of Being charge to have accounted for Heidegger's explicit inclusion of Aquinas among the guilty.[18]

Lotz' attempt to situate Heidegger in terms of Aquinas achieves certain insights which come close to the heart of the matter,[19] but it must be said that this is done at the cost of blurring certain distinctions and insights which lie at the center of Thomism. We must say to him what Maritain said to Sertillanges: "Ambiguity is not a philosophical instrument, and the conciliation of Thomism with certain modern systems would be too dearly paid for were it to be bought at the price of equivocal language."[20]

In another recent article on "Heidegger's Theory of Being," Thomas F. Rukavina submits "a fresh attempt toward an easier understanding of Heidegger's views on Being, by using a schema of interpretation which, unusual as it may seem, recaptures, I am confident, the dynamics of Heidegger's thinking and provides, I hope, a rather simple insight into the otherwise opaque content of his doctrine of Being."[21] One admires Professor Rukavina's confidence, but fears that his hopes were dashed from the beginning.

[16] *Ibid.*, pp. 18, 36 fn. 32, 37 fn. 51, 43 fn. 82.

[17] See *ibid.*, p. 43 fn. 83. The closest he comes to this is by way of metaphor pure and simple. "There is ignorance in knowledge as well as knowledge in not-knowing. Thus the *tension* between the conceptual grasp and superconceptual manifestation is always with us. We might circumscribe the problem better by saying that the *superconceptual* manifestation is *knowledge in the guise of not-knowing* since Being as expressly or conceptually known is necessarily borne and colored by Being as inexpressibly manifested. . . . In manifestation Being's plenitude is revealed, but it is not really thought out; in the concept Being is truly thought out but its fulness is never attained (pp. 24-5)." Just how equivocal this 'identification' is in terms of Heidegger is shown unmistakably when Lotz remarks in a later note (p. 43 fn. 83) that the core of the "treasure of knowledge" is "hoc principium per se notum, quod affirmatio et negatio non sunt simul vera."

[18] See Martin Heidegger, *Einführung in die Metaphysik* (Tübingen: Max Niemeyer Verlag, 1966), p. 14. English translation by Ralph Manheim, *An Introduction to Metaphysics* (New Haven, Conn.: Yale University Press, 1959), p. 17. Hereafter this text will be referred to as EM; the German page reference will be followed by a / and the corresponding reference in Manheim's translation.

[19] See Lotz, *art. cit.*, esp. pp. 19-24.

[20] "L'ambiguïté n'est pas un instrument philosophique, et ce serait payer trop cher la conciliation du thomisme avec certains systèmes modernes que de l'obtenir d'un langage équivoque." (DS, p. 843/429).

[21] *The New Scholasticism*, XL (October, 1966), 425.

Like Gilson, Rukavina touches on a decisive insight, then loses the contact before a paragraph is finished: "Richardson takes Heidegger's concept of Truth as 'lighting process,' as the essence of what Heidegger has had to tell us about the nature of Being. . . . The idea of Truth as lighting process is certainly the most adept metaphor for clarifying the nature of knowledge, but as a means of making clear the nature of Being it succeeds only in raising grave questions."[22]

Thus between my seminar paper and this study a great deal of reading and thought intervened to convince me of the need for locating the focus of Heidegger's thought in the context of Aquinas without doing violence to either. All that I said in that earlier paper has remained with me; but what has become increasingly clear is the very great need of showing the *precise* character of the relation which may be established organically, that is, as an *inner* (not simply a verbal) continuity between the analyses of Aquinas and the Thought of Being which Heidegger elaborates. The newness of Heidegger's way is in one sense or another apparent to all. The problem is that human intelligence is of such a nature that it cannot enter into an understanding of the new until it has succeeded somehow in accurately relating this novelty to the already-considered. It is never a question of reduction, but precisely of relating. Thus, if Maritain is correct in seeing the true progress of philosophy consist in continuous deepening of insights, then to say that Heidegger's dominating insight is in Aquinas (contextualized and emphasized differently, of course) is not to 'pigeon-hole' and dismiss the thought of Heidegger: for the proper question is not whether Heidegger's central insight and concern was touched on by Aquinas; but rather, the question is whether this insight, though not perhaps alien to Thomism, is deepened as it is recovered (in the sense of "considered anew") through Heidegger. In this way the historical character of Thomas' thought may be scrupulously respected, while its philosophical character is likewise maintained.

Why do I say there is a very great need for an analysis of this kind? We will see why at a number of places along our path, but here at its very beginning we must at least point out that in dealing with a thought such as Heidegger's, that is, a thought endowed with a literally inexhaustible complexity and subtlety, we are in one sense free to pursue just about any line of discussion which might strike our fancy. Interesting and lively as such exchanges might be, their value would be very much diminished if we do not first take the greatest care to achieve a basic orientation within the Heideggerean problematic; and not indeed *a* basic orientation, but *Heidegger's*

[22] *Ibid.,* p. 424.

basic orientation. And to do this an accurate perspective within the considerations of previous philosophy is required, a proper acoustical setting for hearing in its uniqueness Heidegger's central theme.

This is not easy to achieve – a fact attested, as we have already seen, by the proliferation of interpretations and adaptations which not only conflict among themselves, but are generally repudiated by Heidegger himself.[23]

This situation is a puzzling one on first encounter. On the one hand, Heidegger claims that the unique thought of Being which he has from the first attempted to express and striven to achieve is something simple.[24] On the other hand, Heidegger himself has not been able to carry through adequately the original project proposed in *Sein und Zeit*. Although there remains a profound continuity between the "early" and "later" Heidegger, so vital that the latter cannot be understood save on the basis of the former, nonetheless there is a hiatus which disrupts the effort at reversal, at shifting the emphasis and focus from Dasein to Being itself.[25] Moreover, how is it that so many men of keen insight and sustained reflection have failed to lay hold of a philosophical perspective which is strange, according to its originator, only in its simplicity?

[23] Cf. Herbert Spiegelberg, *The Phenomenological Movement* (2nd ed.; The Hague: Martinus Nijhoff, 1965), Vol. I, 288ff.

[24] See Martin Heidegger, "Über den 'Humanismus': Brief an Jean Beaufret, Paris," in *Platons Lehre von der Wahrheit mit einem Brief Über den Humanismus* (Bern: Francke Verlag, 1947), pp. 78 and 116. "Letter on Humanism," trans. by Edgar Lohner, *Philosophy in the Twentieth Century*, ed. by William Barrett and Henry D. Aiken (New York: Random House, 1962), Vol. III, pp. 283 and 302. Hereafter referred to as HB: German page references followed by / and corresponding page numbers in Lohner's translation.

[25] In a recent book, *Heidegger's Philosophy* (New York: Macmillan, 1964), p. 33, Magda King gives this succinct characterization of the difference between Heidegger I and II: "What changes in Heidegger's later works is his way of 'getting into the circle': Being is no longer approached through man's understanding, but rather it is man's understanding which is approached through the manifestations of Being."

CHAPTER II

THE PROBLEM OF LANGUAGE AND THE NEED FOR A RETRIEVE

> "Indes bleibt alles Formelhafte mißverständlich. Gemäß dem in sich mehrfältigen Sachverhalt von Sein und Zeit bleiben auch alle ihn sagenden Worte wie Kehre, Vergessenheit und Geschick mehrdeutig. Nur ein mehrfältiges Denken gelangt in das entsprechende Sagen der Sache jenes Sachverhalts.
>
> "Dieses mehrfältige Denken verlangt zwar keine neue Sprache, aber ein gewandeltes Verhältnis zum Wesen der alten."
>
> M. Heidegger, "Vorwort" to Fr. Richardson's *Heidegger: Through Phenomenology to Thought*, p. XXIII.

From the very outset, Heidegger realized clearly that his thought threatened to founder on the shoals of language.[1] Thus in the very "Introduction" to *Being and Time* he made this significant observation:

With regard to the awkwardness and "inelegance" of expression in the analyses to come, we may remark that it is one thing to give a report in which we tell about *beings*, but another to grasp beings in their *Being*. For the latter task we lack not only most of the words, but, above all, the "grammar".[2]

Twenty years later, looking back over the mighty intellectual effort formally initiated with *Being and Time*, Heidegger felt constrained to remark not altogether happily:

---

[1] See Spiegelberg, I, 273, 310-11, and 351.

[2] "Mit Rücksicht auf das Ungefüge und 'Unschöne' des Ausdrucks innerhalb der folgenden Analysen darf die Bemerkung angefügt werden: ein anderes ist es, über *Seiendes* erzählend zu berichten, ein anderes, Seiendes in seinem *Sein* zu fassen. Für die letztgenannte Aufgabe fehlen nicht nur meist die Worte, sondern vor allem die 'Grammatik'." *Sein und Zeit* (8th ed.; Tübingen: Max Niemeyer Verlag, 1963), pp. 38-9. Cf. *Being and Time*, trans. by John Macquarrie and Edward Robinson (New York: Harper and Row, 1962), p. 63. Hereafter referred to as SZ. Since the Macquarrie-Robinson translation has the pagination of the later German editions (which differs but slightly from that of the earlier ones) indicated in its margins, only reference to the German text will be made in subsequent footnotes.

Thinking which tries to think forward into the truth of Being in the struggle of the first breakthrough expresses only a small part of this entirely different dimension. ... In order to make this attempt of thinking recognizable and understandable within philosophy, it was possible at first to speak only within the horizon of the existing philosophy and within the usage of the terms familiar to it.

In the meantime I have come to be convinced that even these terms must immediately and inevitably lead astray. For the terms and their corresponding conceptual language were not rethought by the readers from the thing which had-to-be-thought first [sc. Being]; instead, this thing was imagined through terms maintained in their usual signification. [3]

This passage contains all the essential clues for establishing an appreciation of the unique character of the Heideggerean problematic, a character which can never be perceived at ground level unless we are first able to step back from the interpretation secured by the categories of traditional scholastic expression. (We will, it is true, reference our discussion by these categories and eventually return to them: but that will be possible only when we have enlarged them.) I say this because the terminology in which the Heideggerean question of Being is initially framed is almost materially identical with the terminology employed by, for example, Thomas Aquinas – we have already seen this through the texts of Gilson and Lotz. The greater number of terms seem at first glance and in some primary sense interchangeable. The fact of the matter is that they are not interchangeable: the secondary meanings of, e.g., the term "being," "ontological," "existential," "world," "meaning" or "sense," as employed by scholasticism in the lineage of Aquinas become the primary meanings in the technical usage of Heidegger. At the same time, their employment by Heidegger is not always technical, especially in the case of the later Heidegger, so that it is not always clear when they have reverted to traditional emphases. Moreover, sensuous metaphors such as Heidegger II employs to characterize the relationship between the essence of man and the truth of Being should, like the myths of Plato, make one suspicious that they cover up a break in the thought.

Accordingly, what I propose for these pages is that we attempt something like what has come to be called a "re-trieve" of the early Heidegger. The

---

[3] "Das Denken, das in die Wahrheit des Seins vorzudenken versucht, bringt in der Not des ersten Durchkommens nur ein Geringes der ganz anderen Dimension zur Sprache. ... Um jedoch diesen Versuch des Denkens innerhalb der bestehenden Philosophie kenntlich und zugleich verständlich zu machen, konnte zunächst nur aus dem Horizont des Bestehenden und aus dem Gebrauch seiner ihm geläufigen Titel gesprochen werden.

"Inzwischen habe ich einsehen gelernt, dass eben diese Titel unmittelbar und unvermeidlich in die Irre führen mussten. Denn Titel und die ihnen zugeordnete Begriffssprache wurden von den Lesern nicht aus der erst zu denkenden Sache wieder-gedacht, sondern diese Sache wurde aus den in ihrer gewohnten Bedeutung festgehaltenen Titeln vorgestellt." (HB, p. 110/297-8).

basic idea here is simple and rich with promise. It gives a precise and formal sense to what we mentioned earlier about the possibility of respecting integrally the historical character of thought without thereby denying or vilipending its philosophical (trans-cultural) validity once it has reached a certain depth of intelligibility:

By the re-trieving of a fundamental problem we understand the disclosure of those original possibilities of the problem which up to the present have lain hidden. By the elaboration of these possibilities, the problem is transformed and thus for the first time is conserved in its proper content. To preserve a problem, however, means to retain free and awake all those interior forces that render this problem in its fundamental essence possible.[4]

Re-trieve is achieved simply by allowing the original awareness or experience of a thinker to come again (future) through what has been said (past), and bringing this experience of 'the way things are' to expression in a renovated discourse (present). This is the basic effort of what the later Heidegger designated "foundational" thought (*das wesentliche Denken*), i.e., the effort of human understanding (*noein*) that lets the unseen plenitude come again through the said.[5]

[4] "Unter der Wiederholung eines Grundproblems verstehen wir die Erschliessung seiner ursprünglichen, bislang verborgenen Möglichkeiten, durch deren Ausarbeitung es verwandelt und so erst in seinem Problemgehalt bewahrt wird. Ein Problem bewahren heisst aber, es in denjenigen inneren Kräften frei und wach halten, die es als Problem im Grunde seines Wesens ermöglichen." Martin Heidegger, *Kant und das Problem der Metaphysik* (Frankfurt: Klostermann, 1951), p. 185. Cf. *Kant and the Problem of Metaphysics*, trans. by James S. Churchill (Bloomington: Indiana University Press, 1962), p. 211. Hereafter referred to as KM: German page reference will be followed by / and the corresponding reference in the Churchill translation.

[5] Some remarks should be added here, even at the risk of running a bit ahead of ourselves. First of all, the notion of re-trieve "is based upon the principle that *Dasein*, as transcendence, transcends first of all and most profoundly the subject-object relationship." – William J. Richardson, "Heidegger and God – and Professor Jonas," *Thought*, XL (Spring, 1965), p. 34. (Hereafter referred to as simply "Heidegger and God.") Consequently, as we remarked on our own right in the text, "thought of this nature that is structured by the unity of future-past-present is profoundly historical thought" (*ibid.*, p. 36). And finally and most importantly, let us remark the provocative correspondence of the structure of a Re-trieve to the structure of Dasein. (The full significance of this correspondence in our context will emerge from the fact that re-trieve is an effort of thought, once we have explained in fuller scope our identification of Dasein with what we shall characterize the "intentional life" of man adequately considered, i.e., considered as the integrity of the life of the human spirit at all three levels, the unconscious and the preconscious as well as the conscious.) "*Dasein* is finite transcendence and its ultimate meaning (that is, the source of its unity) is time. As transcendence, *Dasein* is continually passing beyond beings to Being, that is, continually coming to Being in such a way that Being is continually coming to *Dasein*. This continual coming is *Dasein's* future. But Being comes to a *Dasein* that already is, and this condition of already-having-been – this is *Dasein's* past. Being, then, comes as future to *Dasein* through *Dasein* as past. Finally, because Being comes to *Dasein* it renders beings manifest, that is, renders them

Our own attempt at something like a re-trieve of Heidegger's original problem-experience is all the more necessary in view of the loss of rigor which characterizes the hermeneutic conceptualizations of the later as compared with the early Heidegger. This must be said in spite of our concurrence with Dondeyne's experience: "In preparing this study we have often had the impression that the most revealing texts on the Heideggerean conception of truth are actually found in the minor works, such as the studies on the origin of the work of art, the original meaning of thing and of technique, the onto-theological structure of metaphysics."[6]

Indeed, even Fr. Richardson admits in prefacing his treatment of Heidegger's *Kant und das Problem der Metaphysik* as "the classic type of what Heidegger I (1929) calls 're-trieve' and what Heidegger II (1950) calls 'dialogue'," that "unless we watch him [Heidegger] go through the process at least once, we might be tempted to think that the 'rigor' (*Strenge*) of which he will speak later is either platitude or sham."[7]

Demske is doubtless right in remarking that "to do justice to Heidegger's total effort one must consider some of what he has written since *Being and Time*"; and doubtless correct in suggesting accordingly that any appraisal of Heidegger's philosophy is incomplete if it is restricted to *Being and Time* alone.[8]

But it is even more correct to remark that any appraisal of Heidegger's philosophy which is not primarily referenced by *Sein und Zeit* will find few thinkers ready to consider seriously its conclusions.

Heidegger makes both points with equal emphasis. He writes to Fr. Richardson:

The distinction you make between Heidegger I and II is justified only on the condition that this is kept constantly in mind: only by way of what Heidegger I has thought does one gain access to what is to-be-thought by Heidegger II. But the thought of Heidegger I becomes possible only if it is contained in Heidegger II.[9]

present to *Dasein* and *Dasein* to them. That is *Dasein's* present. Now the unity of future-past-present constitutes the unity of time so that the source of unity of *Dasein* is the unity of time itself" (*ibid.*, pp. 33-4).

[6] "En préparant cette étude nous avons eu plusieurs fois l'impression que les textes les plus révélateurs sur la conception heideggerienne de la vérité se trouvent en réalité dans les oeuvres mineures, telles les études sur l'origine de l'oeuvre d'art, la signification originaire de la chose et de la technique, la structure onto-théologique de la métaphysique." – "La différence ontologique chez M. Heidegger," *Revue Philosophique de Louvain*, LVI (1958), 272.

[7] William J. Richardson, *Heidegger: Through Phenomenology to Thought* (The Hague: Martinus Nijhoff, 1963), p. 106. Hereafter abbreviated to H:TPT.

[8] James M. Demske, "Heidegger's Quadrate and Revelation of Being," *Philosophy Today*, 7 (Winter, 1963), 245, 255-6 fn. 1.

[9] "Ihre Unterscheidung zwischen 'Heidegger I' und 'Heidegger II' ist allein unter der

Does this not accord strictly with what Bergson had to tell us about the nature of philosophical intuition? – "the first step the philosopher takes, when his thought is still faltering and there is nothing definite in his doctrine, is to reject certain things definitively. Later he will be able to make changes in what he affirms; he will vary only slightly in what he denies."

Heidegger is separated from Aristotle and Aquinas phenomenologically (as we shall see) by the "gulf between the conditions or mode of thought and the conditions or mode of the thing" (the transobjective subject),[10] and metaphysically by the chasm of act/potency (as we shall also see);[11] but his original flash of intuitivity into *Sein* as *die Sache des Denkens*, into the *praecognitum* priority of *intentionale* over *entitativum* (see chapters V, VI and VII below, esp. pp. 72-73) never ceased to forbid him to accept the Being-question formulated by scholasticism as accurately rendering into language his original problem-experience. Probably the most consistent explanation of the inner necessity of Heidegger's "reversal" (*Kehre*) is the one given by Ralph Powell, that it consists in the gradual elimination of the covert act-potency distinctions which were key threads in the fabric of *Sein und Zeit*.[12] The fact remains that if left to rest solely on the post-*Sein und Zeit* writings, the philosophical stature Heidegger has achieved would soon diminish spectacularly, if not vanish altogether. If indeed as Fr. Richardson states the whole of Heidegger II is "a re-trieve of Heidegger I,"[13] then it would serve a real purpose if this un-said could be retrieved somewhat differently than Heidegger himself has done, for the ambivalence of metaphorical formulations can hardly provide adequate guidelines for any serious attempt to philosophically reference a theological project. Indeed, in reading certain sections of such a book as *The Later Heidegger and Theology*, one sometimes gets the impression of a man muttering "My God!" as he stands bewildered in the midst of a Sahara sandstorm. "Yet the more a philosopher is surrounded by confusion, the more inescapable is his obligation to try, with even

Bedingung berechtigt, dass stets beachtet wird: Nur von dem unter I Gedachten her wird zunächst das unter II zu Denkende zugänglich. Aber I wird nur möglich, wenn es in II enthalten ist." ("Vorwort" to H:TPT, p. XXIII).

[10] Cf. Maritain, DS, p. 167/86: ". . . il y a un abîme entre les conditions ou le mode de la pensée et les conditions ou le mode de la chose."

[11] Sêe fn. 25 for Chapter III below.

[12] Here we must mention three studies, only one of which is as yet available in printed form: "Has Heidegger Destroyed Metaphysics," *Listening*, 2 (Winter, 1967), 52-9; "Heidegger's Retreat from a Transcultural Structure of Dasein" (circa November, 1966); and "The Late Heidegger's Omission of the Ontic-Ontological Structure of Dasein," scheduled for publication as one of the major papers in connection with the Symposium on the Philosophy of Martin Heidegger held at Duquesne University, October 15-16, 1966.

[13] H:TPT, p. 625.

greater persistence, to clarify matters."[14] It is all well and good to talk about Being, with or without a capital "b"; but unless one has a determinate specification or two to boundary the discussion, it is difficult to see how much can really be accomplished.

In any event, the effort of re-trieve which defines foundational thinking rests on the fact that in whatever is *said*, a hidden plenitude is left *unsaid*. Heidegger claims to have made a new departure in Western thought by raising a radically new problem. Our effort in this essay therefore must aim at a disclosure of what this problem is, and how it differs from the central problem of traditional philosophy. How is it that when Heidegger raises questions about the ontological status of the world, centered on inquiry into the Being of the things that are, there is a radically new problematic nascent? Has it not always been the central concern of philosophy to inquire into being? Indeed, St. Thomas identifies philosophy in its most proper sense with Metaphysics, and by Metaphysics he understands the study of *ens inquantum ens*.

The fact is however that Heidegger from the very first never moved on the level of metaphysical inquiry in the sense given it by Aquinas, though the converse cannot be said without some decisive clarifications – as we shall see. It cannot even be said (in response to Fr. Richardson's query[15]), at least as far as Thomistic thought is concerned, that Heidegger's task may be unequivocally characterized as "laying the foundation (digging the ground) for metaphysics." Gradually, Heidegger himself came to a similar realization. One sees this awareness dawn rather dramatically in following the reissues of his 1929 lecture, "*Was ist Metaphysik*?", which first defined itself as a discussion of a definitely metaphysical question. In 1943 a "Postscript" was added to the essay, wherein it is suggested that instead of posing a decidedly metaphysical question, the essay had arisen rather "from a way of thinking which has already entered into the overcoming of metaphysics."[16]

[14] Jacques Maritain, "Freudianism and Psychoanalysis," in *Scholasticism and Politics*, trans. by Mortimer J. Adler (New York: Image Books, 1960), p. 139.

[15] "Would it not be possible . . . that the entire problematic of Heidegger, placed as it is on a different level, might leave intact the traditional questions concerning essence-existence, substance-accident, etc., and, if it succeeds, simply serve to lay the indispensable ground(work) for them?" (H:TPT, p. 154). In the present study, the reason why a negative answer must finally be made to this question will be pointed up in a number of ways, e.g., in Chapter VIII, esp. p. 121; Chapter X, esp. pp. 165 and 166; and Appendix II.

[16] "Die Frage, 'Was ist Metaphysik?' fragt über die Metaphysik hinaus. Sie entspringt einem Denken, das schon in die Überwindung der Metaphysik eingegangen ist." "Nachwort" to *Was ist Metaphysik?*, p. 43, Cf. "What is Metaphysics: Postscript," trans. by R. F. C. Hull and Alan Crick, in *Existence and Being*, Werner Brock, ed. (Chicago: Gateway, 1949), pp. 349-50. Hereafter referred to as WM: Ep; German page reference will be followed by / and the corresponding pages of the English text.

And finally, in adding in 1949 an "Introduction" to the text, Heidegger discloses the full realization that his thinking (in contrast to metaphysical
thinking) "is directed toward a different point of origin," and "with its first
step it immediately leaves the realm of all ontology"[17] in the traditional sense
of that word.

The metaphysical Being-question as St. Thomas framed it and the phenomenological one which Heidegger poses are radically different, and everything
depends on their being recognized as such. Their origins are diverse and
their terms are not the same. Neither can be judged true or false relative to
the other in any direct way because their terms in principle need never coincide. Metaphysics grounds its inquiry into *ens commune* on things-which-
exist, which exercise *esse*, "as if it were taken for granted that the truth of
Being could be set up over causes and basic explanations or, what is the same
thing, over their incomprehensibility."[18] Phenomenology seeks to ground
its determination of the sense of *Sein* in the transcendence of Dasein where
alone the concealing-revealing manifestation of things-in-Being takes place.

For Heidegger, the question of Being is primarily, or at least, was first of
all, the question of man in terms of Dasein. With Aristotle, it was far otherwise:

> The question which was raised of old and is raised now and always, and is always
> the subject of doubt, viz., what being is, is just the question, what is substance
> (*ousia*)? . . . And so we also must consider chiefly and primarily and almost ex-
> clusively what that *is* which is in *this* sense.[19]

Similarly for St. Thomas, the problem of securing an understanding of the
nature of being was principally one of ascertaining and specifying the nature
of the fundamental units structuring the natural world as they are in their
own right independent of human awareness and secondary circumstances.
Thus he followed Aristotle in removing from the principal consideration of
Metaphysics being as supported in existence by virtue of fundamental
natural units and being according as it signifies that which is true.[20]

---

[17] ". . . in eine andere Herkunft gewiesen ist." (WM: In, p. 13/212). "Indessen hat das
Denken an die Wahrheit des Seins als der Rückgang in den Grund der Metaphysik den
Bereich aller Ontologie schon mit dem ersten Schritt verlassen." (WM: In, p. 21/219).

[18] "Als ob es denn so ausgemacht sei, dass die Wahrheit des Seins sich überhaupt auf
Ursachen und Erklärungsgründe oder, was das Selbe ist, auf deren Unfasslichkeit, stellen
lasse." (HB, p. 60/274).

[19] *Metaphysica*, Book VII, ch. 1, 1028b2-7 (Ross translation).

[20] "Postquam Philosophus removit a principali consideratione huius scientiae ens per
accidens et ens secundum quod significat verum, hic incipit determinare de ente per se, de
quo est principalis consideratio huius scientiae." (*In VII Met.*, lect. 1, n. 1245).
   I am not forgetting the advance secured by Aquinas in recognizing that Aristotle, by
equating substance with the subject of metaphysics simply, had been caught in a confusion

The vocabulary proper to the Metaphysics of St. Thomas, to Thomistic "thought of being," has to do directly only "with the operations and means of knowledge taken in their relation to extramental being,"[21] i.e., to what taken in itself "does not belong to the realm of logic or to that which is properly constituted by the life of reason" *taken in any phase or at any level.*[22] The Being of entities which Heidegger wishes to thematize, however, *das Sein des Seienden*, precisely *lacks* as yet a developed and recognizably proper vocabulary, and is bound up intrinsically and essentially with the revelation of beings in human awareness – with "ens secundum quod significat verum" (not, to be sure, at the derivative level of *judicium*, but) at the level of original possibility.

[A]. The "nature of reality" as elucidated by a rightly understood Thomism involves "both the intuition of *my* existence and of the existence *of things*; but first and foremost of the existence of things."[23] [B]. Being, then, as that within which a given entity, man, mountain, rock, tree, star, maintains and exercises "that sovereign activity *to be* in its own way, in an independence from *me* which is total, totally self-assertive and totally implacable,"[24] refers "to the act of existing insofar as it grounds and centers the intelligible structure of reality, as it expands into activity in every being, and as, in its supreme, uncreated plenitude, it activates and attracts to itself the entire

or conflation of the fundamental with the formal subject of First Philosophy, which is not *ens per se* (*substantia*), but *ens commune*, and which is not arrived at by abstraction and hence transcends confinement to the basic categories of finite being, the *decem praedicamenta* (which is also why metaphysical conceptions are never as such univocal, to the distress of the purely logical mind!). I have made all these points expressly elsewhere ("Finitude, Negativity, and Transcendence: The Problematic of Metaphysical Knowledge," *Philosophy Today*, XI [Fall, 1967], pp. 184-206). But for the purposes of the present study, such differences, however important in themselves (they do indeed place Thomistic metaphysics on a different plane than the work of Aristotle), are subordinate to the point in which Aquinas and Aristotle in nowise differ, namely, principal concern with *id quod existit extra et independens ab anima*. Cf. further Ch. VIII below, esp. around fn. 59.

[21] ". . . le vocabulaire de la métaphysique. . . se rapporte aux opérations et aux moyens de connaissance pris dans leur rélation a l'être extramental . . ." (DS, p. 792/398).

[22] "Les modernes, d'une façon générale, se donnent l'*objet* comme pur objet, détaché en lui-même de toute *chose* où il aurait l'existence, je dis une existence indépendante de mon *cogito*, posée pour soi avant mon acte de pensée et sans lui: existence qu'on appelle en ce sens-là extramentale, sans que l' 'extériorité' dont il s'agit ait la moindre signification spatiale, et qu'on pourrait appeler aussi prémentale, c'est-à-dire précédant la connaissance que nous en avons, ou encore métalogique, non en ce sens que pour la connaître il faudrait répudier la logique ou user d'une autre logique que la logique, mais en ce sens qu'elle-même n'appartient pas à la sphère du logique ou de ce qui est constitué en propre par la vie de la raison, à la sphère du *connu en tant même que connu*, elle est 'au delà' de cette sphère." (DS, pp. 177-8/91-2).

[23] Jacques Maritain, *The Range of Reason* (New York: Charles Scribner's Sons, 1952), p. 88.

[24] *Ibid.*

dynamism of nature."[25] [C]. "Thus, the inner dynamism of the intuition of existence or of the intelligible value of Being, causes me to see that absolute existence or Being-without-nothingness transcends the totality of nature – and makes me face the existence of God."[26]

With Phenomenology (as thought through in principle by Heidegger), the emphasis of that first implication [A] is reversed, and from that inversion eventuates a consistent transposition of the sense of the entire sequence:

[A]. "The nature of reality" as elucidated by Heidegger is "reality" as experienced by the phenomenologist, wherein beings "are" insofar as they are manifest, insofar as they appear to man. [B]. Being, then, as that which enables beings to become manifest, is essentially revelation – revelation of a secular kind. [C]. It should not be surprising that the revelation continues as long as beings are, nor that it should be "of this world." This is why Heidegger has insisted so strongly from the beginning that Being itself, as he has experienced it, is not and cannot be God.[27]

The language of the former metaphysical task is long established (how well or accurately is another question); but "for the latter task we lack not only most of the words, but, above all, the 'grammar'."[28] Thus in 1957 Heidegger writes:

The difficulty is one of language. Our occidental languages are in one way or another languages of metaphysical thought.[29]

Heidegger asks "What is called Being?" and with this initial step engages a problematic which, he considers, has never been engaged in these words before. That this is really possible is a consequence of what has been recognized by all thinkers as the poverty of language.[30] The whole structure and possibility of the Heideggerean re-trieve can be found liminally in St. Thomas' study *De veritate*:

A word which comes to expression in us by reason of an actual consideration, issuing as it were from some consideration of principles or at least from habitual

[25] *Ibid.*, p. 87.
[26] *Ibid.*, p. 89.
[27] Richardson, "Heidegger and God," p. 30.
[28] "Für die letztgenannte Aufgabe fehlen nicht nur meist die Worte, sondern vor allem die 'Grammatik'." (SZ, p. 39).
[29] "Das Schwierige liegt in der Sprache. Unsere abendländischen Sprachen sind in je verschiedener Weise Sprachen des metaphysischen Denkens. . ." *Identität und Differenz* (Pfüllingen: Neske, 1957), p. 72. Cf. *Essays in Metaphysics*, trans. by Kurt F. Leidecker (New York: The Philosophical Library, 1960), p. 66. Hereafter referred to as ID; German reference followed by / and corresponding page number in Leidecker's translation. See Richardson, "Heidegger and God," pp. 37-8.
[30] E.g., see Cajetan, *Commentaria in summam theologicam*, I, q. 25, art. 1. Also Karl Menninger, *The Human Mind* (New York: Knopf, 1964), pp. 297-8. And Mortimer Adler, *How to Read a Book* (New York: Simon & Schuster, 1940), p. 186. Cf. too Plato's Seventh Epistle.

knowledge, does not take possession of all that is in that from which it arose: for the intelligence expresses in the conception of a word only some facet of what it holds in an habitual awareness. Similarly, in reflection upon a conclusion, the entire force of a principle is never expressed.[31]

Consequently, if we are to achieve a foundational clarification and understanding of the Heideggerean problematic, we must give ourselves over to the experience which gave the original impetus to Heidegger's thought. We must determine this experience in the light of Heidegger's texts, surely; but this obviously involves more than what any given text directly says. Heidegger's lines must be read against the realities of sharable human experience over which they were initially drawn, in terms of which alone can his experience be re-captured – and subsequently re-trieved for expression in a renovated discourse. In short, a philosophical reading – that is, a thoughtful reading – must penetrate to what does not stand in the words and is nevertheless said, to the unspoken which is entangled in the spoken, to the culturally expressed reality which is not itself entirely cultural.

Our understanding of this difficult thinker will not be a true one if it takes over a perspective into which the prima facie sense of the words channel it, especially if this perspective or line of sight is taken to be correct since it presents itself as comfortable (familiar) and self-evident (agreeing with what we have long thought to be the case). On the contrary, we must relentlessly question the seemingly customary perspective because conceivably – in this case actually – this line of sight does not lead to what Heidegger himself has directly in view: even our preliminary, cursory comparison of the phenomenological with the metaphysical sense of the Being-question is enough to ensure us of this! However relentless, our effort will not succeed unless we ourselves really ask Heidegger's initial (therefore determining) questions and in this very asking create our own perspectives as it were for the first time. In scholastic circles, we say that an answer is transcendentally related to its question. Well, Heidegger provides a rare opportunity to discover what this really implies.

We shall no doubt work a certain violence on Heidegger's thought in terms of its temporal maturation through our attempt to lay hold of the original problematic of this philosopher in its proper specification and ex-

---

[31] "Verbum enim quod in nobis exprimitur per actualem considerationem, quasi exortum ex aliqua principiorum consideratione, vel saltem cognitione habituali, non totum in se recepit, quod est in eo a quo oritur: non enim quidquid habituali tenemus cognitione, hoc exprimit intellectus in unius verbi conceptione, sed aliquid eius. Similiter in consideratione unius conclusionis non exprimitur totum id quod erat in virtute principii." (Q. 4, art. 4, "Respondeo").

periential fulness. But such 'violence', as Heidegger himself acknowledges, is an essential characteristic of any genuine re-trieve:

> What is essential in all philosophical discourse is not found in the specific propositions of which it is composed but in that which, although unstated as such, is made evident through these propositions.
>
> It is true that in order to wrest from the actual words that which these words "intend to say," every interpretation must necessarily resort to violence. This violence, however, should not be confused with an action that is wholly arbitrary. The interpretation must be animated and guided by the power of an illuminative idea. Only through the power of this idea can an interpretation risk that which is always audacious, namely, entrusting itself to the secret élan of a work, in order by this élan to get through to the unsaid and to attempt to find an expression for it. The directive idea itself is confirmed by its own power of illumination.[32]

We shall say: Heidegger's investigation of the sense and meaning (*Sinn*) of Being, *das Sein des Seiendes*, leads to the notion of man's Intentional Life considered in its integrity and at its source as the only notion able to penetrate the twofold ambiguity that plagues Heideggerean thought concerning the relationship between Dasein and Being on the one hand, and that between Dasein and man on the other.[33] If, in evaluating our efforts, one should

---

[32] ". . . wie denn überhaupt in jeder philosophischen Erkenntnis nicht das entscheidend werden muss, was sie in den ausgesprochenen Sätzen sagt, sondern was sie als noch Ungesagtes durch das Gesagte vor Augen legt.

"Um freilich dem, was die Worte sagen, dasjenige abzuringen, was sie sagen wollen, muss jede Interpretation notwendig Gewalt brauchen. Solche Gewalt aber kann nicht schweifende Willkür sein. Die Kraft einer vorausleuchtenden Idee muss die Auslegung treiben und leiten. Nur in Kraft dieser kann eine Interpretation das jederzeit Vermessene wagen, sich der verborgenen inneren Leidenschaft eines Werkes anzuvertrauen, um durch diese in das Ungesagte hineingestellt und zum Sagen desselben gezwungen zu werden. Das aber ist ein Weg, auf dem die leitende Idee selbst in ihrer Kraft zur Durchleuchtung an den Tag kommt." (KM, pp. 182-3/206-7).

[33] "If fundamental ontology is not an anthropology, it is and remains an interrogation of There-being insofar as this is the ontological structure of man in his intrinsic finitude. It will be easy, then, to see why There-being is spoken of so often as the equivalent of man (KM, p. 206; WW, pp. 14-17; WG, pp. 46-50, passim). . . . But it could be exceedingly misleading to reduce this intimacy between There-being and man to the simple identification of There-being and the individual, still more to consider the ontological dimension as a *property* of man, more precisely of his intellect. Rather, the There-being is the ontological structure of man, ontologically prior (*ursprünglicher*) to man, and it is the finitude of There-being as an intrinsically finite comprehension of Being that is the ground of the finitude of man. . . . Hence the There-being, rather than a mere synonym for man, is essentially a coming-to-pass that takes place *in* man. Of course, this poses problems. If There-being takes place *in* man, what is the precise relation between the two? For that matter, what man are we talking about? *There is an obscurity, then,* not only concerning the relationship between There-being and Being but concerning the relationship between There-being and man – all the more, then, between Being and man." (Richardson, H:TPT, pp. 45-6: the last emphasis is supplied. To get some idea of how thoroughly this double ambiguity permeates Heidegger's thought, see also pp. 67, 97, 141, 146, 192, 241-2, 248, 279, 347, 349, 350-53, 357, 409, 413, 437, 486, 495, 536-7, 539-40, 627, 635.).

accuse us of doing violence to "that which is said" (*das Gesagte*), he would miss the point completely. He would fail to grasp the whole sense of an effort at re-trieve, which is to say what an author did not say, could not say, but somehow made manifest. The only legitimate evaluative approach is to precise and criticize the fundamental idea which commands this 'violence' and gives it in a profound way its sense. What is at stake is nothing less than the difference between a comparative textual analysis and a philosophical study:

A genuine commentary never understands the text better than the author of the text, but it does understand the text otherwise. Only this "otherwise" must be such that it touches the very same thing that the text commented on considers.[34]

Besides, with the appearance of such a masterful study as Fr. Richardson's *Heidegger: Through Phenomenology to Thought*, which traces the stages of Heidegger's development with tireless attention to its full complexity, detail, and subtlety, the danger of distortion in our own very different effort is pretty well allayed.[35] Let us consider directly, then, the experience which first set Heidegger along the paths of philosophy.

---

[34] "Eine rechte Erläuterung versteht jedoch den Text nie besser als dessen Verfasser ihn verstand, wohl aber anders. Allein dieses Andere muss so sein, dass es das Selbe trifft dem der erläuterte Text nachdenkt." – Martin Heidegger, *Holzwege* (Frankfurt: Klostermann, 1950), p. 197. See also p. 235. Hereafter referred to as HW.

[35] De Waelhens, himself a student of Heidegger's thought for over two decades, feels justified in saying: "Fr. Richardson's book will probably constitute an epoch in the history of Heideggerian thought. For the first time, indeed, and at the very moment when this thought approaches its decline, the itinerary of this long quest has been retraced for us in its totality and presented in a sense which for today and for a long time to come seems to be definitive." – "Reflections on Heidegger's Development: Apropos of a Recent Book," *International Philosophical Quarterly*, V (September, 1965), 475.

CHAPTER III

THE FORGOTTENNESS OF BEING

> "Wo immer und wie weit auch alle Forschung das
> Seiende absucht, nirgends findet sie das Sein. Sie trifft
> immer nur das Seiende, weil sie zum voraus in der Absicht
> ihres Erklärens beim Seienden beharrt. Das Sein jedoch
> ist keine seiende Beschaffenheit an Seiendem. Das Sein
> lässt sich nicht gleich dem Seienden gegenständlich vor-
> und herstellen. Dies schlechthin Andere zu allem Seienden
> ist das Nicht-Seiende. Aber dieses Nichts west als das
> Sein."
> M. Heidegger, *Was ist Metaphysik*, p. 45.

Philosophy, it has been said, takes rise from attentiveness to the mystery of totality as such. This is at least verified in the case of Heidegger's philosophy, and it explains perhaps why he at first confused his probing of the Being-question with a formally metaphysical inquiry.

Man poses questions which "react" even against the privileged role of the questioner himself, in that these peculiar questions regard all things equally (including therefore the questioner himself) inasmuch as they are. Such are the so-called metaphysical questions, questions which go beyond this or that region of the real to interrogate beings as such. Well and good, said the young Heidegger, but don't overlook the fact that such questioning "has always to be based on the essential situation of existence which puts the question."[1] In other words, Heidegger asks, what about the fact that the placing of a metaphysical question exhibits a twofold nature? It not only points toward the existence of the rocks, trees and stars, but simultaneously points "back" to to the phenomenon which makes such a question possible in the first place.

---

[1] "Hieraus entnehmen wir die Anweisung: das metaphysische Fragen muss im Ganzen und aus der wesentlichen Lage des fragenden Daseins gestellt werden." *Was ist Metaphysik*, p. 24; cf. p. 38. Cf. also the English translation, "What is Metaphysics?" by R. F. C. Hull and Alan Crick, *Existence and Being*, W. Brock, ed. (Chicago: Gateway, 1949), pp. 325 and 344. Hereafter this text of Heidegger's will be referred to as WM; German page references will be followed by a and corresponding references to the Hull-Crick translation.

This phenomenon consists in the awareness that "in some way or another, the human mind is all things" (*anima est quodammodo omnia*);[2] and Heidegger was so struck by this realization that he called it "the ground phenomenon of our Dasein," i.e., of the condition of human awareness.[3]

As certainly as we shall never comprehend absolutely the totality of beings, it is equally certain that we find ourselves placed in the midst of beings and that they are somehow revealed in totality. Ultimately there is an *essential difference* between *comprehending* the totality of beings and *finding* ourselves in the midst of beings-in-totality. The former is absolutely impossible. The latter is going on in existence all the time.[4]

In a certain sense, one can discern in this "essential difference" the entire preoccupation of Heidegger I, because in meditating this difference one comes to realize in an initial way what Heidegger means by the forgottenness of Being.

In the course of lived experience we find ourselves in the midst of what-is-in-totality (*das Seiende im Ganzen*), wholly pervaded by it. However distracting our daily preoccupations may become (the "everydayness of Dasein"), they are still maintained within the unity of a whole, within a World-horizon.

It goes without saying that *the World* is not identified simply with the *sum* of all beings. First of all, such a sum cannot be easily thought about: how add up things, values, institutions, ideas, men? Besides, such a sum would not add anything to the factors that compose it. Now we ought to say of each one of these beings (though in different senses) that they are, whether to the World or within the World. It is necessary, then, to give to World a particular signification, which the notion of sum does not even begin to suggest.[5]

For if we attend to this phenomenon of World carefully, we discover the rather startling fact that our awareness of it is permeated by a peculiar concealment or negativity: the fact that beings always stand out from a background of totality, despite the fact that we never comprehend this totality in

---

[2] St. Thomas Aquinas, *In II de anima*, lect. 13, n. 787; *Summa theologica*, I, q. 16, art. 3; *De veritate*, q. 1, art. 1; *et alibi*.

[3] ". . . das Grundgeschehen unseres Da-seins." (WM, p. 31/334 and 41/348). Cf. SZ, pp. 13-14. Also *Vom Wesen der Wahrheit* (Frankfurt: Klostermann, 1954), pp. 20-21; English translation cf. by R. F. C. Hull and Alan Crick, "On the Essence of Truth," in *Existence and Being*, p. 315. Hereafter referred to as WW, with English page references following the German reference.

[4] "So sicher wir nie das Ganze des Seienden an sich absolut erfassen, so gewiss finden wir uns doch inmitten des irgendwie im Ganzen enthülten Seienden gestellt. Am Ende besteht ein wesenhafter Unterschied zwischen dem Erfassen des Ganzen des Seienden an sich und dem Sichbefinden inmitten des Seienden im Ganzen. Jenes ist grundsätzlich unmöglich. Dieses geschieht ständig in unserem Dasein." (WM, p. 30/333).

[5] A. De Waelhens, "Reflections on Heidegger's Development," p. 481.

an actual way, culminates in the realization that even though Being reveals itself in revealing beings or "entities," it cannot be seized for and by itself in any positive way, and therefore conceals itself in the very beings to which it somehow "gives rise". Heidegger discovered that this "concealment" aspect of the disclosure of beings, though certainly implicated in the question of the nature of Being, was ignored in all the philosophers whose works he could lay his hands on: "So it happened that the first experience of the Being-question was followed quickly by the experience of the forgottenness of Being."[6]

This peculiar "reticence" of Being is a striking phenomenon, and it is perhaps surprising that it had never been thematized as such prior to Heidegger. We may remark, however, that it did not go entirely unnoticed in traditional philosophizing. St. Thomas described this striking phenomenon in an equally striking formula: the "contraction" of Being into the modes of discourse, that is, the categories of language.[7] It is worth noting that this formula of St. Thomas is roughly equivalent to what Heidegger characterizes

[6] Richardson, "The Place of the Unconscious in Heidegger," *Review of Existential Psychology and Psychiatry*, V (Fall, 1965), 269.

[7] *De veritate*, q. I, art. I; *In V Met.*, lect. 9, nn. 889-894, esp. n. 890. According to Heidegger, the Not ("non potest esse et non esse simul") doesn't come into Being through negation as an "intentional act" of some "knowing subject": rather, negation as a conscious intentional act is only possible on the basis of the Not which derives from the nihilation of Nothing, i.e., from the "withdrawal" of the totality, i.e., the contraction of Being into a language-category (see WM, pp. 28-9/331, 34/338, 36-7/341-2). "As Heidegger goes about meditating the process of *a-letheia*, this strange paradox (hidden from the metaphysician) that Being contracts into the beings it makes manifest and hides by the very fact that it reveals, never loses its fascination for him. He interrogates Being precisely inasmuch as it is hidden always in *on* (yet different from *on*), for it is 'upon the hidden [dimension] of *on* that metaphysics remains grounded (WM, p. 20).' We find striking confirmation of this in the inaugural lecture at Freiburg (1929), when, in posing the question that gives the lecture its title, 'What is Metaphysics?', he meditates the sense of Non-being (*Nichts*). The hiddenness of Being (in beings) is, then, for Heidegger as essential a part of his experience as Being itself.

"What we call here the 'hiddenness' of Being (in beings) may be understood in terms of a 'not' that contracts Being in beings and at the same time differentiates it from them. Since the function of Being is simply to en-light-en beings, then this contracting 'not' is intrinsic to its very nature. For want of a better word, let us call the 'not' – character of Being 'negativity'. Then the manifestive power that shines forth in beings as beings we may call 'positivity'. Once we comprehend this fusion of positivity and negativity into the unity of a single process, we begin to grasp what Heidegger understands as the process of truth. For truth, understood in the radical sense of *a-letheia*, is literally non-(*a-*) concealment (*lethe*). Being as the process of non-concealment is that which permits beings to become non-concealed (positivity), although the process is so permeated by 'not' that Being itself remains concealed (negativity). To think Being in its truth, then, is to think it in terms of both positivity and negativity at once.

"In the simplest of terms: Heidegger's whole effort is to interrogate the positive-negative process of *a-letheia*, insofar as it gives rise to metaphysics." (Richardson, H:TPT, pp. 8-9).

as "the permeation of Dasein by nihilating modes of behavior," which "behavior" alone "brings Dasein face to face with beings as such."[8] We have here some first indication that to think Being as such (in Heidegger's sense), then, will be to think it as in some manner (as yet unspecified) concealed: what permeates the Horizon of Totality as the definition of its comprehensibility as such and in every particular sector? Hence Heidegger's otherwise puzzling remark: "In the disclosure and explication of Being, Beings are in every case our preliminary and accompanying theme (*das Vor- und Mitthematische*); but our real theme is Being."[9] The remark points out that although Being cannot *be* except in beings, it can manifest itself sufficiently *as* itself to permit us to discern it in its *difference* from beings.[10]

This same realization can be achieved in a number of ways. The notion of Being, insofar as it is manifested (or "verified") in any particular being, has a confused intelligibility which indistinctly mingles everything that is actually found in the entity. We must go so far as to say that entities as particular beings could not even be experienced "factually" unless Being itself were previously grasped in a way that is very different from conceptualizations of this or that kind of being.[11]

Only because Being is 'in the consciousness' – that is to say, only because it is understandable in Dasein – can Dasein also understand and conceptualize such characteristics of Being as independence, the 'in-itself', and Reality in general. Only because of this are 'independent' beings, as encountered within-the-world, accessible to circumspection.[12]

Thus, while everything that we can know, feel, or experience in any way is understandable to us in terms of its state of Being, Being itself transcends, goes beyond any possible beings or class of beings. Yet this transcending

---

[8] "Diese Möglichkeiten des nichtenden Verhaltens – Kräfte, in denen das Dasein seine Geworfenheit trägt, wenngleich nicht meistert – sind keine Arten des blossen Verneinens. Das verwehrt ihnen aber nicht, sich im Nein und in der Verneinung auszusprechen. Dadurch verrät sich freilich erst recht die Leere und Weite der Verneinung. Die Durchdrungenheit des Daseins vom nichtenden Verhalten bezeugt die ständige und freilich verdunkelte Offenbarkeit des Nichts, das ursprünglich nur die Angst enthüllt." (WM, p. 37/343). ". . . das Wesen des ursprünglich nichtenden Nichts liegt in dem: es bringt das Da-sein allererst vor das Seiende als ein solches." (WM, p. 34/339). "Da-sein heisst: Hineingehaltenheit in das Nichts." (WM, p. 35/339).

[9] "In der Erschliessung und Explikation des Seins ist das Seiende jeweils das Vor- und Mitthematische, im eigentlichen Thema steht das Sein." (SZ, p. 67).

[10] See H:TPT, pp. 578-9.

[11] See John of St. Thomas, *Cursus Phil.*, II, q. 1, art. 3. SZ, p. 315.

[12] "Nur weil Sein 'im Bewusstsein' ist, das heisst verstehbar im Dasein, deshalb kann das Dasein auch Seinscharaktere wie Unabhängigkeit, 'Ansich', überhaupt Realität verstehen und zu Begriff bringen. Nur deshalb ist 'unabhängiges' Seiendes als innerweltlich Begegnendes umsichtig zugänglich." (SZ, pp. 207-8).

Being itself is (in this similar to the beings it is transcendent relative to) essentially finite "because it appears *only* in a plurality of beings that it cannot abolish as a plurality. Presence and what is present in this Presence never coincide."[13]

Being in its manifestations is necessarily finite. Hence it withdraws behind the beings to which it imparts presence, concealing itself in its own revelations. This self-concealing revealment is precisely what Heidegger understands by the mystery of Being.[14]

Gazing out through the revelation of what-is (present) at any moment into the mystery (of Presence itself), says Heidegger, "is a questioning in the sense of the only question that exists: What is that which is as such in totality?"[15] Being turns all attention from itself and directs Dasein's gaze toward beings. The "empirically" present beings, on the other hand, are revealed *as* so present by reason of the effulgence of Being, as that which is Non-being.

How comprehend this mysterious reticence which is mutual to both Non-being and beings, each revealed by reason of what it is *not*? This "not" which separates beings and Non-being is difference, sc. the ontological difference. And it is precisely here, it would seem, that the full weight of the question mark falls.[16]

Heidegger's Being regarded entitatively, i.e., from the standpoint of beings (entities), is Non-being (*das Nichts und das Nicht-Seiende*). Yet this horizon of objectivity (of transobjective subjects in the sense of *das Seiende,* beings or "things" as present in awareness) designated as Non-being admits of a positive description in terms of Being itself, *das Sein des Seiendes.*[17] "This helps us to see that the entire problematic of revealment-concealment in Being is nothing more than the problem of the 'not' which constitutes the ontological difference as such."[18] That which must be rendered thematic is the Being of beings in its difference (Non-being) from beings, and indeed in its difference from what may be said about the beings precisely as such. "Being always must be contracted (therefore negatived) to beings, hence comports the risk of being considered only *as* a being and thereby of being

---

[13] De Waelhens, p. 496.

[14] H:TPT, p. 448.

[15] "Die Entbergung des Seienden als eines solchen ist in sich zugleich die Verbergung des Seienden im Ganzen. Im Zugleich der Entbergung und Verbergung waltet die Irre ... Der Ausblick in das Geheimnis aus der Irre ist das Fragen im Sinne der einzigen Frage, was das Seiende als solches im Ganzen sei. Dieses Fragen denkt die wesentlich beirrende und daher in ihrer Mehrdeutigkeit noch nicht gemeisterte Frage nach dem *Sein* des Seienden." (WW, p. 23/319).

[16] Richardson, H:TPT, p. 203. See also p. 234.

[17] Cf. H:TPT, p. 200.

[18] *Ibid.*, p. 565.

forgotten completely."[19] The central problem of philosophy – as Heidegger takes it over – is a problem of discerning Being *for* itself, even if not *by* itself.[20] One begins to feel the justice of Fr. Richardson's counsel to be "extremely cautious in seeing a correlation between what Heidegger means by Being and any sense that the scholastics, such as St. Thomas Aquinas, gave to the term."[21]

For Heidegger, "that which never and nowhere 'is' discloses itself as that which differs from everything that 'is', i.e., what we call 'Being'."[22] For Heidegger, "Being is not an existing quality of beings, nor, unlike beings, can Being be conceived and established objectively. This, the purely 'Other' than everything that 'is', is that-which-is-not (*das Nicht-Seiende*). Yet this 'Nothing' functions as Being,"[23] and "shows itself as essentially belonging to beings while they are slipping away in totality."[24]

This unusual manner of articulating Being (as the comprehensibility of things, or the ground of awareness' every level) gives us the widest possible concept of beings as such: they are something and not nothing. A delusion, the meaning of a poem, God, an isolated love, hope, thinking, seeming, becoming, feeling, dreaming... are evidently something and not nothing, although they are not concrete, sensible things in the (metaphysically) primary sense of the word – i.e., although they are not 'substances'. Starting from the idea of something, a "real thing" is no longer played off against an "ideal thing" and the one measured by the other: both are set off against Nothing (*das Nichts*) as the totally other to all things, and understood in their most fundamental character as "not nothing". Heidegger's idea of Being formulates the demand that the "thought of Being" start from the widest and deepest of all distinctions – the difference between something and nothing.[25] With this start, the problem of the nothing is drawn into the very

[19] *Ibid.*, p. 432.

[20] See *ibid.*, pp. 562-5, "The Case of the Altered Epilogue." Also pp. 424, 432, 439, 501, 542, 554, 563, 582 fn. 14.

[21] *Ibid.*, p. 320 fn. 27.

[22] ". . . was nie und nirgends ein Seiendes ist, sich entschleiert als das von allem Seienden Sichunterscheidende, das wir das Sein nennen." (WM: Ep, p. 45/353).

[23] "Das Sein jedoch ist keine seiende Beschaffenheit an Seiendem. Das Sein lässt sich nicht gleich dem Seienden gegenständlich vor- und herstellen. Dies schlechthin Andere zu allem Seienden ist das Nicht-Seiende. Aber dieses Nichts west als das Sein." (WM: Ep, p. 45/353).

[24] ". . . bekundet sich das Nichts eigens mit und an dem Seienden als einem entgleitenden im Ganzen." (WM, p. 33/338).

[25] Regarding this methodologically grounded (as we shall see later) manner of drawing the distinction of "something" over against "nothing", and allowing for all the very real and deep differences between the Phenomenology of Heidegger and that of Husserl, the criticism levelled by Maritain makes several telling points: "En définitive il semble que dès l'origine la phénoménologie ait procédé à une sorte d'hybridation contre nature entre

center of the philosophical project – and yet this "nothing" is the veil of Being itself.[26]

When Heidegger asks, "Why are there beings, why is there anything at all, rather than nothing?", and characterizes this as the most far-reaching,

l'ontologique et le logique. Il est grave pour une philosophie de ne pouvoir pas distinguer entre l'*ens reale* et l'*ens rationis*. Elle risque de s'engager, en dépit de toutes ses protestations contre le constructivisme, dans l' 'élucidation' d'un univers de fictions, et de laisser de côté le devoir propre d'une honnête philosophie, qui est d'assigner les raisons du donné et d'en acquérir l'intelligence. D'autres inconvénients devaient surgir. En écartant le sujet transobjectif [in Husserl's case, by way of a specially designed *epoche* or 'suspension of belief'; in Heidegger's case, simply by virtue of a more pure methodological conception which, as we suggested already and will consider in some detail, determined the very inner character of his 'Thought of Being' even through its 'reversal'], on introduit dans le monde lui-même des essences intelligibles et de l' 'a-priori' les effets propres de la matérialité, et c'est en vain qu'on essaie de ne pas traiter ce monde à la facon empiriste, comme ceux qui méconnaissent les nécessités intelligibles et qui pensent avec leurs yeux et leur mains traitent le monde du concret sensible. (Footnote: Si la phénoménologie se donne essentiellement pour une analyse ou description 'eidétique', c'est bien, semble-t-il, pour remédier à cet inconvénient. Mais le remède reste insuffisant. En faisant varier librement, par l'imagination, l'objet des diverses fonctions intentionnelles pour ne retenir que l'*eidos* de celles-ci, on ne dégage pas devant l'esprit une nécessité de droit saisie dans une essence, on constate seulement une nécessité de fait de la vie intentionnelle, succédané de la véritable nécessité intelligible. La remarque de Victor Delbos, que la phénoménologie risque de soumettre la pensée à l'indétermination du sublogique, trouve ici même une de ses vérifications.) Car si l'intelligence en sa vie propre est pure, je ne dis pas des apports expérimentaux d'où elle tire tous ses biens, je dis de toute coaction matérielle et de toute servilité empirique, c'est parce que tout le contingent, le potentiel et le matériel, toute la masse d'inertie qui peut se définir par la résistance à l'intelligibilité, fait partie du monde auquel elle s'applique et qu'elle connaît, mais est situé hors d'elle comme ce monde lui-même. D'autre part, du fait que les essences perçues par l'esprit ne sont plus saisies en des sujets transobjectifs existant hors de l'esprit et engagés eux-memes dans le flux du temps, les objets extra-temporels de l'intelligence se trouvent, par un retour inattendu de platonisme, séparés de l'existence réelle et temporelle; et pour rejoindre celle-ci il ne restera plus qu'à invertir l'intelligence en donnant au temps le pas sur l'être, soit qu'on cherche avec M. Bergson a substituer le temps à l'être, soit qu'on cherche avec M. Heidegger à asseoir l'être sur le temps. Ce qui est assurer le réalisme en en détruisant le premier fondement." (DS, pp. 206-8/106-7). The positive factors of Heideggerian methodological consideration which such criticism necessarily leaves out of account we shall try to highlight throughout our study, though in the end it will be plain that they are not sufficient to nullify the full thrust of the criticism.

[26] Adapted from King, *Heidegger's Philosophy*, p. 11. See also WM, p. 41/347-8: "Einzig weil das Nichts im Grunde des Daseins offenbar ist, kann die volle Befremdlichkeit des Seienden über uns kommen. Nur wenn die Befremdlichkeit des Seienden uns bedrängt, weckt es und zieht es auf sich die Verwunderung. Nur auf dem Grunde der Verwunderung – d. h. der Offenbarkeit des Nichts – entspringt das 'Warum?'. Nur weil das Warum als solches möglich ist, können wir in bestimmter Weise nach Gründen fragen und begründen. Nur weil wir fragen und begründen können, ist unserer Existenz das Schicksal des Forschers in die Hand gegeben.

"Die Frage nach dem Nichts stellt uns – die Fragenden – selbst in Frage. Sie ist eine metaphysische."

deepest, and most fundamental of all questions (because through this question what-is-in-totality, *das Seiende im Ganzen*, "is for the first time opened up *as such* with a view to its possible ground, and in the act of questioning it is kept open"[27]), he means thereby:

How is it possible that beings (independently of "where" they might have come from, "who" or "what" may have "caused" them, as metaphysics understands these terms) can *be* (manifest) as beings. In other words, it is a question about the coming-to-pass of the lighting-process of *a-letheia*, which we now understand as the emergence of the ontological difference. What is more, it is a question about this process as permeated by negativity. Heidegger himself expands the question thus: ". . . How does it come about that everywhere [about us] beings have the primacy . . . while that which is not a being, which is thought of as Non-being in the sense of Being itself, remains forgotten?. . ."[28]

Being for Heidegger is precisely that (ground of comprehensibility or awareness-possibility) which, from the ontic (entitative) standpoint of things (beings) is Non-being.[29] Conversely, Non-being (for Heidegger) is Being itself stated in other than ontic terms. This experience of the forgotten-ness of Being was brought clearly into language by Heidegger in 1949. "In its answers to the question concerning beings as such, metaphysics operates

[27] "Wenn wir daher die Frage 'Warum ist überhaupt Seiendes und nicht vielmehr Nichts?' in ihrem Fragesinn recht vollziehen, müssen wir die Hervorhebung von jeglichem besonderen, einzelnen Seienden unterlassen, auch den Hinweis auf den Menschen. . . . Innerhalb des Seienden im Ganzen ist kein Rechtsgrund zu finden für die Hervorhebung gerade *des* Seienden, das man Mensch nennt und zu dem wir selbst zufällig gehören.

"Aber insofern das Seiende im Ganzen jemals in die genannte Frage gerückt wird, tritt zu ihm das Fragen und es zu diesem Fragen doch in eine ausgezeichnete, weil einzigartige Beziehung. Denn durch dieses Fragen wird das Seiende im Ganzen allererst *als ein solches* und in der Richtung auf seinen möglichen Grund eröffnet und im Fragen offengehalten." (EM, p. 3/4). See also pp. 1/1 and 2/2-3.

[28] Richardson, H:TPT, p. 14. Cf. "Heidegger and God," pp. 27-8: "For Leibniz, of course, the formula asks effectively about a Supreme Being that grounds all other beings and therefore is an eminently metaphysical question. For Heidegger, the question means: How is it possible that beings, independently of 'where' they might have come from, 'who' or 'what' may have caused them as metaphysics understands these terms, can *be* (manifest) as beings? In other words, it is a question about the coming-to-pass of the nonconcealment of beings, about the emergence of the ontological difference."

[29] *Ibid.*, pp. 200, 424, 564, 572. Also Dondeyne, p. 278: "Comme il a été dit plus haut, c'est parce que l'homme se tient en quelque sort dans le néant, qu'il peut rencontrer l'étant, e 'laisser être', lui laisser dire ce qu'il a à dire (entgegen-stehen-lassen). Ce néant n'est pas le 'Nichts schlechthin', avons-nous vu, la suppression par la pensée de la totalité de l'étant, mais la possibilité toute positive, originelle et transcendentale de se tenir ouvert pour la rencontre de l'étant, ou, ce qui revient au même, de 'former', de 'projeter', de 'tenir ouvert l'horizon dans lequel l'étant pourra être rencontré dans son être'. Ce pouvoir fondamental de 'se tenir ouvert en projetant un horizon de rencontre', Heidegger l'appelle: 'das Grund-vermögen einer entgegenstehenlassende Zuwendung zu. . .'. Il est le correspondant de la corrélation transcendentale kantienne, la 'Beziehung auf den Gegenstand überhaupt = X'."

with a prior conception of Being."[30] Oblivious to the peculiar nature of this prior conception, this "preontological" comprehension which is precisely not rooted in the order of pure reason (*Vernunft*) but "below" it, metaphysics is cut off from the truth of Being: "To metaphysics, the nature of truth always appears only in the derivative form of the truth of knowledge."[31]

Being metaphysics, it is by its very nature excluded from the experience of Being; for it always represents beings (*on*) only with an eye to what of Being has already manifested itself as beings (*a on*). But metaphysics never pays attention to what has concealed itself in this very *on* insofar as it became unconcealed.[32]

Perhaps this is sufficient to effect the first phase of our re-trieve of the early Heidegger, scil., the re-call of the experience of the forgottenness of Being.

Heidegger's guide-question is: What is it that is called Being? "If it does not concern itself with beings and inquire about their first cause among all beings, then the question must begin from [i.e., designate] that which is not a being. And this is precisely what the question names, and it capitalizes the word: the Nothing,"[33] or, as we might write it, "the No-thing". The point is clear:

If Being is not a being, nor the sum total of them, the process of nonconcealment (truth or truth-ing) has a built-in "not" character to it that contracts, constricts, or hides it within the beings it lets be (manifest). As a result, if we try to describe Being merely in terms of the beings that it is not, then the most we can say about it, perhaps, is that it is not a being; and if for a moment, and simply for purposes of exposition, we call every being a "thing," then Being is not a thing, it is No-thing, it is Nothing (*Nichts*). Being (*Sein*) and Nothing (*Nichts*) are one.[34]

That will suffice then for purposes of exposition, for purposes of re-trieving the initial problem-experience and flash of intuitivity which forbid Heidegger

[30] "Die Metaphysik hat in ihren Antworten auf ihre Frage nach dem Seienden als solchem vor diesem schon das Sein vorgestellt. Sie spricht Sein notwendig aus und darum ständig. Aber die Metaphysik bringt das Sein selbst nicht zur Sprache, weil sie das Sein nicht in seiner Wahrheit und die Wahrheit nicht als die Unverborgenheit und diese nicht in ihrem Wesen bedenkt." (WM: In, p. 10/210).

[31] "Das Wesen der Wahrheit erscheint der Metaphysik immer nur in der schon abkünftigen Gestalt der Wahrheit der Erkenntnis und der Aussage dieser." (WM: In, pp. 10-11/ 210).

[32] "Als Metaphysik ist sie von der Erfahrung des Seins durch ihr eigenes Wesen ausgeschlossen; denn sie stellt das Seiende (*on*) stets nur in dem vor, was sich als Seiendes (*a on*) schon von diesem her gezeigt hat. Die Metaphysik achtet jedoch dessen nie, was sich in eben diesem *on*, insofern es unverborgen wurde, auch schon verborgen hat." (WM, p. 20/218).

[33] "Wenn sie nicht beim Seienden anfragt und für dieses die erste seiende Ursache erkundet, dann muss die Frage bei dem ansetzen, was nicht das Seiende ist. Solches nennt die Frage und schreibt es gross: das Nichts . . . ." (WM: In, p. 22/220).

[34] Richardson, "Heidegger and God," p. 25.

to accept the formulation of the Being-question given by Aristotle. But *"to keep to* the problem of Nothing" as the problem of Being itself (or 'as such'), "necessitates changing man into his Dasein."[35] Heidegger I came to regard as a decisive factor in the effort to recover Being from its forgottenness "the essential experience that only in and from Dasein, as a thing to which we have entry, can any approximation to the truth of Being evolve for historical man."[36] Why so? For an altogether fundamental reason:

The Being of beings is comprehensible – and in this lies the innermost finitude of transcendence – only if Dasein by virtue of its very nature constrains itself within the Nothing. Holding oneself to the Nothing is no arbitrary and casual attempt to "think" about this Nothing, but an event which underlies all finding oneself in the midst of beings already on hand. The intrinsic possibility of this event must be clarified in a fundamental-ontological analytic of Dasein.[37]

Yet how does such a constrainment within the Nothing by virtue of the very nature of Dasein become in the first place possible? And in what sense does it provide the necessary avenue for an analytic which is guided from the outset solely by the question about the sense and truth of Being? Nothing less than a clarification in principle of how man is "changed" into his Dasein can establish the bounds of the question in *Sein und Zeit,* and therewith the possible ways in which Being can be thought in its "mittent" character (*Geschick*), i.e., as it emerges in Heidegger II,[38] without foregoing the rigor of the preliminary analyses.

By what method then was Heidegger able to effect this "essential transformation" of man, to precise the notion of Dasein as the focus for any progress in formalizing the Being-question? The entire character of the Heideggerean problematic is at stake with this question. The remaining chapters will attempt to clarify and deal with the problem systematically, i.e., in an adequate manner. We may point out immediately two counts which

[35] "Wie steht es um das Nichts?" (WM, p. 33).
"Die für unsere Absicht zunächst allein wesentliche Antwort ist schon gewonnen, wenn wir darauf achthaben, dass die Frage nach dem Nichts wirklich gestellt bleibt. Hierzu wird verlangt, dass wir die Verwandlung des Menschen in sein Da-sein. . ." (WM: Ep, p. 33/337).
[36] "Das im Vortrag versuchte Denken erfüllt sich in der wesentlichen Erfahrung, dass erst aus dem Da-sein, in das der Mensch eingehen kann, eine Nähe zur Wahrheit des Seins für den geschichtlichen Menschen sich vorbereitet." (WW, p. 27/323).
[37] "Das Sein des Seienden ist aber überhaupt nur verstehbar – und darin liegt die tiefste Endlichkeit der Transzendenz – wenn das Dasein im Grunde seines Wesens sich in das Nichts hineinhält. Dieses Sichhineinhalten in das Nichts ist kein beliebiges und zuweilen versuchtes 'Denken' des Nichts, sondern ein Geschehen, das allem Sichbefinden inmitten des schon Seienden zugrundeliegt und in einer fundamental-ontologischen Analytik des Daseins nach seiner inneren Möglichkeit aufgehellt werden muss." (KM, pp. 214-5/246).
[38] See the remarks on this point in the Introduction to the present study.

make the understanding of this question decisive. First of all because the preliminary notion of Dasein can hardly be appreciated rightly except through a clear insight into Heidegger's understanding of the nature of phenomenological research. And secondly, as was already suggested, because much of the difficulties of Heidegger II in explaining the involvement of Being in human nature are the consequence of his failure to clarify the relation between man in his Dasein and man as entity (*animal rationale*), that is, the ontico-ontological structural interarticulation which gives rise to the possibility of a categorical *as well as* an existentialistic understanding of the human reality.[39] For this it is not sufficient merely to note:

Metaphysical thinking does, of course, inquire about the being which is the source and originator of this light [of Being]. But the light itself is considered sufficiently illuminated as soon as we recognize that we look through it whenever we look at beings . . . The truth of Being may thus be called the ground in which metaphysics, as the root of the tree of philosophy, is kept and from which it is nourished.
But what still appears as ground from this point of view is presumably something else, once it is experienced in its own terms – something as yet unsaid, according to which the essence of metaphysics, too, is something else and not metaphysics.[40]

The inadequate sufficiency of this perspective will have to be shown. For now let us simply restate in a summary way this first step of re-trieving Being from its forgottenness. The experience of the forgottenness of Being "involves the crucial conjecture that in view of the unconcealedness of Being the involvement of Being in human nature is an essential feature of Being"[41] – for if Being as Presence and what is present in this Presence (namely, beings) never coincide, yet neither can Presence be such save in the essential nature of a being that has openness for encounter with beings as its Being. Once this has been grasped,

we can no longer accept the claim of metaphysics that it takes care of the fundamental involvement in "Being" and that it decisively determines all relations to beings as such. [For whenever the question about what beings are is raised, beings

_____

[39] A possibility readily recognized by Heidegger himself: cf. SZ, pp. 45, 54-5, 118, *inter alia.*

[40] ". . . fragt das metaphysische Denken allerdings nach der seienden Quelle und nach einem Urheber des Lichtes. Dieses selbst gilt dadurch als erhellt genug, dass es jeder Hinsicht auf das Seiende die Durchsicht gewährt . . . Die Wahrheit des Seins kann deshalb der Grund heissen, in dem die Metaphysik als die Wurzel des Baumes der Philosophie gehalten, aus dem sie genährt wird.
Allein das, was so noch als Grund erscheint, ist vermutlich, wenn es aus ihm selbst erfahren wird, ein Anderes und noch Ungesagtes, demgemäss auch das Wesen der Metaphysik etwas anderes ist als die Metaphysik." (WM: In, pp. 7/9-207-9).

[41] ". . . die . . . Erfahrung der Seinsvergessenheit schliesst die alles tragende Vermutung ein, gemäss der Unverborgenheit des Seins gehöre der Bezug des Seins zum Menschenwesen gar zum Sein selbst." (WM: In, p. 13/212).

as such are in view – which view was possible in the first place thanks only to the light of Being. Yet this light itself does not fall within the purview of questioning into what beings are in their transobjective or metalogical subjectivity.] But this "overcoming of metaphysics" does not abolish metaphysics. As long as man remains the *animal rationale* he is also the *animal metaphysicum*. As long as man understands himself as the rational animal, metaphysics belongs, as Kant said, to the nature of man. But if our thinking should succeed in its efforts to go back into the ground of metaphysics, it might help to bring about a change [in the conception of] human nature, accompanied by a transformation of [the task of] metaphysics.[42]

It is a transformation of the idea of human nature that marks the first step away from the forgottenness of Being toward the determination of the sense of Being. The step is possible once it is clearly realized that what is most basic in man as man is not a specific trait in the ontic (entitative) order, but rather something which precisely does not reside in man after the manner of an "accident" or "inherent property", something that does not correspond in any way with an observable fact, something that cannot be fitted into a substance/accident or subject/object ontology according to what is most proper and formal to it, something which in fact belongs to an order fundamentally distinguished from the ontic (entitative) order and which lies as the prior possibility for any subject-object "field" as such, namely, man's comprehension of Being. Man is before and during all else the Comprehendor of Being, the being endowed from his source with a comprehension of Being. This comprehension is not at all present in him under the guise of a knowledge that is either completely achieved or conceptually explicit, yet it is always at issue in whatever man does. Self-awareness, *prise de conscience*, is but an ontic and therefore essentially inadequate expression of the ontological truth that man is the being for whom, in his Being, there is concern for Being. The "comprehension" in question is the ontological "reality" lying behind man's ontic distinctiveness as radically other than any specific ontic traits which are at most secondary consequences, mediate derivatives of the ontological dimension of the human reality – it is this ontological dimension belonging essentially to the order of *intentionale* (in the non-Husserlian sense yet to be determined) that Heidegger has in mind when he uses the term Dasein (There-being) to designate the Being of man.

[42] "Der Anspruch der Metaphysik, den tragenden Bezug zum 'Sein' zu verwalten und alles Verhältnis zum Seienden als solchem massgebend zu bestimmen, wird hinfällig. Doch diese 'Überwindung der Metaphysik' beseitigt die Metaphysik nicht. Solange der Mensch das animal rationale bleibt, ist er das animal metaphysicum. Solange der Mensch sich als das vernünftige Lebewesen versteht, gehört die Metaphysik nach dem Wort Kants zur Natur des Menschen. Wohl könnte dagegen das Denken, wenn ihm glückt, in den Grund der Metaphysik zurückzugehen, einen Wandel des Wesens des Menschen mitveranlassen, mit welchem Wandel eine Verwandlung der Metaphysik einherginge." (WM:In, p. 9/209).

In the transforming of the conception of essential human nature required by the perspectives arising directly from the re-collection of Being in its forgottenness, this pre-conceptual grasp of Being which is always at issue for man in his Dasein "will be called *preontological*"; and the accompanying transformation of the metaphysical task in this re-trieved perspective on the Being-question will be a turning away from the concern with transobjective subjects of *esse* in order to engage immediately in the explicitation of this pre-ontological understanding of Being "by raising it to the level of concepts."[43] "But in that case the question of Being is nothing other than the radicalization of an essential tendency-of-Being which belongs to Dasein itself – the pre-ontological comprehension of Being."[44]

"More original than man is the finitude of Dasein in him,"[45] as that structure which lets beings be manifest to man (including himself as a being among beings), thereby rendering all encounter and comportment with beings in the first instance possible. "More original than man is the finitude of Dasein in him," as the There of Being among beings "which is the source of unity between the Being-question and the finitude of man who poses it."[46]

But with all this we have still done no more than describe an initial experience and sketch the requirements for dealing with it philosophically. The question of meeting those requirements methodologically remains open. Granted that the changing of man into his Dasein calls for a transformation in the notion of essential human nature (with a consequent transformation in the fundamental task of ontology) based on man's comprehension of Being, it still remains for us to clarify in principle what is at stake in any notion of human nature which prescinds from the ontic or entitative dimension of man. To what extent and along what lines is such a precision possible? Even assuming the basis for such a distinction, how fundamental would it be? The transformation of essential human nature which Heidegger calls for is not something that explains itself – indeed, *Selbstverständlich* is practically a term of philosophical opprobrium for Heidegger.

So far our discussion has not demonstrated Dasein's priority, nor has it shown decisively whether Dasein may possibly or even necessarily serve as the primary being to be interrogated. But indeed something like a priority of Dasein has announced itself.[47]

[43] De Waelhens, p. 476.
[44] "Die Seinsfrage ist dann aber nichts anderes als die Radikalisierung einer zum Dasein selbst gehörigen wesenhaften Seinstendenz, des vorontologischen Seinsverständnisses." (SZ, p. 15).
[45] "Ursprünglicher als der Mensch ist die Endlichkeit des Daseins in ihm." (KM, p. 207/237). Heidegger italicizes the entire sentence.
[46] Richardson, H:TPT, p. 45.
[47] "Mit dem bisher Erörterten ist weder der Vorrang des Daseins erwiesen, noch über

Let us consider this change of man into Dasein as carefully as it requires in order to become transparent in principle. When we have done this, the question as to whether Heidegger's own method is not in the end inadequate to secure in the mode of being human the very conception which it first creates, will arise of its own accord – and ineluctably. We will treat it directly only then. We may say in advance however that to understand Dasein is to understand the power and limits of phenomenological philosophy which has reached maturity, as well as its organic relation to traditional philosophy.

seine mögliche oder gar notwendige Funktion als primär zu befragendes Seiendes ent-schieden. Wohl aber hat sich so etwas wie ein Vorrang des Daseins gemeldet." (SZ, p. 8).

CHAPTER IV

FROM MAN AND THE "COGITO SUM" TO DASEIN

> "What is all-important to realize – and I have never seen this brought out directly in any of the English literature – is that Dasein is a phenomenal structure (therefore Being likewise), that is, it designates that aspect of the phenomenon of man which the phenomenological gaze first encounters when it enters upon research into the human condition as such: *animal rationale* and the *res cogitans* constitute the phenomenon of man; but it is *Dasein* alone which is the phenomenological phenomenon of man."
> John N. Deely, "The Situation of Heidegger in the Tradition of Christian Philosophy," *The Thomist*, xxxi (April, 1967), p. 175 fn. 35.

Heidegger struggled over a long period of years with the problem of formalizing his basic experience of the forgottenness of Being in such a way that the materials of this experience could be rendered suitable for research into the meaning (or "sense") of Being itself. In other words, he struggled with the problem of reducing or converting his primal intuitions into a *status quaestionis*.

"To gain this clarity," Heidegger informs us, "three insights were decisive, though, to be sure, not yet sufficient for the venture of analysing the Being-question as a question about the sense of Being."[1] The first of these was his personal encounter with Husserl, which brought him his first acquaintance with Phenomenology. The second insight derived from a renewed study of the Aristotelian texts (especially Book IX of the *Metaphysics* and Book VI of the *Nichomachean Ethics*), and consisted in the interpretation of the Greek concept of (original) truth "as a process of revealment (*alētheuein*) and in the characterization of truth as non-concealment, to which all self-

---

[1] "Dafür waren drei Einsichten entscheidend, die freilich noch nicht ausreichten, um eine Erörterung der Seinsfrage als Frage nach dem Sinn von Sein zu wagen." (Heidegger's "Vorwort" to H:TPT, p. XI).

manifestation of beings pertains."[2] The third decisive insight was the recognition of the fundamental trait of *ousia*, the Being of beings, as Presence, because "the disquieting, ever watchful question about Being under the guise of Presence (Present) developed into the question about Being in terms of its time character":[3]

In being present there moves, unrecognized and concealed, present time and duration – in one word, Time. Being as such is thus unconcealed owing to Time. Thus Time points to unconcealedness, i.e., the truth of Being. But the Time of which we should think here is not experienced through the changeful career of beings. Time is evidently of an altogether different nature which neither has been recalled by way of the time concept of metaphysics ["tempus nihil aliud est quam numerus motus secundum prius et posterius"] nor ever can be recalled in this way. Thus Time becomes the first name, which is yet to be heeded, of the truth of Being, which is yet to be experienced.[4]

But before these three insights became sufficient for even the initial formalization of the Being-question as "a question about the sense (*Sinn*) of Being," it was necessary that they first come together and take on a unified consistency as Heidegger's grasp of the meaning and scope of the principle of phenomenological research, "to the things themselves" ("*zu den Sachen selbst!*"), tightened in his actual employment of the phenomenological method. It is true that Heidegger eventually broke with Husserl and even came to dissociate himself from the general phenomenological movement; but one must realize that this dissociation was called for only by what Heidegger regards to this day as "a more faithful adherence to the principle of Phenomenology."[5]

---

[2] "Ein erneutes Studium der Aristotelischen Abhandlungen (im besonderen des neunten Buches der 'Metaphysik' und des sechsten Buches der 'Nikomachischen Ethik') ergab den Einblick in das *aletheuein* als entbergen und die Kennzeichnung der Wahrheit als Unverborgenheit, in die alles Sichzeigen des Seienden." (*Ibid.*, pp. XI-XIII).

[3] "Die beunruhigende, ständig wache Frage nach dem Sein als Anwesenheit (Gegenwart) entfaltete sich zur Frage nach dem Sein hinsichtlich seines Zeitcharakters." (*Ibid.*, p. XIII).

[4] "Im Anwesen waltet ungedacht und verborgen Gegenwart und Andauern, west Zeit. Sein als solches ist demnach unverborgen aus Zeit. So verweist Zeit auf die Unverborgenheit, d. h. die Wahrheit von Sein. Aber die jetzt zu denkende Zeit ist nicht erfahren am veränderlichen Ablauf des Seienden. Zeit ist offenbar noch ganz anderen Wesens, das durch den Zeitbegriff der Metaphysik nicht nur noch nicht gedacht, sondern niemals zu denken ist. So wird Zeit der erst zu bedenkende Vorname für die allererst zu erfahrende Wahrheit des Seins." (WM: In, pp. 17-18/216).

[5] ". . . wurde 'die Phänomenologie' im Sinne Husserls zu einer bestimmten, von Descartes, Kant und Fichte her vorgezeichneten philosophischen Position ausgebaut. Ihr blieb die Geschichtlichkeit des Denkens durchaus fremd (. . .).
"Gegen diese philosophische Position setzte sich die in 'Sein und Zeit' entfaltete Seinsfrage ab und dies auf grund eines, wie ich heute noch glaube, sachgerechteren Festhaltens am Prinzip der Phänomenologie." (Heidegger's "Vorwort" to H:TPT, p. XV).

Thus Richardson remarks that "it is singularly important to realize that Heidegger never abandons the phenomenological attitude that seeks only to let the phenomenon manifest itself";[6] and this is so because "his conception of Being in the later period is as rigorously phenomenological as ever it was in *Sein und Zeit*. By that I mean that whatever is said about it is said in terms of that process of *a-lētheia* that lets beings be un-concealed to *Dasein*."[7] It is this attitude which altogether determines the orientation of the original Heideggerean problematic in relation to the Being-question and makes possible the initial conception of man in terms of There-being, Dasein. Precisely because it is secured in principle by the phenomenological method, Dasein is a *phenomenal* structure (the precise designation of this term will be brought forward only when we have determined in a later chapter the unique nature of phenomenological research). The ramifications of this we will draw out with care, since they are decisive; but we cannot do so more rapidly than the intrinsic difficulty of the matter to be thought allows. The first point to be noted is simply this: whatever the relation of Dasein as a phenomenal structure (*ontologisch und nicht ontisch, intentionale et non entitativum*) to man as an entity or ontic reality may be, "man is the There through whose Being the manifestive irruption among beings takes place" *only* "on the basis of [his preontological or preconceptual or 'presuppositional'[8]] comprehension of Being."[9] This means that in posing the question of the Being of things-in-Being Heidegger is concerned only with the process by which beings are lit up and reveal themselves as what they are for and to man. The point is capital. "What about beings before There-being discovers them" – the traditional interpretation[10] of the Being-question? "The question cannot be asked" without abandoning the attitude of phenomenology as Heidegger understands it.[11]

---

[6] H:TPT, p. 47. See also pp. 627-631.

[7] "Heidegger and God," p. 68.

[8] Cf. SZ, p. 8.

[9] "Auf dem Grunde des Seinsverständnisses ist der Mensch das Da, mit dessen Sein der eröffnende Einbruch in das Seiende geschieht. . ." (KM. p. 206/237),

[10] ". . . nous ne pouvons penser de l'être [dit Jacques Maritain] qu'en le pensant distinct du connaître. . ." (DS, p. 448/226).

[11] Richardson, H:TPT, p. 44. See also *ibid.*, pp. 109 fn. 8, 149-50, 392, 419, and 627. " 'The nature of reality' as elucidated by Heidegger is 'reality' as experienced by the phenomenologist, wherein beings 'are' insofar as they appear to man." (Richardson, "Heidegger and God," p. 30). Heidegger himself, in WG, makes this point about as emphatically as one could imagine it being made: "Wenn man heute 'Ontologie' und 'ontologisch' als Schlagwort und Titel für Richtungen in Anspruch nimmt, dann sind diese Ausdrücke recht äusserlich und unter Verkennung jeglicher Problematik gebraucht. Man lebt der irrigen Meinung, Ontologie als Frage nach dem Sein des Seienden bedeute 'realistische' (naiv oder kritische) 'Einstellung' gegenüber der 'idealistischen'. Ontologische

Being then is the lighting-process by which beings are "lit up"; and whether these beings be subjects (men) or objects (things), the light itself is neither one nor the other but "between" them both, as the possibility for encounter.[12] Thus Dasein "*is luminosity*, but this luminosity supposes another which the light illumines at the same time as this light itself. No revelation can be a light unto itself alone."[13]

We may attempt (careful the while not to push the attempt too far) to illustrate this with an analogy. Imagine a streetlight casting its glow in a heavy fog. The illumination suffuses the fog itself, lighting it up, and discloses perhaps the outline of certain buildings or other objects that lie within the circle of illumination the lamp casts. On this analogy, the fog (as suffused) would symbolize the World; the buildings, etc., would symbolize what-is, scil., *das Seiende*; the lamp itself would stand for man; Being is the very lighting up, the very suffusion-which-discloses; and the circle of illumination would represent Dasein. Thus both Dasein (as horizon) and Being (as ground of revealment) stand between man and the beings. "*Dasein* is transcendent, that is, it passes beyond all beings (including itself [as entitative or 'ontic']), beyond that level where beings are conceived as objects opposed to subjects (that is, beyond all subject-object polarity) to the Being of Beings."[14] Notice that, phenomenologically speaking, the circle of illumination presents itself as a constitutive state of the lamp, yet it is *not disclosed as originating in the lamp*. What the light, i.e., the illumination, in itself is or what the lamp (the projecting "There") in itself might be, independently of the (disclosive or manifestive) process (scil., of World and of beings-as-in-the-World) in which they cooperate, is simply not a part of the phenomenologically articulated problem.[15]

Problematik hat so wenig mit 'Realismus' zu tun, dass gerade *Kant* in und mit seiner *transzendentalen* Fragestellung den ersten entscheidenden Schritt seit *Plato* und *Aristoteles* zu einer *ausdrücklichen* Grundlegung der Ontologie vollziehen konnte. Dadurch dass man für die 'Realität der Aussenwelt' eintritt, ist man noch nicht ontologisch orientiert. 'Ontologisch' – in der populär-philosophischen Bedeutung genommen – meint jedoch – und darin bekundet sich die heillose Verwirrung – das, was vielmehr ontisch genannt werden muss, d.h. eine Haltung, die das *Seiende* an ihm selbst sein lässt, was und wie es ist. Aber damit ist noch kein *Problem des Seins* gestellt, geschweige denn das Fundament für die Möglichkeit einer Ontologie gewonnen." (WG, p. 15 fn. 14).

    [12] See Heidegger, HB, pp. 101/293 and 106/296. Also Richardson, H:TPT, pp. 6, 101, 154-5, 176, 386, 478, 486, 488.
    [13] De Waelhens, p. 487.
    [14] Richardson, "Heidegger and God," p. 33.
    [15] "The tradition has spoken of the *lumen naturale* in man. This is an effort to express by what Heidegger considers an image of the ontic order what is in fact the ontological structure of There-being, sc. that it is in such a way as to be There (see SZ, p. 133)," i.e., luminosity: the luminosity of the There which is There-being's innermost constitution is the disclosedness of the World. (Richardson, H:TPT, pp. 58-9). "When Heidegger calls

Thus Heidegger "overcomes" the subject-object dichotomy not, as some imagine to be adequate, by simply refusing to talk in terms of it (as though refusal to discuss an issue constituted a philosophical resolution of the difficulties involved!), but thanks to a methodological conception which in principle precludes entitative (or "ontic") polarizations as primary data. Being comes to light in Dasein, and Dasein is always "mine." Yet it lies prior to any subject-object structured field of awareness not because one *says* it does, or because one can talk *as though* it does, but because it is structurally (therefore in principle) prior: "If man is only man on the basis of the Dasein in him, then the question as to what is more primordial than man can, as a matter of principle, not be an anthropological one."[16] In the phenomeno-ogically structured approach to man, human nature is transformed in such wise that *animal rationale* is "displaced" by Dasein: the rational animal among other animals, both "rational" and non, gives way to the place (*Da*) of Being (*Sein*) among beings.

And just as the problematic is not subjective, so neither can it be objective. More subjective than any subject, the transcendence of Dasein to Being (Non-being) is likewise more objective than any object:

There-being is not a subject in relation to an object but it is this relation itself, sc. that which is 'between' subject and object. This 'between' is not derived from, and therefore subsequent to, the juxtaposition of subject and object, but is prior to the emergence of this relation, rendering it possible. The problem of transcendence, consequently, is not to explain how a subject goes out of itself in order to establish contact with an object, where object, understood as the totality of objects, is identified with the world, but how it comes-to-pass that There-being as to-be-in-the-World encounters other beings and then, once having discovered them, constitutes them as objects.[17]

And yet the entire problematic is constituted philosophically possible as problematic (that is, as a series of interrelated questions ordered about a specifying focus according to a definite sequence of primacy) by Phenom-

---

lumen naturale an ontic image, we can discern in inchoative form the entire polemic against subjective thinking. He does not deny, rather he endorses the image, but since in the tradition this refers to a characteristic of the human intellect, it implies for him an opposition between a being-subject (*intellectus*) and a being-object (*intelligible*) [see Chapter X of the present study, esp. p. 159,] hence remains in the order of beings, sc. is ontic. His entire effort is to try to transcend this opposition by conceiving There-being in a completely ontological dimension as a being whose Being is to be the luminosity of the World." (H:TPT, p. 59 fn. 58). See in the present study pp. 57-60, 85-86, 152ff., *inter alia*.

[16] "Wenn der Mensch nur Mensch ist *auf dem Grunde des Daseins in ihm*, dann kann die Frage nach dem, was ursprünglicher ist als der Mensch, grundsätzlich keine anthropologische sein. Alle Anthropologie, auch die philosophische, hat den Menschen schon als Menschen gesetzt." (KM, p. 207/237-8).

[17] Richardson, H:TPT, p. 101.

enology which "understands itself," that is to say, the philosophical formulation of the re-trieved *Seinsfrage* only became possible after "the
meaning and scope of the principle of Phenomenology, 'to the things themselves,' became clear"[18] in its properly and uniquely phenomenological
sense:

> This maxim, one may rejoin, is abundantly self-evident, and it expresses, more-
> over, the underlying principle of any scientific knowledge whatsoever. Why should
> anything so self-evident be taken up explicitly in giving title to a branch of research?
> In point of fact, the issue here is a kind of 'self-evidence' which we should like to
> bring closer to us. . .[19]

In point of fact, the kind of "self-evidence" at issue in the phenomenological
import of "the things themselves" remained unrealized for Husserl himself,
nor has it become generally clear for phenomenologists since.[20] Here again
an altogether decisive issue is at stake. We shall be obliged accordingly to
render transparent the full phenomenological import of "the things themselves" as an essential factor in any re-trieve of the original Heideggerean
problematic. We shall see that although the intentionality of consciousness
in the transcendental ego is a threshold that must be crossed in interrogating
the sense of Being, to halt research and confine it to that level would be
tantamount to falling back into onticity, a failure in the end to leave that
order of entitative categories which the sense of Being first appears only by
way of opposition to. With such a confinement, the sense of the phenomenological research-principle is diluted and its power and scope correspondingly diminished in an artificial way. These points will stand out sharply
when we come to examine Phenomenology directly as the medium of the
Being-question. For the present, concerned as we are only with rendering in-
disputable the phenomenological origin of Dasein as Heidegger's ground-
concept for critically departing research into the meaning of Being (the
content of the Dasein notion therefore must likewise await a later treatment),
we need only take this preliminary note with Heidegger:

> If, indeed, phenomenology, as the process of letting things manifest themselves,
> should characterize the standard method of philosophy, and if from ancient times

---

[18] "Mit der vorläufigen Aufhellung von *aletheia* und *ousia* klärten sich in der Folge Sinn
und Tragweite des Prinzips der Phänomenologie: 'zu den Sachen selbst'." (Heidegger's
"Vorwort" to H:TPT, p. XIII).

[19] "Diese Maxime ist aber doch – möchte man erwidern – reichlich selbstverständlich
und überdies ein Ausdruck des Prinzips jeder wissenschaftlichen Erkenntnis. Man sieht
nicht ein, warum diese Selbstverständlichkeit ausdrücklich in die Titelbezeichnung einer
Forschung aufgenommen werden soll. Es geht in der Tat um eine 'Selbstverständlichkeit',
die wir uns näher bringen wollen. . ." (ZS, p. 28).

[20] Cf. Heidegger's "Vorwort" to H:TPT, pp. XII-XVII.

the guide-question of philosophy has perdured in the most diverse forms as the question about the Being of beings, then Being had to remain [for phenomenology maturely conceived] the first and last thing-itself of thought.[21]

Agreement with Fr. Richardson on this score is necessary for anyone who understands Heidegger in more than a surface (i.e., terminological) way:

It would be hard to exaggerate the importance of Heidegger's conception of phenomenology for the evolution of foundational thought. Clearly it is not simply one method arbitrarily chosen from among others equally possible. It is imposed by his conception of the Being-process itself as that which renders beings manifest in a negatived way. If phenomenology is the method chosen for the meditation upon There-being which is to prepare a way to interrogate the sense of Being itself, this means that it is the way that the Heidegger of 1927 goes about the *thinking of Being*.[22]

Now what about this way to the thought of Being which is first prepared by meditation on the Dasein in man? Being is not a being, because it is that which enables beings to be (present) to man and men to each other. It is nearest to man, because it makes him (via Dasein) to be what he is and enables him to enter into comportment with other beings. Yet it is farthest removed from him because it is not a being with which he, structured as he is to deal directly only with beings, can comport himself.[23]

From the point of view of beings, Being encompasses them all, just as a domain of openness encompasses what is found within it. Being is a domain of openness precisely because it is the lighting process by which beings are lit up. If these beings be 'subjects' or 'objects' then the light itself is neither subject nor object but 'between' them both, enabling the encounter between the subject and object [trans-objective subject] to come about.[24]

The preliminary notion of Being is that there is something "which determines beings as beings" for and in awareness; and "that on the basis of which beings are understood, however we may discuss them in detail," is precisely

---

[21] "Wenn anders die Phänomenologie als das Sichzeigenlassen der Sache selbst die massgebende Methode der Philosophie bestimmen soll und wenn die Leitfrage der Philosophie sich von alters her in den verschiedensten Gestalten als die Frage nach dem Sein des Seienden durchhielt, dann musste das Sein die erste und letzte Sache selbst für das Denken bleiben." (Heidegger's "Vorwort" to H:TPT, p. XV).

[22] H:TPT, p. 47.

[23] "Das 'Sein' – das ist nicht Gott und nicht Weltgrund. Das Sein ist weiter denn alles Seiende und ist gleichwohl dem Menschen näher als jedes Seiende, sei dies ein Fels, ein Tier, ein Kunstwerk, eine Maschine, sei es ein Engel oder Gott. Das Sein ist das Nächste. Doch die Nähe bleibt dem Menschen am weitesten... Denn im Lichte des Seins steht schon jeder Ausgang vom Seienden und jede Rückkehr zu ihm." (HB, p. 76/282). See Richardson, H:TPT, p. 6, and "Heidegger and God," p. 25.

[24] Richardson, "Heidegger and God," p. 25.

what we provisionally term "Being."[25] In any question as to the meaning of this Being, however, we must point out at once that "there is no 'circular reasoning' but rather a remarkable 'relatedness backward or forward' which what we are asking about (Being) bears to the enquiry itself as a mode of Being [i.e., a way of comportment which is itself virtual and implicit in any field of awareness as such] of a being [spec., man, *animal rationale*, in his Dasein]."[26]

How may we begin to explicitate the meaning of this preliminary notion to which Phenomenology turned towards *réalité humaine* as such gives rise? "Insofar as Being constitutes what is asked about, and 'Being' means [in the first instance] the Being of beings, then beings themselves turn out to be *what is interrogated* [again, in the first instance]."[27] But "everything we talk about, everything we have in view, everything towards which we comport ourselves in any way is being."[28] "Being lies in the fact that something is, and in its being the way it is."[29] Hence in principle we must face the problem: "In *which* beings is the *meaning* of Being to be discerned?"[30] The question is capital, for if the characteristics of the Being of beings, i.e., of their comprehensibility or intelligible structure as beings (revealed), can indeed be yielded without falsification, "then those beings must, on their part, have become accessible as they are in themselves."[31] In other words, "when we come to what is to be interrogated [beings with respect to their Being, i.e., their visibility in *noein*], the question of Being requires that the right way of access to beings shall have been obtained and secured in advance,"[32] and for no arbitrary reason, but because "a being can show itself from itself in many ways, depending in each case on the kind of access we have to it."[33]

---

[25] "*Das Gefragte* der auszuarbeitenden Frage ist Sein, das, was Seiendes als Seiendes bestimmt, das, woraufhin Seiendes, mag es wie immer erörtert werden, je schon verstanden ist." (SZ, p. 6).

[26] "Nicht ein 'Zirkel im Beweis' liegt in der Frage nach dem Sinn von Sein, aber eine merkwürdige 'Rück- oder Vorbezogenheit' des Gefragten (Sein) auf das Fragen als Seinsmodus eines Seienden." (SZ, p. 8).

[27] "Sofern das Sein das Gefragte ausmacht, und Sein besagt Sein von Seiendem, ergibt sich als das *Befragte* der Seinsfrage das Seiende selbst." (SZ, p. 6).

[28] "Seiend ist alles, wovon wir reden, was wir meinen, wozu wir uns so und so verhalten, seiend ist. . ." (SZ, pp. 6-7).

[29] "Sein liegt im Dass- und Sosein. . ." (SZ, p. 7).

[30] "An *welchem* Seienden soll der Sinn von Sein abgelesen werden. . ." (SZ, p. 7).

[31] "Soll es aber die Charaktere seines Seins unverfälscht hergeben können, dann muss es seinerseits zuvor so zugänglich geworden sein, wie es an ihm selbst ist." (SZ, p. 6).

[32] "Die Seinsfrage verlangt im Hinblick auf ihr Befragtes die Gewinnung und vorherige Sicherung der rechten Zugangsart zum Seienden." (SZ, p. 6).

[33] "Seiendes kann sich nun in verschiedener Weise, je nach der Zugangsart zu ihm, von ihm selbst her zeigen." (SZ, p. 28).

If the question about Being is to be explicitly formulated and carried through in such a manner as to be completely transparent to itself, then any treatment of it in line with the elucidations we have given requires us to explain how Being is to be looked at, how its meaning is to be understood and conceptually grasped; it requires us to prepare the way for choosing the right being for our example, and to work out the genuine way of access to it.[34]

Now for Heidegger only phenomenological research (for reasons we shall bring to light) can *in principle* achieve necessary and explicit access to beings in terms of their Being. Hence "if our analysis is to be authentic, its aim is such that the prior task of assuring ourselves 'phenomenologically' of that being which is to serve as our example, has already been prescribed as our point of departure."[35] But since "the way in which Being and its structures are encountered in the mode of [ascertainably ontological] phenomenon is one which must first of all be *wrested* from the objects of Phenomenology,"[36] we fulfill the "prior task" of achieving an adequately secured ('critically departured' in the phenomenological sense) basis for investigating the sense of Being only if our investigation proceeds from that point at which Being first (with a priority of nature) comes out of concealment, i.e., from that being for whom Being is first revealed and always at issue. That is why Dasein is "in every case mine", why one must always use a personal pronoun when speaking in terms of it.[37]

Not only can we be assured on this exclusive basis of beginning our analysis with a *phenomenological* phenomenon rather than with some appearance or semblance, but only in this way does it become possible for the philosophical project to render itself self-critical in a positive sense.[38]

[34] "Wenn die Frage nach dem Sein ausdrücklich gestellt und in voller Durchsichtigkeit ihrer selbst vollzogen werden soll, dann verlangt eine Ausarbeitung dieser Frage nach den bisherigen Erläuterungen die Explikation der Weise des Hinsehens auf Sein, des Verstehens und begrifflichen Fassens des Sinnes, die Bereitung der Möglichkeit der rechten Wahl des exemplarischen Seienden, die Herausarbeitung der genuinen Zugangsart zu diesem Seienden." (SZ, p. 7).

[35] "Die Voraufgabe einer 'phänomenologischen' Sicherung des exemplarischen Seienden als Ausgang für die eigentliche Analytik ist immer schon aus dem Ziel dieser vorgezeichnet." (SZ, p. 37).

[36] "Die Begegnisart des Seins und der Seinsstrukturen im Modus des Phänomens muss den Gegenständen der Phänomenologie allererst *abgewonnen* werden." (SZ, p. 36).

[37] "Das Seiende, dessen Analyse zur Aufgabe steht, sind wir je selbst. Das Sein dieses Seienden ist *je meines*. Im Sein dieses Seienden verhält sich dieses selbst zu seinem Sein. Als Seiendes dieses Seins ist es seinem eigenen Sein überantwortet. Das *Sein* ist es, darum es diesem Seienden je selbst geht." (SZ, pp. 41-2). "Das Ansprechen von Dasein muss gemäss dem Charakter der *Jemeinigkeit* dieses Seienden stets das *Personal*pronomen mitsagen: 'ich bin', 'du bist'." (SZ, p. 42).

[38] "Jeder ursprünglich geschöpfte phänomenologische Begriff und Satz steht als mitgeteilte Aussage in der Möglichkeit der Entartung... Die Möglichkeit der Verhärtung

And finally, "in this way the ordinary conception of phenomenon becomes phenomenologically relevant."[39] The point is of no less significance than the others which have been made concerning the "prior task" of any thought of Being which is to be authentic (this stricture, let it be noted, is Heidegger's own), because it introduces as a constitutive element of the original problematic-structure the observation that thought never becomes so detached from the entitative dimension of Dasein that it has nothing to do with entities. An inauthentic philosophical analysis is initially characterized by Heidegger as one which is forgetful of Being, one which restricts its attention to the ontic ("existentiell") dimension of man and the world. "Heidegger in this context assumes that the only type of inauthenticity of There-being is that which forgets its own ontological dimension. Would not There-being be equally inauthentic if it forgot its *ontic* dimension and lost itself in a pure mysticism or mythicism of Being?"[40] The question will be a decisive one for the Interpretation we are working out.

What is of immediate import in all this however is the vindication of the point we have taken such care to stress, spec., that even the preliminary notion of the essential nature of the *réalité humaine* as Dasein presupposes a solid understanding of the nature of Heideggerean Phenomenology as the very ground from which the preliminary notion springs: "the very *point of departure* for our analysis [of Being] requires that it be secured by the proper method, just as much as does our *access* to the phenomenon, or our *passage* through whatever is prevalently covering it up"[41] – i.e., in order to make the ordinary of "formal" notion of phenomenon phenomenologically relevant in explicitating the Being-question (and we must do this since man is directly structured to deal only with beings), the authenticity and aim of our analysis are such "that the prior task of assuring ourselves 'phenomenologically' of that being [sc. man in his Dasein] which is to serve as our example, *has*

---

und Ungriffigkeit des ursprünglich 'Griffigen' liegt in der konkreten Arbeit der Phänomenologie selbst. Und die Schwierigkeit dieser Forschung besteht gerade darin, sie gegen sich selbst in einem positiven Sinne kritisch zu machen." (SZ, p. 36).

[39] "Und so wird der vulgäre Phänomenbegriff phänomenologisch relevant." (SZ, p. 37).

[40] Richardson, H:TPT, p. 51 fn. 67. See SZ, p. 316: "Die ontologische 'Wahrheit' der existenzialen Analyse bildet sich aus auf dem Grunde der ursprünglichen existenziellen Wahrheit. Nicht jedoch bedarf diese notwendig jener." This statement is capital for our context. It should be kept in mind. Ontological truth, i.e., the truth resulting from existential analysis, is developed on the basis of fundamental existentiell truth, i.e., the truth resulting from predicamental (categorial!) analysis. The former analysis, *Sein und Zeit* suggests, presupposes the validity of the latter, but not *e converso* – and yet it is the former which is to provide the fundament for *all* ontology!!!

[41] "Daher fordern des *Ausgang* der Analyse ebenso wie der *Zugang* zum Phänomen und der *Durchgang* durch die herrschenden Verdeckungen eine eigene methodische Sicherung." (SZ, p. 36).

already been prescribed as our point of departure":[42] the point must be respected because it discloses an essential formal element of the question of Being as it arises for Phenomenology.

The *starting point* from which a disclosure of Being can take place is *not* (cannot be) *optional*. For "whenever an ontology takes for its theme beings whose character of Being is other than that of Dasein, it has its own foundation and motivation in Dasein's own ontical [or entitative] structure, in which a pre-ontological [i.e., preconceptual] understanding of Being is comprised as a definite characteristic."[43] The meaning of Being can only be disclosable in that realm of beings (or entities) where Being is an issue, a matter of concern (if only of, for the most part, modal – existentiell – concern). And since Being, as the comprehensible guise (Reality) of the Real[44] becomes an issue of concern (*cura*) only where a question springs up authentically; since moreover the very placing of a question is a being's mode of Being[45] and as such derives its essential character from that which is inquired about – namely, Being (whether as such or as "the Being of. . ."[46]), the very working out of the Being-question of itself (*per se*) requires that we make a particular entity, spec., the inquirer as that being which inquires, transparent in its own Being. The force of this requirement derives too from the nature of our enterprise as one of understanding (*noein*), that is, of determining "how Being is to be looked at, how its meaning is to be understood and conceptually grasped."[47] (Moreover, it is a requirement suggested even in the derivative perspectives of "traditional" epistemology, where the true root of the "problem of knowledge" shows itself as nothing other than that

---

[42] "Die Voraufgabe einer 'phänomenologischen' Sicherung des exemplarischen Seienden als Ausgang für die eigentliche Analytik ist immer schon aus dem Ziel dieser vorgezeichnet." (SZ, p. 37).

[43] "Wissenschaften sind Seinsweisen des Daseins, in denen es sich auch zu Seiendem verhält, das es nicht selbst zu sein braucht. Zum Dasein gehört aber wesenhaft: Sein in einer Welt. Das dem Dasein zugehörige Seinsverständnis betrifft daher gleichursprünglich das Verstehen von so etwas wie 'Welt' und Verstehen des Seins des Seienden, das innerhalb der Welt zugänglich wird. Die Ontologien, die Seiendes von nicht daseinsmässigem Seinscharakter zum Thema haben, sind demnach in der ontischen Struktur des Daseins selbst fundiert und motiviert, die die Bestimmtheit eines vorontologischen Seinsverständnisses in sich begreift." (SZ, p. 13).

[44] See SZ, pp. 202ff. Also fn. 40 in Chapter IX of the present study.

[45] Cf. SZ, p. 12.

[46] See ID, pp. 59/54 and 61/56.

[47] "Wenn die Frage nach dem Sein ausdrücklich gestellt und in voller Durchsichtigkeit ihrer selbst vollzogen werden soll, dann verlangt eine Ausarbeitung dieser Frage nach den bisherigen Erläuterungen die Explikation der Weise des Hinsehens auf Sein, des Verstehens und begrifflichen Fassens des Sinnes, die Bereitung der Möglichkeit der rechten Wahl des exemplarischen Seienden, die Herausarbeitung der genuinen Zugangsart zu diesem Seiendem." (SZ, p. 7).

of "the phenomenon of knowing as such and the kind of Being which belongs to the knower."[48])

To restate then: "If we are to formulate our question explicitly and trans-
parently, we must first give a proper explication of a being (Dasein) with
regard to its Being."[49] "This being which each of us is himself and which includes inquiring as one of the possibilities of its Being, we shall denote by
the term 'Dasein'."[50] And "we have chosen to designate this being as
'Dasein', a term which is purely an expression of its Being," because "we
cannot define Dasein's essence by citing a 'what' of the kind that pertains to
a subject-matter, and because its essence lies rather in the fact that in each
case it has its Being to be, and has it as its own."[51]

Consequently "the question about the meaning of the Being of a being
takes as its theme the 'upon which' of that comprehension of Being which
underlies all *Being* of beings," or, as the earlier editions of *Sein und Zeit*
expressed it (and it is not without significance that this direct concession to
the mutual irreducibility of the ontic and ontological dimensions in the
mode of being human was supressed in the later editions), "all ontical *Being
towards* beings" – "des allem ontischen *Sein zu* Seiendem."[52] It follows that
"the meaning of Dasein's Being is not something free-floating which is
other than and 'outside of' itself, but is the self-comprehending Dasein itself."[53] The question becomes: "What makes possible the Being of Dasein,
and therewith its factical existence?"[54] "The issue is one of *seeing* a primordial structure of Dasein's Being – a structure in accordance with whose
phenomenal content the concepts of Being must be Articulated," and which

[48] ". . . welche Instanz entscheidet denn darüber, *ob* und *in welchem Sinne* ein Erkennt-
nisproblem bestehen soll, was anderes als das Phänomen des Erkennens selbst und die
Seinsart des Erkennenden?" (SZ, p. 61).
[49] "Die ausdrückliche und durchsichtige Fragestellung nach dem Sinn von Sein verlangt eine vorgängige angemessene Explikation eines Seienden (Dasein) hinsichtlich seines
Seins." (SZ, p. 7).
[50] "Dieses Seiende, das wir selbst je sind und das unter anderem die Seinsmöglichkeit des
Fragens hat, fassen wir terminologisch als *Dasein*." (SZ, p. 7).
[51] ". . . weil die Wesensbestimmung dieses Seienden nicht durch Angabe eines sachhal-
tigen Was vollzogen werden kann, sein Wesen vielmehr darin liegt, dass es je sein Sein als
seiniges zu sein hat, ist der Titel Dasein als reiner Seinsausdruck zur Bezeichnung dieses
Seienden gewählt." (SZ, p. 12).
[52] "Die Frage nach dem Sinn des Seins eines Seienden macht das Woraufhin des allem
Sein von Seiendem zugrundeliegenden Seinsverstehens zum Thema." (SZ, p. 325). See
Macquarrie-Robinson translation, p. 372 fn. 1.
[53] "Der Seinssinn des Daseins ist nicht ein freischwebendes Anderes und 'Ausserhalb'
seiner selbst, sondern das sich verstehende Dasein selbst." (SZ, p. 325).
[54] "Was ermöglicht das Sein des Daseins und damit dessen faktische Existenz." (SZ, p.
325).

structure "cannot be grasped by the traditional ontological categories"[55] for the very good reason that it does not, according to what is proper to it, fall within any entitative categories. But what would the entitative consequences, the ontic implications or even (analytical) presuppositions for such a structure be, if any? The investigation of such a question is methodologically ruled out by the phenomenological research mode. But the interesting point is that it should arise therein to begin with. Can the concept of Dasein be adequately worked out within methodological restrictions which cut short inquiry into structural implications which appear in the concept from the very first, and essentially so? To admit that it cannot would be to deny that only as Phenomenology is philosophy possible. At this stage we only mention the question.

Suffice it to note now in this regard that the Being of Dasein, upon which the structural whole as such is ontologically supported, will become accessible to us only when and if we look (*noein*) "all the way *through* this whole *to a single* primordially unitary phenomenon which is already in this whole in such a way that it provides the ontological foundation for each structural item in its structural possibility."[56] For this reason the question of Being itself chiefly and primarily "is nothing other than the radicalization of an essential tendency-of-Being which belongs to Dasein itself – the pre-ontological understanding of Being."[57]

Yet granting this, what manner of determination should our explication of the preliminary notion of Being, secured thanks to Dasein, work toward? Obviously the meaning or sense of Being as such will not be disengaged by defining beings as such through their ontic causes, as if Being had the character of some possible entity. No:

Being, as that which is asked about, must be exhibited in a way of its own, essentially different from the way in which beings are discovered. Accordingly, *what is to be found out by the asking* – the meaning of Being – also demands that it be con-

---

[55] "Weil es . . . um das *Sehen* einer ursprünglichen Seinsstruktur des Daseins geht, deren phänomenalem Gehalt gemäss die Seinsbegriffe artikuliert werden müssen, und . . . diese Struktur durch die überkommenen ontologischen Kategorien grundsätzlich nicht fassbar ist. . ." (SZ, pp. 54-5).

[56] "Zugänglich wird uns das Sein des Daseins, das ontologisch das Strukturganze als solches trägt, in einem vollen Durchblick *durch* dieses Ganze *auf ein* ursprünglich einheitliches Phänomen, das im Ganzen schon liegt, so dass es jedes Strukturmoment in seiner strukturalen Möglichkeit ontologisch fundiert." (SZ, p. 181).

[57] "Wenn die Interpretation des Sinnes von Sein Aufgabe wird, ist das Dasein nicht nur das primär zu befragende Seiende, es ist überdies das Seiende, das sich je schon in seinem Sein zu *dem* verhält, wonach in dieser Frage gefragt wird. Die Seinsfrage ist dann aber nichts anderes als die Radikalisierung einer zum Dasein selbst gehörigen wesenhaften Seinstendenz, des vorontologischen Seinsverständnisses." (SZ, pp. 14-15).

ceived in a way of its own, essentially contrasting with the concepts in which entities acquire their determinate signification.[58]

The point is decisive. "Basically, all ontology, no matter how rich and firmly compacted a system of categories it has at its disposal, remains blind and perverted from its ownmost aim, if it has not first adequately clarified the meaning of Being, and conceived this clarification as its fundamental task."[59] "Therefore *fundamental ontology*, from which alone all other ontologies can take their rise, must be sought in the existential analytic of Dasein," and this only inasmuch as this analytic is guided and determined beforehand by question of the sense of Being as such;[60] "so that Dasein functions as that being which in principle is to be *interrogated* beforehand as to its Being."[61]

Let this be enough to bear out our key contention that the distinction between man as *animal rationale* and man as Dasein is one that is drawn phenomenologically. If there is to be a transformation of the notion of essential human nature in line with the requirements of the Being-question which phenomenological philosophy poses, then this transformation must itself be brought about phenomenologically; and so decisive is this transformation for any authentic investigation of the sense of Being that Heidegger calls it the "prior task" for thought of Being. Whatever may be the shift in emphasis for the "later" Heidegger, we are talking here about an intrinsic exigency of the original problematic. It is no overstatement therefore when we say that the understanding of the initial concept of Dasein as a phenomenal structure, as the immediate "precipitate", so to speak, which results from beholding the human reality through a purely phenomenological gaze is all-important for grasping the original sense of Heidegger's

---

[58] "Sein als das Gefragte fordert daher eine eigene Aufweisungsart, die sich von der Entdeckung des Seienden wesenhaft unterscheidet. Sonach wird auch das *Erfragte*, der Sinn von Sein, eine eigene Begrifflichkeit verlangen, die sich wieder wesenhaft abhebt gegen die Begriffe, in denen Seiendes seine bedeutungsmässige Bestimmtheit erreicht." (SZ, p. 6).

[59] "Alle Ontologie, mag sie über ein noch so reiches und festverklammertes Kategoriensystem verfügen, bleibt im Grunde blind und eine Verkehrung ihrer eigensten Absicht, wenn sie nicht zuvor den Sinn von Sein zureichend geklärt und diese Klärung als ihre Fundamentalaufgabe begriffen hat." (SZ, p. 11). Heidegger italicizes this entire sentence.

[60] "Daher muss die *Fundamentalontologie*, aus der alle andern erst entspringen können, in der existenzialen Analytik des Daseins gesucht werden." (SZ, p. 13). "Die existenzialzeitliche Analyse des Daseins verlangt ihrerseits eine erneute Wiederholung im Rahmen der grundsätzlichen Diskussion des Seinsbegriffes." (SZ, p. 333).

[61] "Jetzt hat sich aber gezeigt, dass die ontologische Analytik des Daseins überhaupt die Fundamentalontologie ausmacht, dass mithin das Dasein als das grundsätzlich vorgängig auf sein Sein zu *befragende* Seiende fungiert." (SZ, p. 14).

Seinsfrage.[62] We might almost say that the very success of our re-trieve ultimately rests on this understanding.

On this way – that is, in the service of the question concerning the truth of Being – it becomes necessary to stop and think about human nature; for the experience of the forgottenness of Being . . . involves the crucial conjecture that in view of the unconcealedness of Being the involvement of Being in human nature is an essential feature of Being. But how could this conjecture, which is experienced here, become an explicit question before every attempt had been made to liberate the determination of human nature from the concept of subjectivity and from the concept of "animal rationale"? *To characterize with a single term both the involvement of Being in human nature and the essential relation of man to the openness ("there") of Being as such, the name of "Dasein" was chosen for that sphere of being in which man stands as man.* . . Any attempt, therefore, to re-think *Being and Time* is thwarted as long as one is satisfied with the observation that, in this study, the term "Dasein" is used in place of "consciousness". As if this were simply a matter of using different words! As if it were not the one and only thing at stake here: namely, to get man to think about the involvement of Being in human nature and thus, from our point of view, to present first of all an experience of human nature which may prove sufficient to direct our inquiry. The term "Dasein" neither takes the place of the term "consciousness" nor does the "object" designated as "Dasein" take the place of what we think of when we speak of "consciousness". "Dasein" names that which should first of all be experienced, and subsequently thought of, as a place – specifically, the location of the truth of Being.[63]

We noted at the very outset of our study that, as Gilson put it, the conception of Dasein has no direct counterpart in the philosophy of St. Thomas.

---

[62] See SZ, pp. 36-7; Richardson, "The Place of the Unconscious in Heidegger," pp. 284-5.

[63] "Auf diesem Weg, und das sagt, im Dienst der Frage nach der Wahrheit des Seins, wird eine Besinnung auf das Wesen des Menschen nötig; denn die . . . Erfahrung der Seinsvergessenheit schliesst die alles tragende Vermutung ein, gemäss der Unverborgenheit des Seins gehöre der Bezug des Seins zum Menschenwesen gar zum Sein selbst. Doch wie könnte dieses erfahrene Vermuten auch nur zur ausgesprochenen Frage werden, ohne zuvor alle Bemühung darein zu legen, die Wesenbestimmung des Menschen aus der Subjektivität, aber auch aus derjenigen des animal rationale herauszunehmen? Um sowohl den Bezug des Seins zum Wesen des Menschen als auch das Wesensverhältnis des Menschen zur Offenheit ('Da') des Seins als solchen zugleich und in einem Wort zu treffen, wurde für den Wesenbereich, in dem der Mensch als Mensch steht, der Name 'Dasein' gewählt . . . Darum wird nun auch jedes Nach-denken verbaut, wenn man sich begnügt festzustellen, in 'Sein und Zeit' werde statt 'Bewusstsein' das Wort 'Dasein' gebraucht. Als ob hier der blosse Gebrauch verschiedener Wörter zur Verhandlung stünde, als ob es sich nicht um das Eine und Einzige handelte, den Bezug des Seins zum Wesen des Menschen und damit, von uns aus gedacht, zunächst eine für das leitende Fragen hinreichende Wesenserfahrung vom Menschen vor das Denken zu bringen. Weder tritt nur das Wort 'Dasein' an die Stelle des Wortes 'Bewusstsein', noch tritt die 'Dasein' genannte 'Sache' an die Stelle dessen, was man beim Namen 'Bewusstsein' vorstellt. Vielmehr ist mit 'Dasein' solches genannt, was erst einmal als Stelle, nämlich als die Ortschaft der Wahrheit des Seins erfahren und dann entsprechend gedacht werden soll." (WM: In, pp. 13-14/212-13).

But enough has been said to now to permit us to observe, by way of approximation, that, if transposed into St. Thomas' perspectives, the notion of Dasein would demand a *thematic* analysis of the Intentional Life of man as such. But we must be careful to point out that "intentional" here must be understood in the Thomistic sense of *esse intentionale* (as developed especially by Martitain), and not in the Husserlian sense of intentionality as the basic structure of consciousness-as-produced or derived from the subjectivity of a transcendental ego.[64] (The locus of intentionality in this latter sense occupies a definitely subordinate position in Heidegger's problematic, and rightly so.[65]) In this transposed perspective, Being as the lighting-process

[64] ". . . la notion même d'intentionalité, en passant des mains des grands réalistes scolastiques [on this historical point, see fn. 9 of Chapter V in this present study] à celles des 'néo-cartésiens' contemporains (comme E. Husserl se designe lui-même dans son dernier ouvrage) a perdu son efficience et sa valeur; comment pouvait-il en être autrement, puisque tout son sens lui vient d'abord de son opposition à l'*esse entitativum* de la chose extramentale? L'intentionalité n'est pas seulement cette propriété de ma conscience d'être une transparence dirigée, de viser des objets au sein d'elle-même, elle est avant tout cette propriété de la pensée, privilège de son immatérialité, par quoi l'être pour soi posé 'hors d'elle', c'est-à-dire pleinement indépendant de son acte à elle, devient existant en elle, posé pour elle et intégré à son acte à elle, et par quoi désormais elle et lui existent en elle d'une seule et même existence supra-subjective.

"Si l'on ne va pas jusque-là, si l'on refuse à l'esprit le pouvoir, qui n'est réel que si l'être lui-même est réel, de 'surmonter' et de s'intérioriser l'être, on matérialise inévitablement la pure transparence de l'intentionalité, en regardant celle-ci comme 'constituante' à l'égard de l'objet par ses 'règles de structure', en lui demandant de constituer *l'autre* et de lui conférer son sens propre 'à partir de mon être à moi' (tandis qu'au contraire elle porte en moi *l'autre* 'à partir' de son altérité même, et me fait être l'autre). Et même si l'on semble, comme il arrive si souvent à E. Husserl, frôler pour ainsi dire la vraie nature de la connaissance, on passe toujours, en fin de compte, à côté du grand secret. On ne voit pas que la connaissance n'a pas à sortir d'elle-même pour atteindre la chose existant ou pouvant exister hors d'elle, – la chose extramentale qu'à cause de ce préjugé on veut exorciser. C'est dans la pensée même que l'être extramental est atteint, dans le concept même que le réel ou métalogique est touché et manié, c'est là qu'il est saisi, elle le mange chez elle, parce que la gloire même de son immatérialité est de n'être pas une chose dans l'espace extérieure à une autre chose étendue, mais bien une vie supérieure à tout l'ordre de la spatialité, qui sans sortir de soi se parfait de ce qui n'est pas elle, – de ce réel intelligible dont elle tire des sens la féconde substance, puisée par eux dans les existants (matériels) en acte. Le moyen de faire évanouir le mystère propre du connaître, c'est précisément d'exorciser l'être extramental, de supprimer ces pour soi ontologiques (métalogiques) pleinement indépendants de ma pensée, que ma pensée fait siens en se faisant eux." (DS, pp. 199-202/ 103-4).

[65] See Richardson, H:TPT, esp. pp. 178-9, but also pp. 98, 146, 153, 206, 253, 339, 370, 380, 420; and Heidegger, WM:In, p. 16/214-5. Cf. Jean-Marc Laporte, "The Evidence for the Negative Judgment of Separation," *The Modern Schoolman*, XLI (November, 1963), 27-8: "The problem of knowledge, of transcendence within immanence, is insoluble on the precritical level of imagination. If a knowing subject imagines himself as some tangible concrete 'thing', the known material object as another tangible concrete 'thing' of the same type, and wonders how the extramental 'thing' can possibly be inside the mind his puzzlement will necessarily turn into the despair of solipsism." Also De Waelhens, *art. cit.*, pp.

would call for an analysis in two directions. It would point on the one side toward the lines of analysis which delineate the nature and function of the illuminating or acting intellect, the *intellectus agens*.[66] These lines of analysis would mark out the character of Being which defines (in the sense of renders comprehensible) the nature of the correlation that links Dasein to man in his facticity. This would amount to a clarification in principle of the essential interrelationship between man as Dasein and man as entity – *subjectum capax essendi*. Is there any other way in which the ambiguity surrounding in Heidegger's thought the relationship between Dasein and man[67] can be penetrated and overcome? Can the ontic-ontological structural interarticulation which gives rise to the possibility of both a categorical and an existentialistic understanding of the human reality be entirely subsumed under phenomenological research purely conceived? For if *existentialia* are the phenomenological parallel to the metaphysical *praedicamenta*, and if these are indeed "the two basic possibilities for characters of Being" in such wise that "the beings which correspond to them require different kinds of primary interrogation respectively,"[68] then how is it possible in the end to authentically and adequately work out the concept of Dasein in order to pursue therefrom the meaning of Being, unless the entitative or ontic dimension of Dasein has also been thematically brought into the problematic as an integral part of that "prior task" which demanded the phenomenological delineation of Dasein's ontological dimension in the first place? Are not different kinds of truly primary interrogation mutually irreducible? In that event, the thematic introduction of the entitative aspect of Dasein has already presup-

---

497ff. Michel Henry, *L'essence de la manifestation* (Paris: Presses Unniversitaires de France, 1964).

[66] This first direction indicated is suggested also by D.M. De Petter, "De oorsprong van de zijnskennis volgens de H. Thomas van Aquino" in *Tijdschrift voor Philosophie* (Juin, 1955), 217, 249. And by Dondeyne, *art. cit.*, pp. 255 fn. 11, 269 fn. 49, 271, and esp. p. 285. "Mais ce n'est pas pour s'évader du monde ou se replier sur lui-même que l'homme est porteur d'un *lumen naturale*, ou, plus exactement, qu'il est porté par lui et en quelque sorte 'retenu en lui'. Il en est de cette lumière comme de l'intellect agent chez Saint Thomas: elle n'est rien sans les étants, encore qu'elle rende possible que les étants 'soient', *au sens phénoménologique de ce terme*, c'est-à-dire au sens de 'devenir manifeste' et se 'montrer comme tel'. Se libérer de l'emprise du milieu environnant et 'laisser-être' (*sein lassen = frei lassen*) les étants, est un seul et même événement: l'avènement de la vérité (Dondeyne, p. 271: my emphasis)." "Si l'on veut trouver dans la scolastique un correspondant de la problématique heideggerienne de l'origine de la vérité, c'est au problème de l'intellect agent qu'il faut songer (*ibid.*, p. 285)." Cf. fn. 15 of this Chapter *supra*.

[67] See fn. 33 of Chapter II, p. 27 *supra*.

[68] "Existenzialien und Kategorien sind die beiden Grundmöglichkeiten von Seinscharakteren. Das ihnen entsprechende Seiende fordert eine je verschiedene Weise des primären Befragens: Seiendes ist *Wer* (Existenz) oder ein *Was* (Vorhandenheit im weitesten Sinne)." (SZ, p. 45).

posed the validity of a metaphysical Interpretation. For even supposing that "the connection between these two modes of the characters of Being cannot be handled until the horizon for the question of Being has been clarified,"[69] their mutual irreducibility would have already been given in advance. And once the horizon of the Being-question has been set up, this problem must be met before the sense of Being can be (authentically) pursued beyond the preliminary stage of the *Daseinsanalyse*, since it presents itself as a formal component of that analysis. But in that case phenomenology is not alone sufficient to meet all the problematic exigencies of the Being-question, not even as it has been phenomenologically re-interpreted or "placed." The exact nature of this deficiency shall have to be examined. This will only be possible after we have determined the priority which the question of Being enjoys in its phenomenological sense. Let us turn our attention here to the second fundamental direction indicated by a notion of Being as the lighting-process when transposed into St. Thomas' perspectives.

If on one side Being as lighting-process calls for delineation of the nature and function of the *intellectus agens*, on another side it would simultaneously point up the need for a thorough reinterrogation of what John of St. Thomas referred to in an important treatise as the "celebrated problem" of the *primum cognitum*.[70] And just as the *intellectus agens* belongs to the ontic dimension of Dasein, so this other side of the interrogation moves directly into the "Being-ontologically" of Dasein. Thus this second line of analysis would seek to penetrate the second crucial ambiguity in Heidegger's thought, that concerning the relationship between Dasein and Being.[71] (We shall see that it is in this direction that the very significant contribution of Heideggerean thought to the progress of philosophy lies, in this direction too that his possible contributions to theological reflection lie.) On this accounting, "beings" would signify extramental reality precisely and only in the measure

---

[69] "Uber den Zusammenhang der beiden Modi von Seinscharakteren kann erst aus dem geklärten Horizont der Seinsfrage gehandelt werden." (SZ, p. 45).

[70] See *Cursus Phil.*, II, q. 1, art. 3. Some indication of the complexities of such a reinterrogation can be garnered from the analysis of conflicting Thomistic views put forward by Laporte, *art. cit.*, pp. 28-35. According to Laporte, two equally legitimate senses should be recognized in the notion of *ens ut primum cognitum*, "one explicit and restricted, the second implicit and transcendental" – a distinction which Laporte suggests as able to resolve the conflicts. Cf. Maritain, DS, p. 215; L. M. Regis, *Epistemology* (New York: Macmillan, 1959), pp. 284-89; G. P. Klubertanz, *Philosophy of Being* (New York: Appleton-Century-Crofts, 1955), pp. 39-40, 45; L. Lachance, *L'être et ses propriétés* (Montréal: Levrier, 1950), pp. 17-40. Several of the relevant texts in St. Thomas must also be noted: *Summa*, I, q. 5, art. 2; q. 79, art. 7; q. 84, art. 7; q. 87, art. 3 ad 1; q. 88, art. 3. *De veritate*, q. 1, arts. 1 and 2 ad 4; q. 8, art. 15; q. 18, art. 8 ad 4. *In Met.*, I, lect. 2, n. 46; IV, lect. 6, n. 605. *De trinitate*, q. 6, art. 4.

[71] See fn. 33 of Chapter II, pp. 311-12 *supra*.

that it had entered upon intentional existence, had become *esse intentionale*, i.e., only as it had entered into the intentional life of man (men). Without being quite sure of Fr. Richardson's own meaning, it is in this sense that we would employ the statement that "it is the 'intentionality of Being' (. . .) that at all times was the unsaid of Heidegger I, rendering possible the entire structure of concern."[72]

We say thus that when these various lines of analyses in both directions are considered together and interwoven, they result in the idea of the Intentional Life of man, and if this Intentional Life be rendered thematic, it yields within the perspectives of Thomistic thought a parallel, more or less equivalent, to the notion of Dasein. We mentioned that "intentional" here must be technically taken and understood in the sense of *esse intentionale*, in something like the authentically Thomistic and developed sense given it by Jacques Maritain, and not at all in the *Intentionalität* sense given it by Edmund Husserl. The matter is difficult and important enough to justify, if not demand, direct treatment, "for a wave of the hand away from Husserl and toward Maritain is not quite enough to supply apodictic evidence. . ."[73]

What is at issue is the fundamental idea which governs our re-trieve.

[72] H:TPT, p. 627.
[73] Fr. Richardson's letter of August 1, 1966.

CHAPTER V

DASEIN AND THE REGRESS TO CONSCIOUS AWARENESS

"Ein Versuch, vom Vorstellen des Seienden als solchen in das Denken an die Wahrheit des Seins überzugehen, muss, von jenem Vorstellen ausgehend, in gewisser Weise auch die Wahrheit des Seins noch vorstellen, so dass dieses Vorstellen notwendig anderer Art und schliesslich als Vorstellen dem Zu-denkenden ungemäss bleibt. Dieses aus der Metaphysik herkommende, auf den Bezug der Wahrheit des Seins zum Menschenwesen eingehende Verhältnis wird als Verstehen gefasst. Aber das Verstehen ist hier zugleich aus der Unverborgenheit des Seins her gedacht. Es ist der ekstatische, d.h. im Bereich, des Offenen innestehende geworfene Entwurf. Der Bereich, der sich im Entwerfen als offener zustellt, damit in ihm etwas (hier das Sein) sich als etwas (hier das Sein als es selbst in seiner Unverborgenheit) erweise, heisst der Sinn (vgl. S. u. Z. S. 151). 'Sinn von Sein' und 'Wahrheit des Seins' sagen das Selbe."
Martin Heidegger, *Was ist Metaphysik*, p. 18.

There is no doubt that for Heidegger the question of Being cannot be resolved in terms of conscious awareness. It is equally certain that the sphere of awareness provides the necessary access to the question. Thus the very title of our chapter is an allusion to the crucial text on "The Idea of Phenomenology"[1] wherein Heidegger sets forth both the prerogatives and limits of

[1] "Versuch Einer Zweiten Bearbeitung. Einleitung. Die Idee der Phänomenologie und der Rückgang auf das Bewusstsein," in *Husserliana*, Band IX, Phänomenologische Psychologie (Den Haag: Martinus Nijhoff, 1962), Herausgegeben von Walter Biemel; Ergänzender Text von Martin Heidegger, pp. 256-63. Hereafter referred to as "Die Idee der Phänomenologie." This is a particularly valuable essay, both for what it says and for the circumstances of its composition.

When Husserl was asked by Encyclopedia Britannica c. 1927 to write the article on Phenomenology, he tried to use this as an occasion to "reconcile" Heidegger to his own (Husserl's) philosophical position. Accordingly, he asked Heidegger to co-author the Britannica article with him. "Die Idee der Phänomenologie" is the draft article which Heidegger drew up in response to Husserl's request. It is called "a second formulation" be-

consciousness as the sphere of access to the question, if not the truth, of Being. Starting with the transcendent Dasein as the only adequate phenomenal base from which to set out in determining the sense of Being, "it is not so much a question of pursuing a study of the intrinsic constitution of transcendence as of elucidating its essential unity with affective tonalities ontologically understood and thrownness," i.e., the referential dependency of Dasein on Beings.[2]

Let us follow this order of questioning across and beyond the threshold of awareness as such, and see for ourselves where it leads.

To be a self is a decisive feature in the nature of (man in his) Dasein as "that being which alone exists" (for in Heidegger the term "existence" denotes exclusively and in sharp contrast with traditional usage "the Being of those beings" – men in their Daseins – "who stand open for the openness of Being in which they stand"[3]); but this existence, this existential nature of

cause it is referenced by Husserl's initial draft for Britannica, which draft was in Heidegger's possession.

Heidegger's attempt at a second formulation was rejected by Husserl, and the Britannica article appeared under Husserl's signature alone. In a letter of December 26, 1927, to Roman Ingarden, Husserl contended that "Heidegger has not grasped the whole meaning of the phenomenological reduction" (Spiegelberg, I, 281). (As a matter of fact, there is reason to contend rather that Husserl, with a less pure insight into the genuine philosophical import of the phenomenological research-principle, failed to grasp the superfluity of the phenomenological 'reduction' – see fn. 25 of Chapter III and also Chapter IX of the present study.)

Thus this essay on "The Idea of Phenomenology" represents the final parting of ways between Heidegger and Husserl, and it gives some fundamental insights into the early Heidegger's methodological conception which have not been adequately incorporated even by so thorough an authority as Fr. Richardson.

[2] "Es gilt nicht so sehr, das Verstehen sogleich bis in die innerste Verfassung der Transzendenz zu verfolgen, als vielmehr seine wesenhafte Einheit mit der Befindlichkeit und Geworfenheit des Daseins aufzuhellen.

"Aller Entwurf – und demzufolge auch alles 'schöpferische' Handeln des Menschen – ist *geworfener*, d. h. durch die ihrer selbst nicht mächtige Angewiesenheit des Daseins auf das schon Seiende im ganzen bestimmt. Die Geworfenheit aber beschränkt sich nicht auf das verborgene Geschehen des Zum-Dasein-kommens, sondern sie durchherrscht gerade das Da-sein als ein solches. Das drückt sich in dem Geschehen aus, das als Verfallen herausgestellt wird. Dieses meint nicht die allenfalls negativ und kulturkritisch abschätzbaren Vorkommnisse im Menschenleben, sondern einen mit dem geworfenen Entwurf einigen Charakter der innersten transzendentalen Endlichkeit des Daseins." (KM, pp. 212-13/244).

[3] "Was bedeutet 'Existenz' in S. u. Z.? Das Wort nennt eine Weise des Seins, und zwar das Sein desjenigen Seienden, das offen steht für die Offenheit des Seins, in der es steht, indem es sie aussteht. . . Das ekstatische Wesen der Existenz wird deshalb auch dann noch unzureichend verstanden, wenn man es nur als 'Hinausstehen' vorstellt und das 'Hinaus' als das 'Weg von' dem Innern einer Immanenz des Bewusstseins und des Geistes auffasst; denn so verstanden, wäre die Existenz immer noch von der 'Subjektivität' und der 'Substanz' her vorgestellt, während doch das 'Aus' als das Auseinander der Offenheit des Seins selbst zu denken bleibt. Die Stasis des Ekstatischen beruht, so seltsam es klingen mag, im

man which makes possible his representation of and consciousness of beings
in the first place,[4] according to what is essential to it "does not consist in
being a self, nor can it be defined in such terms,"[5] for the fundamental
reason that Dasein, as "Being-in-the world cannot be reduced to a relation
between subject and object," which self-hood (unlike "mineness") necessarily implies. "It is, on the contrary, that which makes such a relation possible,
insofar as transcendence carries out the projection of the Being of beings."[6]

Now if we ask ourselves where for St. Thomas the subject-object dichotomy is transcended, where it at once disappears in order to become derivatively (analytically) possible, it must be answered that subject-object considerations are "swallowed up" in that unique kind of existence which is
neither the proper act of existence of the subject knowing or subject known
as such (object), nor of their accidents (a kind of existence, therefore, which,
like the "existence" of which Heidegger speaks, is sharply distinguished
from the usual metaphysical sense of *esse* which refers "to the reality of
anything at all that is [entitatively] real, from God to a grain of sand.")[7]).
This altogether and irreducibly unique order of things was called by St.
Thomas the intentional order, the sphere of *esse intentionale*, sometimes
esse immateriale or (less properly) *esse spirituale*. Subject-object thinking is
not adequate to the problematic constituted by question directly interrogating the *ens* of *esse intentionale* precisely because intentionality in its proper
office is neither a thing in itself (substance) nor the modification of some
thing (accident). The incommensurability of subject-ist thinking to this
order of things is clear on two counts. First of all, "even when *esse intentionale* has nothing to do with the world of knowledge, it is already a way
for forms to escape from [entitative] entombment in matter";[8] and secondly,

---

Innestehen im 'Aus' und 'Da' der Unverborgenheit, als welche das Sein selbst west...
Das Seiende, das in der Weise der Existenz ist, ist der Mensch. Der Mensch allein existiert." (WM:In, p. 15/214).

[4] "Das existenziale Wesen des Menschen ist der Grund dafür, dass der Mensch Seiendes
als ein solches vorstellen und vom Vorgestellten ein Bewusstsein haben kann." (WM:In, p.
16/214).

[5] "Ein Selbst zu sein, kennzeichnet zwar das Wesen desjenigen Seienden, das existiert,
aber die Existenz besteht weder im Selbstsein, noch bestimmt sie sich aus diesem." (WM:
In, p. 16/215).

[6] "Das In-der-Welt-sein ist aber nicht erst die Beziehung zwischen Subjekt und Objekt,
sondern das, was eine solche Beziehung zuvor schon ermöglicht, sofern die Transzendenz
den Entwurf des Seins von Seiendem vollzieht." (KM, p. 212/243-4).

[7] "... in der Sprache der Metaphysik das Wort 'Existenz' ... meint, nämlich die Wirklichkeit jedes beliebigen Wirklichen von Gott bis zum Sandkorn ..." (WM:In, p. 14/213).

[8] "L'*esse intentionale*, même quand il ne concerne pas le monde de la connaissance, est
déjà pour les formes une manière d'échapper à l'ensevelissement dans la matière." (DS, p.
223/115). And Maritain goes on to add: "Nous pensons qu'il y aurait grand intérêt pour
les philosophes à étudier le rôle qu'il joue dans le monde physique lui-même, où sans doute

even when *esse intentionale* is considered relative to the world of knowledge as the kind of existence which defines its very possibility, "St. Thomas has never made understanding consist in the intellect's being (entitatively) informed by the word or representative quality, but rather in its being (intentionally) informed by the object or *res intellecta*" *by means of* the word as vicar of the object and *medium quo* of knowledge.[9] Even in the context of thought and knowledge therefore "it is a capital mistake to confuse the (intentional) information of the intellect by the object, thanks to the concept, with the (entitative) information of the intellect by the concept."[10] Everything depends on this point being unshakably grasped. It means:

The act of knowing is none of the actions we customarily observe round about us; it is not part of the category *agere* – nor of the category *pati* – in Aristotle's table. Taken purely in itself, it does not consist in the production of anything, even within the knowing subject. To know is to advance oneself to an act of existing that, in itself, does not involve production.

relève de lui cette sorte d'animation universelle par laquelle le mouvement met dans les corps plus qu'ils ne sont, et colore la nature entière d'un semblant de vie et de sentiment. Quoi qu'il en soit, ce qui nous importe ici, c'est son rôle dans la connaissance et dans les opérations immatérielles de celle-ci, c'est la présence intentionelle de l'objet dans l'âme et la transformation intentionnelle de l'âme en l'objet, fonction l'une et l'autre de l'immatérialité (imparfaite pour le sens, absolue pour l'intelligence) des facultés cognitives." (DS, pp. 223-4/115). As we shall see in Chapter VII, this resolute dichotomy between sense and intellect is resolved and overcome at the single root of the soul's powers.

[9] See John of St. Thomas, *Cursus Theol.*, I P., q. 27, disp. 12, art. 5, n. 11. In his *History of the Phenomenological Movement*, vol. I, p. 40 fn. 2, Spiegelberg gives a brief presentation of the sense of intentionality according to the usage, supposedly, of St. Thomas Aquinas. It is unfortunate but perhaps inevitable that in such an encompassing work of scholarship occasional caricatures will occur. They cannot for that reason be pardoned, the less so the more fundamental they are. It must be said that the presentation of St. Thomas' usage by Spiegelberg bears no readily recognizable relation to St. Thomas' actual usage. And the relation does not become any more discernible with a second scrutiny. Many of the pertinent texts from St. Thomas' works which treat of this matter have been gathered together by Jacques Maritain in the first *Annexe* to *Les degrés du savoir*, "A propos du concept," pp. 769-819/387-417. A careful reading even of these selected texts renders inadmissable Spiegelberg's characterization of the scholastic *intentionale* as "a kind of distillate from the world outside"; or his statement that *secunda intentio* refers "to logical categories"; or his claim that, as regards the various kinds of *intentio* distinguished by Aquinas, "Never is there any suggestion of a reference to an object as the distinguishing characteristic of these 'intentions' "; and even his claim that the notion of an "intentional relation" has "no standing among the genuine Scholastics." In short, every point mentioned in his footnote is eccentric – literally "off center". It is regrettable that Professor Spiegelberg should have chosen, even indeliberately, the easy method of historical distortion in order to bring out Brentano's originality in appropriating the term "intentional."

[10] "Comme nous le notons dans nos *Réflexions sur l'intelligence* (p. 67), c'est une erreur capitale . . . de confondre l'information (intentionelle) de l'intelligence par l'objet grâce au concept, avec l'information (entitative) de l'intelligence par le concept." (DS, pp. 800-801/404).

In fact, there is a production of an image in sensitive knowledge and of a mental word, or concept, in intellectual knowledge; but that inner production is not formally the act itself of knowing. It is at once a condition and a means, and an [entitative] expression [or derivative] of that act.[11]

For all these reasons the ancients said that the act of knowing "is a properly immanent action, a perfectly vital action, belonging to the category 'quality'."[12] But it fits even into this entitative category (which is after all what the *praedicamenta* were designed to be) only derivatively, and not according to what is most formal and "proper" to it. What we want to bring out in this chapter is that the irreducibility of the order of *esse intentionale* can be understood strictly, in such wise that *esse intentionale* cannot really be fitted into a substance-accident ontology (which is not quite the same, Heidegger notwithstanding, as an act-potency Metaphysics) except it be considered not in the pure line of knowing but in the line rather of the conditions for knowledge in finite beings. It will be apparent that this strict interpretation has

---

[11] "L'acte de connaissance n'est aucune des actions que nous avons coutume d'observer autour de nous, il ne fait pas partie du prédicament 'action' – ni du prédicament 'passion' – de la table d'Aristote; pris purement en lui-même, il ne consiste pas dans la production de quelque chose, ... Connaître, c'est se porter soi-même à un acte d'exister d'une perfection suréminente, cela ne comporte pas, de soi, production.

"De fait il y a production d'une image dans la connaissance sensitive, d'un verbe mentale ou concept dans la connaissance intellectuelle; mais cette production intérieure n'est pas formellement l'acte lui-même de connaissance, elle est à la fois une condition et un moyen, et une expression de cet acte." (DS, p. 220/113).
Compare these observations of Dondeyne: "Pour Heidegger, l'expérience donatrice originaire du 'faire-être' se situe à un niveau autre que l'action productrice au sens habituel de ce terme; elle se confond avec notre expérience originaire de présence-au-monde et le 'Sein-lassen' libérateur qui en constitue en quelque sorte l'essence intime. C'est dire déjà qu'elle est de l'ordre de la 'parole' ou, ce qui revient au même, de la 'vérité' entendu au sens heideggerien de *aletheia* (dévoilement: *Entbergung*). L'avènement de la vérité (*das Geschehen der Wahrheit*), grâce au laisser-être libérateur (*Sein-lassen*) est, pour Heidegger, l'*événement significatif premier* (*das Urgeschehen*): c'est là que tout d'abord quelque chose 'se passe', 'se produit'. Là réside le fondement de toutes les modalités du produire et des innombrables sens que l'expression 'faire être', 'fonder' peut revêtir: '*Im Entbergen gründet* jedes Her-vorbringen' (Die Frage nach der *Technik* dans *Vorträge und Aufsätze*, Günther Neske Pfullingen, 1954, p. 20). C'est pourquoi l'activité réalisatrice par excellence n'est pas la fabrication des machines mais la création de l'oeuvre d'art, le dire des poètes et la pensée du penseur original. Ce n'est pas sans raison que, pour désigner ces formes soidisant improductives de l'action, le langage courant se soit toujours servi du terme 'création'." (*Art. cit.*, p. 266).
[12] "C'est pourquoi les anciens disaient que l'acte de connaître est une action proprement immanente, et parfaitement vitale, qui appartient au prédicament 'qualité'." (DS, p. 221/113). Concerning the intellect as productive, that is, on the production of the mental word by the act of intellection, an act which, though immanent as such, is yet virtually productive, see Cajetan, *In sum. theol.*, I, q. 27, art. 1; q. 34, art. 1 ad 2; also John of St. Thomas, *Cursus Phil.*, III P., q. 11, art. 1; *Cursus Theol.*, I P., q. 27, disp. 12, art. 5 (Vives, T. IV). Also DS, pp. 393, 395, 409, 411.

never been rendered fully thematic in Thomism, and we shall show that it must become so if Thomism is to incorporate and *realize* within itself the measure of truth in Heidegger's philosophy, in order that that truth as such may become seizable and demonstrable, formed and organically articulated as a definitive step in the progress of philosophy.

We note then that the kind of existence which defines not only the possibility of thought and knowledge but their actuality as well, *die Sache des Denkens* for St. Thomas, is *esse intentionale*, that order of reality wherein subject and object are united in a single, suprasubjective mode of existing, in an *actus perfecti* which is precisely other than the actuality either of the subject known or of the subject knowing – other even from the mind (*anima*) of the subject (actually or possibly) knowing. Having noted that, let us proceed to set down several points of remarkable coincidence which turn up along a line of analysis terminologically not indicated by the usual thrust (*ad ens quod est extra animam*) of properly metaphysical analyses; points that may serve to aid us in seeing aright the unusual perspective Heidegger is seeking to establish through and (he would almost say) in spite of "metaphysical" terminology, terminology which, directed as it is straight to the beings in the first instant, precisely does not primordially intend that which *Denken des Seins* must keep principally in view.

Suppose we were to say that Heidegger is concerned with the inner nature and root possibility of that which we call thought or knowledge, as Fr. Richardson suggests is the case;[13] and suppose we were to make some preliminary assessment of the analytic approaches which Thomistic philosophy affords for this problem (in the present chapter we shall consider principally approaches to the first part of the problem, the inner nature of thought, taking up in the next chapters the problem of its root possibility – but without ruling out in advance on the dubious grounds of methodological purity whatever entitative considerations may prove essentially bound up, however secondarily and derivatively, with an integral delineation of that root possibility). What would such an assessment show? To keep our inventory within reasonable length, we will base the comparative assessment principally on two sources, Maritain's *Les degrés du savoir* and Heidegger's *Sein und Zeit*.

In any such assessment, it would have to be noted at once that "it is a kind of existence which defines knowledge"[14] that the scholastics called "*esse intentionale*",[15] the very notion and whole meaning of which "first came to it

[13] H:TPT, p. 16.
[14] "C'est une sorte d'existence qui définit la connaissance." (DS, pp. 218-219/112-113).
[15] DS, p. 219/114.

from its opposition to the *esse entitativum* of the extramental thing"[16] (*das Sein als das Nicht-Seiende*?); moreover, this original notion of *esse intentionale* is not "an explanatory factor already known and clarified by some other means";[17] for everything our intellect knows "it knows by referring it in some way to the sensible things of nature"[18] which are precisely not "intentionalia" (ontic and not ontological?) – i.e., the *ens* of *esse intentionale* is never given directly in our experience of entities, "rather, it is anything that *makes known*, before itself being a known object. More exactly, let us say it is something that, before being known as object by a reflective act, is known only by the very knowledge that brings the mind to the object through its mediation. In other words, *it is not known by 'appearing' as object but by 'disappearing' in the face of the object* [ontological difference?], for its very essence is to bear the mind to something other than itself."[19] Thus, thought "has no need to get outside of itself to attain the thing that exists or can exist outside knowledge. . . because the very glory of the immateriality of thought is not to be a thing in space exterior to another extended thing, but rather a life which is superior to the whole order of space. . . a higher life which perfects itself by that which is not it, itself, even without going outside itself."[20] Similarly, "When Dasein directs itself toward something and grasps it, it does not somehow first get out of an inner sphere in which it has proximally been encapsulated, but its primary kind of Being is such that it is always 'outside' alongside beings which it encounters and which belong to a world already discovered."[21] The *esse intentionale* of thought therefore "is

[16] ". . . tout son sens lui vient d'abord de son opposition à l'*esse entitativum* de la chose extramentale." (DS, p. 200/103).

[17] ". . . la notion . . . n'est [pas] pour le philosophe un élément d'explication déjà connu ou déjà élucidé par ailleurs." (DS, pp. 224-5/115).

[18] ". . . tout ce que notre intelligence connait . . . elle le connaît en le rapportant en quelque façon aux choses sensibles de la nature." (DS, p. 256/132).

[19] ". . . c'est quelque chose qui fait connaître avant d'être soi-même objet connu, disons plus précisément, quelque chose qui avant d'être soi-même connu comme objet par un acte réflexif, n'est connu que de la connaissance même qui par son moyen porte l'esprit à l'objet, en d'autres termes, est connu non en 'apparaissant' comme objet mais en 'disparaissant' devant l'objet, parce que son essence même est de rapporter l'esprit à autre chose que soi." (DS, p. 232/119-20).

[20] ". . . la connaissance n'a pas à sortir d'elle-même pour atteindre la chose existant ou pouvant exister hors d'elle . . . parce que la gloire même de son immatérialité est de n'être pas une chose dans l'espace extérieure à une autre chose étendue, mais bien une vie supérieure à tout l'ordre de la spatialité, qui sans sortir de soi se parfait de ce qui n'est pas elle." (DS, pp. 201-2/104).

[21] "Im Sichrichten auf. . . und Erfassen geht das Dasein nicht etwa erst aus seiner Innensphäre hinaus, in die es zunächst verkapselt ist, sondern es ist seiner primären Seinsart nach immer schon 'draussen' bei einem begegnenden Seienden der je schon entdeckten Welt." (SZ, p. 62).

not only that property of my consciousness of being directed transparency, of aiming at objects in the depths of itself. Above all, intentionality is a property of thought, a prerogative of its immateriality, whereby being in it-self, posited 'outside it', i.e., being which is fully independent of the act of thought, becomes a thing existing within it, set up for it and integrated into its own act through which, from that moment, they both exist in thought with a single, self-same suprasubjective existence."²² And this responds rather directly to Heidegger's question:

Whither and whence and in what free dimension could the intentionality [taken as no more than that property of my consciousness of aiming at objects in the depths of itself – the Husserlian sense which is only a limited aspect of Thomistic *esse in-tentionale*, as Maritain indicates] of consciousness move, if instancy [i.e., 'the open-standing standing-in in the unconcealedness of Being, from Being, in Being'] were not the essence of man in the first instance? What else could be the meaning ... of the word *Sein* in the terms *Bewusstsein* (conscious awareness) and *Selbst-bewusstsein* (self-consciousness) if it did not designate the existential nature of that which is in the mode of existence?²³

It is neither (man) the knower as such nor still less the "real" thing known, not therefore either term of a relationship but the *esse intentionale* con-stitutive of the relationship itself and as such, which is the Being of the There and has accordingly the fundamental structure of what Heidegger chooses to term "existence" (*Existenz*, later *Ek-sistenz*): "This 'Being' of the There, and only this, has the fundamental structure of ek-sistence, sc. taking a stance ecstatically within the truth of Being."²⁴

In short, for our assessment "it is within thought itself that extramental being is grasped,"²⁵ but precisely and only insofar as this "extramental being" has entered upon the intentional mode of existence: "Thus we must distinguish between the thing as thing – as existing or able to exist for itself [*secundum esse entitativum*] – and the thing as object – when it is set before

---

²² "L'intentionalité n'est pas seulement cette propriété de ma conscience d'être une transparence dirigée, de viser des objets au sein d'elle-même, elle est avant tout cette pro-priété de la pensée, privilège de son immatérialité, par quoi l'être pour soi posé 'hors d'elle', c'est-à-dire pleinement indépendant de son acte à elle, devient existant en elle, posé pour elle et intégré à son acte à elle, et par quoi désormais elle et lui existent en elle d'une seule et même existence supra-subjective." (DS, p. 200/103).

²³ "Wohin und woher und in welcher freien Dimension sollte sich denn alle Intentiona-lität des Bewusstseins bewegen, wenn der Mensch nicht schon in der Inständigkeit sein Wesen hatte? Was anderes kann, falls man je ernstlich daran gedacht hat, das Wort '-sein' in den Namen 'Bewusstsein' und 'Selbstbewusstsein' nennen als das existenziale Wesen dessen, das ist, indem es existiert?" (WM:In, p. 16/215).

²⁴ "Dieses 'Sein' des Da, und nur dieses, hat den Grundzug der Ek-sistenz, das heisst des ekstatischen Innestehens in der Wahrheit des Seins." (HB, p. 69/278).

²⁵ "C'est dans la pensée même que l'être extramental est atteint. . ." (DS, p. 201/104).

the faculty of knowing and made present to it [*secundum esse intentionale per modum speciale specei expressae*]."[26] Heidegger writes: "Beings *are*, quite independently of the experience by which they are disclosed, the acquaintance in which they are discovered, and the grasping in which their nature is ascertained. But Being 'is' only in the understanding of those beings to whose Being something like an understanding of Being belongs."[27]

If our cognition as finite must be receptive intuition, then it is not sufficient merely to establish this fact, for the problem now arises: What does the possibility of this by no means self-evident reception of the being entail?

Obviously this: that the being by itself can come forward to be met, i.e., appear as ob-jective. However, if the presence of the being is not subject to our control, then our being-dependent on its reception requires that the being have in advance and at all times the possibility of becoming an object.

A receptive intuition can take place only in a faculty which lets something become an object in an act of orientation toward. . ., which alone constitutes the possibility of a pure correspondence. And what is it that we, by ourselves, let become an object? It cannot be something entitative. If not a being, then a Nothing (*Nichts*). Only if the act of objectification is a holding oneself into Nothing can an act of representation within Nothing let, in place of it, something not Nothing, i.e., a being, come forward to be met, supposing such to be empirically manifest. Naturally, this Nothing of which we speak is not the *nihil absolutum*.[28]

Nor is it the (knowing subject's) act of objectification as such; so that "if it is proper to the knower to be another thing than what it is, we must needs, to

[26] ". . . il nous faut donc distinguer la chose en tant que chose, existant ou pouvant exister pour elle-même, et la chose en tant qu' objet, posé devant la faculté de connaître et rendu présent à elle." (DS, p. 176-91).

[27] "Seiendes *ist* unabhängig von Erfahrung, Kenntnis und Erfassen, wodurch es erschlossen, entdeckt und bestimmt wird. Sein aber 'ist' nur im Verstehen des Seienden, zu dessen Sein so etwas wie Seinsverständnis gehört." (SZ, p. 183).

[28] "Wenn sonach unser Erkennen als endliches ein hinnehmendes Anschauen sein muss, dann genügt es nicht, dies nur einzugestehen, sondern jetzt erwacht erst das Problem: was gehört denn notwendig zur Möglichkeit dieses keineswegs selbstverständlichen Hinnehmens von Seiendem?

"Doch offenbar dieses, dass Seiendes von sich aus begegnen, d. h. als Gegenstehendes sich zeigen kann. Wenn wir aber des Vorhandenseins des Seienden nicht mächtig sind, dann verlangt gerade die Angewiesenheit auf das Hinnehmen desselben, dass dem Seienden im vorhinein und jederzeit die Möglichkeit des Entgegenstehens gegeben wird.

"Allein in einem Vermögen des Gegenstehenlassens von. . ., in der eine reine Korrespondenz allererst bildenden Zuwendung-zu. . ., kann sich ein hinnehmendes Anschauen vollziehen. Und was ist es, was wir da von uns aus entgegenstehen lassen? Seiendes kann es nicht sein. Wenn aber nicht Seiendes, dann eben ein Nichts. Nur wenn das Gegenstehenlassen von. . . ein Sichhineinhalten in das Nichts ist, kann das Vorstellen anstatt des Nichts und innerhalb seiner ein nicht Nichts, d. h. so etwas wie Seiendes begegnen lassen, falls solches sich gerade empirisch zeigt. Allerdings ist dieses Nichts nicht das nihil absolutum. Welche Bewandtnis es mit diesem Gegenstehenlassen von... hat, gilt es zu erörtern." (KM, p. 71/76-7).

avoid absurdity, distinguish two ways of having existence; we have to conceive of an *esse* that is not the proper act of existing of the subject as such or of its accidents."[29] There is an entitative order of things, according to which things are isolated unto themselves alone, not in an absolute independence, to be sure, but in such wise that "this is not that," in such wise that plurality and individuation are characteristic features of beings, in such wise that beings *are*, quite independently of the experience by which they are disclosed, the acquaintance in which they are discovered, and the grasping in which their nature is ascertained. It was to secure a basic understanding of this entitative or "ontic" order of beings that Aristotle worked out the table of *praedicamenta*. But this entitative order does not as such embrace the ambit of the real. Consider: Being "is" only in the comprehension of those beings to whose Being something like an understanding of Being belongs.

We are forced, if we would conceive of knowledge without absurdity, to introduce the notion of a very special kind of existence, which the ancients called *esse intentionale*, intentional being, and which is opposed to *esse naturae*, i.e., to the being a thing possesses when it exists in its own nature [*secundum esse subjectivum*].
An existence according to which the known will be in the knower and the knower will be the known, *an entirely tendential and immaterial existence, whose office is* not *to posit a thing outside nothingness* for itself and as a subject, but, on the contrary, *for another thing and as a relation.*[30]

Not "*in* a relation" but "*as* a relation": the *esse intentionale* is the relationship itself and as such, but, according to what is most formal and proper to it, it is neither of the terms of the relation, no more in an "accidental" way way than in a "substantial" way. It simply belongs to an order other than the entitative (ontic). "How understand, then, the relationship between Being and ek-sistence?" asks Fr. Richardson. To answer the question, he cites a text from Heidegger: "Being is not just a term of the relation but itself *is* the relationship, '. . .insofar as it sustains ek-sistence in its existential,

---

[29] "Car enfin les scandales soufferts par le principe d'identité ne peuvent être qu'apparents, et il est sûr que si le propre du connaissant est d'être autre chose que ce qu'il est, nous devons, pour éviter l' absurdité, distinguer deux manières d'avoir l'existence, concevoir un *esse* qui ne soit pas l'êxister propre d'un sujet comme tel ou de ses accidents." (DS, p. 221/114).
[30] ". . .on est contraint, si l'on veut concevoir sans absurdité la connaissance, d'introduire la notion d'une sorte d'existence toute particulière, que les anciens appelaient *esse intentionale*, être intentionnel, et qui s'oppose à l'*esse naturae*, à l'être qu'une chose possède quand elle existe en sa propre nature.
. . . une autre sorte d'existence, selon laquelle le connu sera dans le connaissant, et le connaissant sera le connu: existence toute tendancielle et immatérielle, qui n'a pas pour office de poser une chose hors du néant pour elle-même et comme sujet, mais au contraire pour autre chose et comme relation . . ." (DS, pp. 221-2/114).

sc. ecstatic, presenc-ing and gathers it unto itself as the domain of the truth of Being in the midst of beings'."[31]

Esse intentionale, then,

is an existence that does not seal up the thing within the bounds of its nature, but sets it free from them. In virtue of that existence, the thing exists in the soul with an existence other than its own existence, and the soul is or becomes the thing with an existence other than *its* own existence. As Cajetan telles us, *intentional being* is there as a remedy for the imperfection essential to every created knowing subject, to wit, the imperfection of possessing a limited natural being and of not being, of itself, everything else.[32]

Thus the possibilities for error and illusion, for "being mistaken" generally, stem "simply from the disparity in the way things exist in these two worlds," the "world" or order of *esse intentionale* and the "world" of nature as *esse entitativum*. "That indicates that thought is not referred to the thing as a material transfer that coincides with its model: there is a gulf between the conditions or mode of thought and the conditions or mode of the thing."[33] Even at the level of explicit and reflexive awareness, precisely as intentionally present (i.e., if we consider the *ens* of its *esse intentionale*), "the concept is *so little a thing* or *object* that to say it is attained by understanding is to say *that the thing*, and not it, *is known as object*. It is known (in the direct act of understanding) only insofar as it is the actualizing form of the understanding of the object."[34] In this way the *ens* of *esse intentionale* has already been grasped preconceptually in the experience of beings as independent entities, as the necessary but not sufficient condition for their being recognized in their independence and known as such; it is known in advance, beforehand, a-priori, and in a non-conceptual or preconceptual manner at a literally pre-conscious level (we shall consider this last point in the seventh chapter).

[31] H:TPT, p. 536. "Das Sein selber ist das Verhältnis, insofern Es die Ek-sistenz in ihrem existenzialen, das heisst ekstatischen Wesen an sich hält und zu sich versammelt als die Ortschaft der Wahrheit des Seins inmitten des Seienden." (HB, p. 77/282).

[32] C'est une sorte d'existence "qui ne scelle pas la chose dans ses limites de nature, mais la dégage de celles-ci; en vertu de laquelle la chose existe dans l'âme selon une autre existence que son existence propre, et l'âme est ou devient la chose selon une autre existence que son existence propre: *être intentionnel*, qui est là, nous dit Cajetan, comme un remède à cette imperfection essentielle à tout sujet connaissant créé, d'avoir un être de nature limité; et de n'être pas par soi tout le reste." (DS, p. 222/114).

[33] "... la possibilité de l'erreur provient simplement de la disparité du mode d'exister des choses en ces deux mondes. Tout cela signifie que la pensée n'est pas à la chose comme un décalque matériel coïncidant avec un modèle: il y a un abîme entre les conditions ou le mode de la pensée et les conditions ou le mode de la chose." (DS, p. 167/86).

[34] "Le concept ... est *tellement peu une chose ou un objet*, que dire qu'il est atteint par l'intellection, c'est précisément dire que non pas lui mais *la chose est connu comme objet*. Il n'est connu (dans l'intellection directe) qu'en tant même qu'il est forme actualisatrice de l'intellection de l'objet." (DS, p. 785/394-5).

All this amounts to saying that the concept [considered in the character of being which is proper to it as manifestive, sc. *esse intentionale*] is a *formal sign*. Like every sign, it is a *praecognitum*, but in this case it is not only necessary to say that the sign is first known, with a simple priority of nature and not of time, but it should be added that it is known *formaliter*, in virtue of its being the actualizing form of knowledge – and not foreknown *denominative* as an object attained by knowledge.[35]

This notion of *esse intentionale* as a-priori in and for our encounter with entities, as a *signum formale praecognitum*, "has been 'made to measure' according to the exigencies of an analysis that respects the proper nature of knowledge. It belongs there and only there."[36] Heidegger says:

Only because Being is 'in the consciousness' – that is to say, only because it is understandable in Dasein – can Dasein also understand and conceptualize such characteristics of Being as independence, the 'in-itself', and Reality in general. Only because of this are 'independent' entities, as encountered within-the-world, accessible to circumspection.[37]

"Hence," for Heidegger, "Being can be something unconceptualized, but it never fails to be comprehended."[38]

But in all of this, most important of all is the observation that *esse intentionale* taken in its proper sense is not an accident, not a modification of a subject. "For after all, the scandals suffered by the principle of identity," which structures the entitative order in *its* proper kind of existing, "can only be apparent, and it is certain that, if it is proper to the knower to be another thing than what it is, we must needs, to avoid absurdity, distinguish two ways of having existence; we have to conceive of an *esse* that is not the proper act of existing of the subject as such or of its accidents."[39] "Taken

---

[35] "Tout cela revient à dire que le concept est *signe formel*. Comme tout signe, il est *praecognitum*, mais ici il ne faut pas seulement dire que le signe est préconnu d'une simple priorité de nature, et non de temps; on doit ajouter qu'il est préconnu *formaliter* à titre de forme actualisatrice de la connaissance, et non pas *denominative*, à titre d'objet atteint par la connaissance." (DS, pp. 783-4/394).

[36] "...cette notion a été taillée 'sur mesure', selon les exigences d'une analyse qui respecte la nature propre de la connaissance, elle ne convient que là." (DS, p. 234/120).

[37] "Nur weil Sein 'im Bewusstsein' ist, das heisst verstehbar im Dasein, deshalb kann das Dasein auch Seinscharaktere wie Unabhängigkeit, 'Ansich', überhaupt Realität verstehen und zu Begriff bringen. Nur deshalb ist 'unabhängiges' Seiendes als innerweltlich Begegnendes umsichtig zugänglich." (SZ, pp. 207-8).

[38] "Sein kann daher unbegriffen sein, aber es ist nie völlig unverstanden." (SZ, p. 183).

[39] "Car enfin les scandales soufferts par le principe d'identité ne peuvent être qu'apparents, il est sûr que si le propre du connaissant est d'être autre chose que ce qu'il est, nous devons, pour éviter l'absurdité, distinguer deux manières d'avoir l'existence, concevoir un *esse* qui ne soit pas l'exister propre d'un sujet comme tel ou de ses accidents." (DS, p. 221/114).

But one must be quick to add the crucial precisions worked out by John of St. Thomas in

purely in itself, [the act of thought and knowing] does not consist in the production of anything, even within the knowing subject."[40] In fact, of course, there is mental productivity and accidental modifications of the soul implicated in all human awareness; but that inner production and modification is not formally the *intentionale* of awareness, not that *esse* which makes thought to be thought. It is precisely in the order of *esse intentionale* that the subject-object relation is maintained without being in any proper sense primary – for a subject-object dichotomy is the immediate product of entitative (ontical) not intentional (ontological) analysis: "St. Thomas warns us that knowledge, taken not as an *accident* of the knower (a condition for the entitative order implied by all creative knowledge) but as a relation to the thing known and in the pure line of knowing, is not in the soul as in a subject in the *entitative* sense of the word 'in'."[41] This is so because it is outside any and every order of the entitative:

Considered with reference to the one who knows, thought is in the knower as an accident is in a substance; and in this context it does not surpass the boundaries of subjectivity, because it is never found anywhere other than in some mind... But considered with reference to that which is knowable... in this context it is not said that thought is in something, but that it is in a relation to something. That which is said by way of relation, however, does not have the defining features of an accident from the fact that there is a relationship, but solely from the quite distinct consideration that it is in (something)... And for this reason thought considered in what is proper to it is not in the soul as in a subject; in this context it goes beyond the confines of subjectivity insofar as something other than the mind is apprehended in the medium (the 'in-between') of thought... And too in this respect there is a certain equality of thought to the mind inasmuch as it embraces everything to which the mind is able to extend itself.[42]

dealing with this question in his *Cursus Philosophicus*, Vol. III, 178a10-179a44 and 185a26-187a42, esp. 186b3-16: "Et quando instatur, quod omnis unio realis vel est accidentalis vel substantialis, *respondetur*, quod in re ita est, quod onmis talis unio vel identice vel formaliter sit accidentalis vel substantialis, sed non requiritur, quod solum formaliter, sicut passiones entis, ut verum et bonum, non sunt formaliter ens, sed identice, alias non essent passiones entis, sed ens ipsum, cui passiones conveniunt. Unio autem objectiva intelligibilis datur ratione ipsius veri seu cognoscibilitatis, quae est passio entis."

[40] "L'acte de connaissance... pris purement en lui-même, il ne consiste pas dans la production de quelque chose, même à l'intérieur du sujet connaissant." (DS, p. 220/113).

[41] "... alors, saint Thomas nous avertit que la connaissance, considérée non pas comme *accident* du connaissant (condition d'ordre entitatif impliquée par toute connaissance créée), mais comme *relation* au connu et dans la pure ligne du connaître, n'est pas dans l'âme comme dans un sujet, en ce sens *entitatif* du mot 'dans' (parce qu'elle est en dehors de tout l'ordre de l'entitatif)." (DS, p. 165 fn. 1/85 fn. 1).

[42] St. Thomas, *Quodlib.*, VII, art. 4: "Secundum quod comparatur ad cognoscentem, notitia... inest cognoscenti sicut accidens in subjecto, et sic non excedit subjectum, quia nunquam invenitur inesse alicui nisi menti... Secundum quod comparatur ad cognoscibile, ... sic non habet quod insit, sed quod ad aliud sit. Illud autem quod ad aliquid

On this last sentence Maritain makes this gloss: "This does not prevent how-ever things known being in the soul in the intentional meaning indicated in the text and not in any entitative sense,"[43] which provides a basis for something very much like the phenomenological World! For to understand this non-entitative presence of things which is dependent upon but not re-ducible to the entitative "world of nature", a way of distinguishing other than that provided by the *praedicamenta* would be needed. Heidegger seeks to work out such another way, and calls his articulations *existentialia*; but the order to which they pertain is the order of *esse intentionale*, for in the original designation "ontological" meant for Metaphysics the entitative order. We will justify this observation in principle when we examine the methodological limits of phenomenological research.

But enough has already been shown to permit us to observe that for the scholastic to inquire thematically and directly into the *ens* of *esse intentionale* would be analogous to Heidegger's *Fundamentalontologie* or *Daseinsanalyse* taken as research into that which renders possible ("ontological truth") our encounter with entities ("ontic truth"), taken as inquiry about *die Sache des Denkens*. The distinction between the entitative and intentional orders, which literally cuts man in two (ontic and ontological dimensions?) – "intel-ligere et esse non sunt idem apud nos," St. Thomas would simply say[44] – is analogous to the ontological difference of Heidegger. And man insofar as he leads an intentional life (how far he does so we will consider in the following chapters) which is defined precisely by way of contradistinction to his existence as "a thing of nature" (and here we underscore that all and only that which has entered upon the modes of intentional existence is capable of contributing to the formation of the knower as such, a principle which holds equally regarding even the awareness of the self by the self[45]) corre-

dicitur, non habet rationem accidentis ex hoc quod est ad aliquid, sed solum ex hoc quod inest... Et propter hoc notitia secundum considerationem istam non est in anima sicut in subjecto; et secundum hanc comparationem excedit mentem inquantum alia a mente per notitiam cognoscuntur... Et secundum hoc etiam est quaedam aequalitas notitiae ad mentem, inquantum se extendit ad omnia ad quae potest se extendere mens." See also *Summa*, I, q. 93; *De veritate*, q. 10.

[43] "Ce qui n'empêche pas que les choses connues sont dans l'âme au sens non pas enti-tatif mais *intentionnel* indiqué dans le texte." (DS, p. 165 fn. 1/85 fn. 2). See fn. 32 of this Chapter *supra*.

[44] *De veritate*, q. 4, art. 4.

[45] According to St. Thomas, even the self becomes knowable only to the extent it enters upon the mode of *esse intentionale*. To maintain otherwise in fact would contravene the entire notion of intentionality as it is found in St. Thomas to begin with. "Quum intellectus noster seipsum intelligit, aliud est esse intellectus, et aliud ipsum eius intelligere; substantia enim intellectus," i.e., esse entitativum seu naturae intellectus, "erat in potentia intelligens antequam intelligeret actu. Sequitur ergo quod aliud sit esse intentionis intellectae, et

sponds to the idea of "*Ek-sistenz*" in Heidegger, to the idea of man's "existential nature."

As a *first approximation* (and no more), we say: the *ens* of *esse intentionale* seems to us to be the Being (*Sein*) of which Heidegger speaks. In the situation of awareness this *ens* (*primum tamquam prae-cognitum*) is hidden, concealed, *lēthe*, in the very beings which emerge into the definiteness of knowledge. Being-as-it-is-in-our-mind then, *ens quod est intra animam*, is the constitutive unity of real beings which are disclosed only insofar as they have entered into the intentional life of man, i.e., insofar as they have been brought into the mode of intentional existence – *sicut habens esse intentionale*.

Entities *are*, quite independently of the experience by which they are discovered, and the grasping in which their nature is ascertained. But Being 'is' only in the understanding of those entities to whose Being something like a comprehension of Being belongs. Hence Being can be something unconceptualized, but it never completely fails to be comprehended. In ontological problematics *Being and truth* have, from time immemorial, been brought together if not entirely identified. This is evidence that there is a necessary connection between Being and understanding, even if it may perhaps be hidden in its primordial grounds.[46]

What, in fine, is the character (*Sinn*) of the *Ens* out of which the *esse* of *esse intentionale* takes rise?

Thus we locate Heidegger in *das Problematik* of scholasticism. Such seems to us the truest sense of Dondeyne's observation:

We see that, with the theme of the ontological difference, Heideggerean thought holds a place in the grand tradition of the *philosophia perennis*. We ought now to examine in what way it distinguishes itself within that tradition.[47]

---

aliud esse intellectus ipsius, quum intentionis intellectae, esse sit ipsum intelligi. Unde oportet quod in homine intelligente seipsum, verbum interius conceptum non sit homo verus, naturale hominis esse habens, sed sit homo intellectus tantum, quasi quaedam similitudo hominis veri ab intellectu apprehensa. . . Intellectus *intelligendo* concipit et *format intentionem* sive rationem intellectam, quae est interius verbum." (*Summa contra gentes*, IV, ch. 11). See DS, pp. 807-8/408-9.

[46] "Seiendes *ist* unabhängig von Erfahrung, Kenntnis und Erfassen, wodurch es erschlossen, entdeckt und bestimmt wird. Sein aber 'ist' nur im Verstehen des Seienden, zu dessen Sein so etwas wie Seinsverständnis gehört. Sein kann daher unbegriffen sein, aber es ist nie völlig unverstanden. In der ontologischen Problematik wurden von altersher *Sein und Wahrheit* zusammengebracht, wenn nicht gar identifiziert. Darin dokumentiert sich, wenngleich in den ursprünglichen Gründen vielleicht verborgen, der notwendige Zusammenhang von Sein und Verständnis. Für die zureichende Vorbereitung der Seinsfrage bedarf es daher der ontologischen Klärung des Phänomens der *Wahrheit*." (SZ, p. 183).

[47] "Nous venons de voir que, par la thème de la différence ontologique, la pensée heidegerienne prend place dans la grande tradition de la *philosophia perennis*. Nous devons examiner maintenant par quoi elle se distingue à l'intérieur de cette tradition." (*Art. cit.*, p. 49).

For it is obvious that the comparisons we have drawn only situate Heidegger: they do not encompass his thought. Before that can be attempted, we shall have to broaden and deepen the problematic of St. Thomas' *esse intentionale* in a way that cannot be accomplished in terms simply of the sphere of conscious awareness.

Yet if man is considered insofar as he leads an intentional life in such wise that we methodologically preclude all entitative considerations, whether they be anterior or concomitant (sine qua non) to this intentional life, in such wise that "one looks away from all psychic functions in the sense of the organization of corporeality, that is to say, away from the psychophysical,"[48] (which, as we shall see, is precisely what phenomenological research as Heidegger conceives it in principle achieves); if moreover we call this intentional life man's ontological dimension, and call his natural or entitative being (in the sense of *suppositum*: the human substance concretely considered as exercising *esse*, therefore as dialectically or "accidentally" modified in countless dynamic ways) his ontic dimension; and if we keep in mind that we are concerned here only with placing Heidegger's thought according to what is proper to it along the main lines of Thomistic philosophy; then it will be seen that we have come a considerable way toward establishing in the language of Thomism the proper sense of Dasein.

Being-in-the-World, transcendence, existence – all these are one, namely, *Dasein*, which, as comprehension of Being, designates the essence of man... It will be noticed that in all these formulae there is implied a double dimension in *Dasein*: that dimension according to which *Dasein* is a being among the rest and like the rest, simply because it is; that dimension according to which *Dasein* differs from all other beings, because it has a privileged com-prehension of Being. Heidegger characterizes this double dimension by two sets of formulae. One set is geared to the word "existence." That dimension according to which *Dasein* is a being like the others is called "existentiell," and that according to which its structure is open to Being is called "existential." The second set of formulae comes from the Greek word for being: *on*. Accordingly, the existentiell dimension is called "ontic," the existential dimension is called "ontological." These two dimensions (levels) of *Dasein* are distinct but not separate. The ontic-existentiell level cannot be at all unless it be structured; reciprocally, unless there is a being for which the existential-ontological may serve as structure, it cannot be a structure.[49]

[48] "Den Erlebnissen zugewendet machen wir die Verhaltungsweisen der 'Seele', das rein Psychische zum Gegenstand. Rein Psychisches wird es genannt, weil im Hinsehen auf die Erlebnisse als solche abgesehen ist von allen seelischen Funktionen im Sinne der Organisation der Leiblichkeit, das heisst vom Psychophysischen. Die genannte phänomenologische Einstellung verschafft den Zugang zum rein Psychischen und ermöglicht die thematische Untersuchung desselben im Sinne einer reinen Psychologie." ("Die Idee der Phänomenologie," p. 258).

[49] Richardson, "The Place of the Unconscious in Heidegger," p. 278.

CHAPTER VI

INTENTIONALITÄT AND *INTENTIONALE:* TWO DISTINCT NOTIONS

"Huiusmodi autem viventia . . . habent duplex esse. Unum quidem materiale, in quo conveniunt cum aliis rebus materialibus. Aliud autem immateriale, in quo communicant cum substantiis superioribus aliqualiter. Est autem differentia inter utrumque esse: quia secundum esse materiale, quod est per materiam contractum, una quaeque res est hoc solum quod est, sicut hic lapis non est aliud quam hic lapis; secundum vero esse immateriale, quod est amplum, et quodammodo infinitum, inquantum non est per materiam terminatum, res non solum est id quod est, sed etiam est quodammodo alia. . . Huiusmodi autem immateriale esse habet duos gradus in istis inferioribus. Nam quoddam est penitus immateriale, sicut esse intelligibile. . . Esse autem sensibile est medium inter utrumque. Nam in sensu res habet esse sine materia, non tamen absque conditionibus materialibus individuantibus, neque absque organo corporali. Et quantum ad hoc duplex esse, dicit Philosophus in tertio huius (nn. 787-8, 790), quod anima est quodammodo omnia."
Saint Thomas Aquinas, *In II de anima*, lect. 5, nn. 282-284.

Still, is there not one severe shortcoming in our characterization thus far of Dasein as Intentional Life of Man? Even though the texts we have cited thus far go beyond subject-object polarity and by that very fact require a non-subject-ist (and a-fortiori non-subject*ive*) analysis, still, insofar as they make reference to the world of awareness, they do so by reference to concepts, elements of explicit awareness (albeit as pure *media quo*). Therefore, though they doubtless indicate a generally unthematized dimension in Thomism, they do so at the level of (what Heidegger would call) our "ontic comportment" with beings. To simply identify Dasein with the intentional life in these terms, at the level of explicit thought, is to destroy the very possibility of an authentic re-trieve of Heidegger I: "Any attempt to re-think *Being and Time* is thwarted as long as one is satisfied with the observation that, in this study, the term Dasein is used in place of 'consciousness';"[1] because "consciousness does not itself create the openness of Beings, nor is it consciousness that makes it possible for man to stand open for beings,"[2] whereas Dasein does. It is not a question of consciousness, but of the Being of consciousness.[3]

Thus Fr. Richardson, in a letter to me criticizing my original seminar paper, made these telling observations:

I would be more willing to concede that "Being-as-it-is-in-the-intellect [see fn. 64, VII]" is probably the closest approximation in Thomistic terms to what Heidegger is talking about than I would that the two problematics are one. . . it seems to me that the openness of *Dasein* (as phenomenal) to Being (as phenomenal) is deeper than (and antecedent to) access of the intelligence to its own *primum cognitum*. It seems to be the openness of the entire man (not just of his intelligence) in his very source (*Wesen*) to that process which lets beings be accessible as beings on any level – even in non-intellectual, i.e. pre-intellectual, contact. In this sense, I think it misleading to speak of *Dasein* as a field of "awareness" for this suggests that *Dasein* is no more than a subject, whereas *In-der-Welt-sein* is profoundly transcendence.[4]

For while (in Heideggerean thought) "it is by the *comprehension* of Being that man is defined. . . this comprehension is not of the order of the understanding, i.e., of what the classical thinkers call reason."[5]

It is necessary to remark here what we have already referred to, namely, that *esse intentionale* as the constitutive Being of a "field of awareness" as such is precisely not, is precisely other than, the proper actuality of the subject known or of the subject knowing, and therefore other than the mind (whether taken as *intellectus, mens,* or *anima*) of the subject (actually or possibly) knowing. But even with that precision in our meaning, the above admonitions are not yet taken seriously enough, because the intentionality (even in the *esse intentionale* sense) of conscious considerations "is not identical with transcendence" – which Dasein in the first place is – "much less the origin of it":[6]

The existential nature of man is the reason why man can represent beings as such, and why he can be conscious of them. All consciousness presupposes ecstatically

---

[1] "Darum wird nun auch jedes Nach-denken verbaut, wenn man sich begnügt festzustellen, in 'Sein und Zeit' werde statt 'Bewusstsein' das Wort 'Dasein' gebraucht." (WM: In, p. 14/213).
[2] "Das Bewusstsein dagegen schafft weder erst die Offenheit von Seiendem, noch verleiht es erst dem Menschen das Offenstehen für das Seiende." (WM:In, p. 16/215).
[3] See SZ, p. 207; WM:In, p. 16/215.
[4] Letter of August 1, 1966.
[5] De Waelhens, p. 482.
[6] Richardson, H:TPT, p. 178.

understood existence as the *essentia* of man – *essentia* meaning that as which man is present insofar as he is man. But consciousness does not itself create the openness of beings, nor is it consciousness that makes it possible for man to stand open for beings. Whither and whence and in what free dimension could the intentionality of consciousness move, if instancy were not the essence of man in the first instance? . . . To be a self is admittedly one feature of that being which exists; but existence does not consist in being a self, nor can it be defined in such terms.[7]

To get to the root of the notion of Dasein we must pass beyond the intentionality of conscious awareness to that which makes the emergence of such awareness a possibility in the first place. "This structure [i.e., Dasein] is to be thought after the manner of an original openness. Whatever is to be said of it in other respects, There-being is open to. . ., or, if one prefers, it is ecstatic."[8] Thus Heidegger denounces almost violently any attempt to interpret his thought on the primary basis of intentionality: "If one characterizes all *comportment* with beings as intentional, then *intentionality* is possible only *on the basis of transcendence*, but it is neither identical with this basis, nor even the inverse possibility of transcendence."[9] Fr. Richardson makes the following gloss on this text:

The remark, innocuous as it appears, yields the following inferences: First of all, the intentionality of consciousness as Husserl describes it (whether this intentionality be explicitly thematized, or remain unthematic and functional) is a relationship between *beings*, i.e., between a being as intentional consciousness and a being as intended as the immanent term of the conscious act. In other words, it is a comportment on the ontic-existentiell level. Secondly, the text suggests that this ontic-existentiell comportment with beings is first made possible by the ontological dimension of *Dasein*, by reason of which *Dasein* is open to the Being of these beings and thus can comport itself with them *as* beings. Thirdly, the text suggests that to conceive of man in Husserlian fashion as merely a being who is the subject of conscious (or, for that matter, unconscious) acts is to forget the true dimension that gives man his primacy among beings, namely, his comprehension of Being it-

[7] "Das existenziale Wesen des Menschen ist der Grund dafür, dass der Mensch Seiendes als ein solches vorstellen und vom Vorgestellten ein Bewusstsein haben kann. Alles Bewusstsein setzt die ekstatisch gedachte Existenz als die essentia des Menschen voraus, wobei essentia das bedeutet, als was der Mensch west, sofern er Mensch ist. Das Bewusstsein dagegen schafft weder erst die Offenheit von Seiendem, noch verleiht es erst dem Menschen das Offenstehen für das Seiende. Wohin und Woher und in welcher freien Dimension sollte sich denn alle Intentionalität des Bewusstseins bewegen, wenn der Mensch nicht schon in der Inständigkeit sein Wesen hätte?. . . Ein selbst zu sein, kennzeichnet zwar das Wesen desjenigen Seienden, das existiert, aber die Existenz besteht weder im Selbstsein, noch bestimmt sei sich aus diesem." (WM:In, p. 16/214-5).

[8] De Waelhens, p. 487.

[9] "Kennzeichnet man alles *Verhalten* zu Seiendem als intentionales, dann ist die *Intentionalität* nur möglich *auf dem Grunde der Transzendenz*, aber weder mit dieser identisch noch gar umgekehrt selbst die Ermöglichung der Transzendenz." *Vom Wesen des Grundes* (Frankfurt: Klostermann, 1955), p. 16. Hereafter referred to as WG.

self (in other words, it is another sign of the forgetfulness of Being). Fourthly, the text suggests that this com-prehension of Being characterizes *Dasein's* structure as a being, and when, as a being, *Dasein* enters into comportment with other beings, thus becoming a conscious subject, it is *Dasein's* ontological structure that lets it be a subject and lets it be conscious, but as structure is not conscious at all. Finally, the text suggests that *Dasein*, as Heidegger conceives it, is a *self*, to be sure, but *not a conscious subject*. It is a presubjective, onto-conscious self.[10]

Intentionality for Heidegger is of course, as Fr. Richardson's commentary suggests, primarily the *intentionalität* of the phenomenologists, and of Edmund Husserl's phenomenology in particular. In this respect (and the text from Heidegger only serves to underscore the point) there can be no questioning the verdict: "In analysing finite transcendence, Heidegger is trying to understand *that which renders all intentionality possible* by explaining the structure of that being which is simultaneously ontic (therefore intentional) and ontological (therefore 'transcendentally constituting')."[11] Taken in its totality and as such, Dasein is a *self* but not a subject. It is "a non-subjective, rather trans-subjective, or even pre-subjective self, sc. transcendence."[12] And if Dasein must be related to the conscious self, then Fr. Richardson's terminology is better than most: Dasein is not (necessarily) a conscious self, nor is it a pre-conscious or unconscious self in the Freudian sense; rather, it is a self that can become conscious as an ego, it is the

---

[10] "The Place of the Unconscious in Heidegger," p. 279.

[11] Richardson, H:TPT, p. 179: my emphasis.

[12] *Ibid.*, p. 101: "This self, however, even in the moment of its authenticity, always remains existentiell as well as existential. This is why we may legitimately speak of it as a 'subject', provided we understand that this terminology is limited to the ontic level and does not include the ontological perspective which constitutes the genuine primacy of There-being (cf., SZ, pp. 110, 111, 227, 229, 382). But such a manner of speaking has nothing to do with subjectivism, if this term be understood to designate an interpretation that restricts itself to the purely ontic dimension of There-being as a subject. '. . . If "subject" be conceived ontologically as existing Dasein, whose Being is grounded in temporality,. . .' then the term 'subjective' has the same sense as 'transcendent' and, in this sense, the World, too, is 'subjective.' '. . . But then this "subjective" World, insofar as it is temporal-transcendent, is more "objective" than any possible "object" (SZ, p. 366)".

"Transcendence, then, is more subjective than any subject and more objective than any object. There-being is not a subject in relation to an object but it is this relation itself, sc. that which is 'between' subject and object. This 'between' is not derived from, and therefore subsequent to, the juxtaposition of subject and object, but is prior to the emergence of this relation, rendering it possible. *The problem of transcendence, consequently, is not to explain how a subject goes out of itself in order to establish contact with an object, where object, understood as the totality of objects, is identified with the world, but how it comes-to-pass that There-being as to-be-in-the-World encounters other beings and then, once having discovered them, constitutes them as objects* (see SZ, pp. 132, 366)." (My emphasis). For Heidegger's own discussion of the emergence of the subject-object relation out of original transcendence, see SZ, pp. 59-62, 148-60, 223-25.

ontological dimension of the conscious subject *as* conscious – it is (if we must call it a "self") the *onto-conscious* self:

It will be perfectly clear to Heideggerean scholars that the term 'onto-conscious' has no textual foundation in Heidegger to recommend it. What it is intended to express, however, is quite simple. *Dasein* as a self that is *not a* (conscious) *subject* is very Heideggerean. It is one of the important themes in *Sein und Zeit*, but to call it simply 'non-subjective' is more misleading than to call it 'pre-subjective,' for it is a self that can *become* conscious as an ego. If by the same reasoning process we call it 'pre-conscious,' we run immediately into difficulty, for 'pre-conscious' (after Freud) has a consecrated meaning that is not at all what is intended here. We say 'onto-conscious' for want of something better, to suggest that the self in question is the ontological dimension of the conscious subject *as* conscious, the Being-dimension of Dasein by reason of which it is the "There" (*Da*) of Being among beings. This dimension is not conscious, therefore may be called '*un*conscious,' for the same reason that Being is not *a* being – in other words, because of the "not" that *differentiates* Being from beings and constitutes what Heidegger calls the 'ontological difference'.[13]

Would not therefore any interpretation of Dasein in terms of man's "intentional life" necessarily fly in the face of Heidegger's entire effort to "loosen up" (*destruieren*) the history of Western ontology, to overcome subjectivism and subjective thinking? Would not, in short, any such interpretation from the first betray itself to the proclivities of subject-ist metaphysics?

By now the proper sense of these questions should have come to the fore: before an affirmative answer ought to be admitted, it would have to be shown that the Thomistic notion of *esse intentionale* is no richer than the *Intentionalität* of Phenomenology. On this score, two points must be recorded from the beginning. First of all, there is no doubt that the intentionality defined by Husserl is incapable of accounting for and assessing any unconscious dimension of the mind, without first being extended and transformed.[14]

Secondly, it must be noted that there have been scholastic authors who saw in the notion of *esse intentionale* little more than the explicit consciousness of Husserl, the presentative thought of Heidegger. Thus Fr. M. D. Simonin considered that "the *intentio intellecta* alone is in *esse intentionale*. . .

---

[13] "The Place of the Unconscious in Heidegger," p. 280. See WG, p. 15.

[14] This is clear from the efforts made along this very line by such competent thinkers as A. De Waelhens, "Réflexions sur une problématique Husserlienne de l'inconscient, Husserl et Hegel," in *Edmund Husserl, 1859-1959* (The Hague: Martinus Nijhoff, 1959), pp. 221-237, esp. p. 225; Paul Ricoeur, "Philosophie de la volonté et de l' action," Proceedings of Second Lexington Conference on "The Phenomenology of Will and Action," Lexington, Ky., May 14-16: 1964: cited according to original French ms., pp. 24-6 (these "Proceedings" are being prepared for publication by Duquesne University Press, Pittsburgh). See also Richardson, "The Place of the Unconscious in Heidegger," p. 288.

Only the word, the term of understanding, belongs to the intentional order."[15] Yet according to the truth of the matter, "if such an assertion were taken literally, it would utterly destroy the whole Thomistic doctrine of knowledge at one stroke of the pen."[16]

No doubt for St. Thomas the concept is the *highest* level of intentional actuation (*saltem in rerum natura*); but that is very different from considering it as the *only* level. In point of fact, Thomistic philosophy requires the immaterial existence of *esse intentionale* for any function of knowing. Let us make the point as forcefully as we can: all and *only* that which has entered upon the mode of *esse intentionale* is capable of contributing to the formation of the knower as such and at every level. And for that very reason alone is there an inner contact between Thomism and the Heideggerean Thought of Being. It has to be said that Heidegger's denunciation of interpretations of his thought referenced by the idea of intentionality only becomes relevant in the Thomistic context if *esse intentionale* is considered according to its entitative implications rather than according to what is irreducibly proper to it (and this is the case whenever *esse intentionale* is considered with reference to the *praedicamenta*).

It is capital to note that consciousness (therefore subjectivity [or *esse intentionale* considered according to its entitative condition of *esse-in*]) is, ontologically speaking, subsequent to the orientation (therefore transcendence [or *esse intentionale* considered according to its proper formal condition of *esse ad*]) of the self which consciousness makes manifest. What is primary is the self, not as subject [*esse naturae seu entitativum*] but as transcendence [*secundum esse intentionale*]. That is why consciousness, ontologically subsequent [to *esse intentionale*], must be explained by something which is ontologically prior, sc. the Being of the self [the *vita*

---

[15] ". . . l'*intentio intellecta* est seule de l'*esse intentionale*. [. . .] Seul le verbe, terme d'intellection, appartient a l'ordre intentionnel." "La notion *d'intentio*," *Revue des Sciences Philosophiques et Theologiques* (juillet, 1930), 456-7.

[16] "Une telle assertion, si on la prenait à la lettre, anéantirait d'un trait de plume toute la doctrine thomiste de la connaissance." (DS, p. 804 fn 1/406 fn. 1). In this connection, see fn. 45 of Chapter V *supra*. The closest analogue in Thomistic scholasticism to the phenomenological ego of Husserl which is "no longer a human ego" (cf. Spiegelberg, I, p. 302) is the notion of "l'*esse cognitum seu objectivum*, selon lequel la chose existe par et pour la pensée, en tant même que connu, est purement idéal n'apporte aucune détermination réelle ni à la chose, ni à l'esprit (sinon présuppositivement, en tant que l'*être pensé* de l'objet suppose le *penser* de l'esprit): existence idéale ou de signifié *reduplicative ut sic*." (DS, p. 238 fn. 1/123 fn. 1). See also DS, p. 258 fn. 1/133 fn. 2. Cf. John of St. Thomas, *Cursus Theol.*, I P., q. 12, disp. 15. art. 3; R. Dalbiez, "Les sources scolastiques de la théorie cartésienne de l'être objectif," *Revue d'Histoire de la Philosophie* (Oct.-Dec., 1929). Similarly, some first indication of the *locus* of the notion of Husserl's eidetic and phenomenological reductions, respectively, in scholasticism is provided by St. Thomas, *In Met.*, I, lect. 2, n. 46; IV, lect. 6, n. 605, lect. 7, n. 616; and *In IV Met.*, lect. 4, nn. 574 and 577.

intentionalis] which consciousness manifests. To reverse the procedure. . . is to distort the whole problematic.[17]

In short, only if we had taken *esse intentionale* in terms of its secondary conditions would our Interpretation thus far have done distorting violence to the sense of Heidegger's texts.

Let us consider a final textual parallel. We opened this chapter with a passage from St. Thomas in which two fundamental conditions of being were distinguished. The first, *esse materiale* in the sense of *entitativum*, is that state according to which a being is itself and no other, according to which "every being is what it is". The second fundamental state or condition, however, *esse immateriale* or *intentionale*, is a state according to which a being is open to the presence of other entities and consequently to a communication with and certain (*quodammodo*) sharing in their being. This second condition attaches only to living, sensate beings (imperfectly, *medium inter*. . .) and to man (perfectly, *penitus immateriale*). St. Thomas is speaking here "metaphysically," i.e., in terms of the *praedicamenta*, but in order to distinguish a condition of being which cannot be adequately considered at the entitative level.

Speaking "phenomenologically," i.e., in terms of *existentialia*, Heidegger distinguishes within the ontic order of things an ontological level which cannot be adequately considered in ontic terms; but he does this precisely in order to locate his own analysis at this properly ontological level and not the level of ontic considerations, or rather, in order to continue his analysis as unmistakably belonging to the "ontological" order. Heidegger is considering Being-in-the-World in general as the basic state of Dasein, and more specifically, he is considering "Being alongside" the world as an *existentiale* founded upon Being-in:

As an *existentiale*, 'Being-alongside' the world never means anything like the Being-present-at-hand-together of Things that occur. There is no such thing as the 'side-by-side-ness' of a being called 'Dasein' with another being called 'world'. Of course when two things are present-at-hand together alongside one another, we are accustomed to express this occasionally by something like 'The table stands "by" the door' or 'The chair "touches" the wall'. Taken strictly, 'touching' is never what we are talking about in such cases, not because accurate re-examination will always eventually establish that there is a space between the chair and the wall, but because in principle the chair can never touch the wall, even if the space between them should be equal to zero. If the chair could touch the wall, this would presuppose that the wall is the sort of thing 'for' which a chair would be *encounterable*. A being present-at-hand within the world can be touched by another being only if by its very nature the latter being has Being-in as its own kind of Being-

[17] Richardson H:TPT, p. 157.

only if, with its being-there, something like the world is already revealed to it, so that from out of that world another being can manifest itself in touching, and thus become accessible in its Being-present-at-hand. When two beings are present-at-hand within the world, and furthermore are *worldless* in themselves, they can never 'touch' each other, nor can either of them '*be*' '*alongside*' the other. The clause 'furthermore are worldless' must not be left out; for even beings which are not worldless – Dasein itself for example – are present-at-hand 'in' the world, or, more exactly, *can* with some right and within certain limits be taken as merely present-at-hand. To do this, one must completely disregard or just not see the existential state of Being-in.[18]

Thus Heidegger distinguishes two states in which entities stand, one according to which they are isolated unto themselves alone (are "worldless" or "present-at-hand" merely); and another, the existential state of Being-in, according to which they, some of them at least and (man in his) Dasein above all, are enabled to become aware not only of themselves but are open to encounter with other entities in the same way as they are able to become aware of themselves (common to *Bewusstsein* and *Seblstbewusstsein* is *das Sein*[19]). Thus, for example, "hardness and resistance do not show themselves at all unless an entity has the kind of Being which Dasein – *or at least something living* – possesses."[20]

Who can doubt that the two texts in question touch, each in their own way, the very same thing?

It is therefore the proper and authentic sense of *esse intentionale*, particul-

---

[18] "Das 'Sein bei' der Welt als Existenzial meint nie so etwas wie das Beisammen-vorhanden-sein von vorkommenden Dingen. Es gibt nicht so etwas wie das 'Nebeneinander' eines Seienden, genannt 'Dasein', mit anderem Seienden, genannt 'Welt'. Das Beisammen zweier Vorhandener pflegen wir allerdings sprachlich zuweilen z. B. so auszudrücken: 'Der Tisch steht 'bei' der Tür, 'der Stuhl 'berührt' die Wand.' Von einem 'Berühren' kann streng genommen nie die Rede sein und zwar nicht deshalb, weil am Ende immer bei genauer Nachprüfung sich ein Zwischenraum zwischen Stuhl und Wand feststellen lässt, sondern weil der Stuhl grundsätzlich nicht, und wäre der Zwischenraum gleich Null, die Wand berühren kann. Voraussetzung dafür wäre, dass die Wand 'für' den Stuhl *begegnen* könnte. Seiendes kann ein innerhalb der Welt vorhandenes Seiendes nur berühren, wenn es von Hause aus die Seinsart des In-Seins hat – wenn mit seinem Da-sein schon so etwas wie Welt ihm entdeckt ist, aus der her Seiendes in der Berührung sich offenbaren kann, um so in seinem Vorhandensein zugänglich zu werden. Zwei Seiende, die innerhalb der Welt vorhanden und überdies an ihnen selbst *weltlos* sind, können sich nie 'berühren', keines kann 'bei' dem andern '*sein*'. Der Zusatz: 'die überdies weltlos sind', darf nicht fehlen, weil auch Seiendes, das nicht weltlos ist, z. B. das Dasein selbst, 'in' der Welt vorhanden ist, genauer gesprochen: mit einem gewissen Recht in gewissen Grenzen als nur Vorhandenes *aufgefasst* werden *kann*. Hierzu ist ein völliges Absehen von, bzw. Nichtsehen der existenzialen Verfassung des In-Seins notwendig." (SZ, p. 55).

[19] Cf. WM:In, p. 16/215.

[20] "Härte und Widerstand zeigen sich überhaupt nicht, wenn nicht Seiendes ist von der Seinsart des Daseins oder zum mindesten eines Lebenden." (SZ, p. 97). See also pp. 105, 114-5, 205, *inter alia*; De Waelhens, p. 480.

arly in its extension beyond as the prior basis for the possibility of conscious awareness, that we intend when we say that Dasein is the intentional life of man. Yet this Intentional Life so taken must moreover be considered not only in its integrity but at its source as well. It is not simply a question of adequating the Heideggerean conception from within Thomistic perspectives, but a question more importantly of realizing within that conception the fulness of its implications. To be rendered fully thematic, we say, Dasein as the Intentional Life of Man must be considered in its integrity and at its source: *in its integrity* – account must be taken of the spiritual unconscious in its priority of nature and time over the logic-dominated sphere of controllable awareness, as well as in its primacy over the automatic unconscious[21]; and *at its source* – the role of the "formative" or "illuminating" or "acting" intellect (*intellectus agens*) must be taken up anew and thematized as such.

With this much clarification of our usage of the notion of intentionality as bulwark against merely terminological misreadings, we are in a position at last to consider the inter- and trans-subjective reality which is Dasein, yet always "mine" and, as such, a self. Not a self in the usual sense of "subject of awareness," and not a self either in the Freudian sense of the unconscious personality-factors which enjoy an autonomous life in such wise that they admit of only mediate introduction into the sphere of conscious awareness, but a self in the sole sense of being the "ontological" dimension (*dimensio intentionalis et non entitativa*) of the conscious subject *as* conscious. We are in a position, in short, to precise for ourselves the sense of Dasein, the sense of an onto-conscious self. The necessity of doing so can be, at this stage, readily appreciated.

The work of our re-trieve thus far has only indicated the possibility of translating the notion of Dasein as Intentional Life. Since this notion of Dasein is the key to the structured problematic of the early Heidegger, the success of our re-trieve as Interpretation depends on the *realization* of the suggested possibility of this translation (Ch. VII). Moreover, if we can demonstrate by reason of such a translation that the structural implications of Dasein insofar as it is ontic as well as ontological demand a prior working out of the categorial meaning of human nature, then we shall have to say that not only is it an overstatement to assert with (the early) Heidegger that "only as Phenomenology is ontology possible";[22] but we shall have to say as well that phenomenological ontology *remains* an *authentic* possibility only

[21] See Jacques Maritain, *Creative Intuition in Art and Poetry* (New York: Pantheon Books, 1953), chapters III and IV, esp. pp. 90-110. Hereafter referred to as CI.
[22] "*Ontologie ist nur als Phänomenologie möglich.*" (SZ, p. 35: Heidegger's italics). See also SZ, p. 38; and Appendix II of this study, as well as Chs. VIII & IX.

on the basis of a metaphysical ontology proceeding according to the *praedica-menta* in terms of act and potency (Ch. VIII; cf. Ch. IV above, p. 52 ad fn. 40). In that case, Phenomenology would be only a part of Metaphysics – albeit the crucial 'critical' part.

Hence the necessity of precising for ourselves the sense of Dasein, of an onto-conscious self.

CHAPTER VII

DASEIN AS THE INTENTIONAL LIFE OF MAN

"Das existenziale Wesen des Menschen ist der Grund dafür, dass der Mensch Seiendes als ein solches vorstellen und vom Vorgestellten ein Bewusstsein haben kann. Alles Bewusstsein setzt die ekstatisch gedachte Existenz als die essentia des Menschen voraus, wobei essentia das bedeutet, als was der Mensch west, sofern er Mensch ist. Das Bewusstsein dagegen schafft weder erst die Offenheit von Seiendem, noch verleiht es erst dem Menschen das Offenstehen für das Seiende. Wohin und woher und in welcher freien Dimension sollte sich denn alle Intentionalität des Bewusstseins bewegen, wenn der Mensch nicht schon in der Inständigkeit sein Wesen hätte? Was anderes kann, falls man je ernstlich daran gedacht hat, das Wort '-sein' in den Namen 'Bewusstsein' und 'Selbstbewusstsein' nennen als das existenziale Wesen dessen, das ist, indem es existiert? Ein Selbst zu sein, kennzeichnet zwar das Wesen desjenigen Seienden, das existiert, aber die Existenz besteht weder im Selbstsein, noch bestimmt sie sich aus diesem."
Martin Heidegger, *Was ist Metaphysik?*, p. 16.

Recalling once again the primary correspondence of Thomas' *entitativum-intentionale* distinction with Heidegger's *ontisch-ontologisch* distinction, the validity of Heidegger's claim to problematic originality stands out at once as verified: "Dasein's ontico-ontological priority was seen quite early, though Dasein itself was not grasped in its genuine ontological structure, and *did not even become a problem in which this structure was sought.*"[1] Thomistic thought recognized full well that "intelligere et esse non sunt idem apud nos."[2] But the main thrust of Thomistic analysis has always been directed to *esse* (*existentia ut exercita*), and to *intelligere* only insofar as it verified

---

[1] "Der ontisch-ontologische Vorrang des Daseins wurde schon früh gesehen, ohne dass dabei das Dasein selbst in seiner genuinen ontologischen Struktur zur Erfassung kam oder auch nur dahinzielendes Problem wurde." (SZ, p. 14).

[2] *De veritate*, q. 4, art. 4.

esse ("Critica"). Is there any need to point out that history, and with it, historical, cultural, social, and psychological determinisms are little more than strangers in the Thomistic house? Human solidarity, personality in culture, subconscious determinisms, creative intuition in art and poetry, the metaphysical character of motivation and meaning – all these are fundamental *data* of the human condition which find their primary basis in the mode of being human precisely not from the side of the *esse* of *existentia ut exercita* but from the side of the *esse* of *ens intentionale*, from the side, that is to say, of a *Daseinsanalyse*.

To see how this is so, it is necessary that we incorporate some decisive but not generally considered textual considerations concerning Intentional Life, not this time in its character as a wholly suprasubjective (therefore neither "subjective" nor "objective" in the usual sense) medium of union, but rather in its source, in the dynamic process of its origin at the single root of the soul's powers. The following texts may be considered most profitably in the comparative context of *Kant und das Problem der Metaphysik* rather than that of *Sein und Zeit*, both by reason of its more traditionally toned terminology, and in view of its articulation of Dasein as the transcendental or "pure" imagination, i.e., as the common source of all that comes to pass in sense and understanding.[3] Beyond this suggestion, these texts we shall cite should call for little comment to those who have followed our lines of Interpretation to now and have pondered well beforehand the Heideggerean writings. These texts should in short serve to justify and clarify adequately what we mean by proposing that the intentional life of man is that area of philosophical reflection where Thomas' analyses and the thought of Heidegger share a common concern. To keep our citations sufficiently brief, we

---

[3] ". . . we find in KM the basic conception of There-being, which was elaborated phenomenologically in SZ, articulated in the more familiar context of Kant's thought according to a language that is more classical and (for most of us) more intelligible. This permits us not only to understand better what Heidegger is trying to say but also to see how we might incorporate his intuitions into other more traditional forms." (Richardson, H:TPT, p. 106).

"The whole burden of *Kant und das Problem der Metaphysik* was the phenomenological reduction of the faculties of intellect and sense into a common root (KM, par. 6); hence intellect as a distinct faculty disappeared. And in *Vom Wesen der Wahrheit*, truth (veritas) as *adaequatio intellectus et rei* was rejected (WW, p. 8) in favor of truth (Wahrheit) as 'the self-hiding uniqueness (Einzige) of the once-happening history of the revealment of meaning – which we call *Sein*'." (Powell, "The Late Heidegger's Omission of the Ontic-Ontological Structure of Dasein," p. 5; printed version, p. 120 [see fn. 78, p. 109 below]).

"Whatever may be said of this masterful book, which profoundly modifies our reading of the Kantian texts, we cannot fail to see in it a very clear confirmation of the same relationships between Being and There-being that *Being and Time* showed us." (De Waelhens, p. 491).

will confine ourselves to their primary source, Jacques Maritain's *Creative Intuition in Art and Poetry*; and we shall make our selection strictly in terms of the originating structure of Intentional Life.

It is difficult to speak of this problem. . . We risk, moreover, being misled by the words we use. I would observe especially that the word *unconscious*, as I use it, does not necessarily mean a purely unconscious activity. It means most often *an activity which is principally unconscious, but the point of which emerges into consciousness.* Poetic intuition, for instance, is born in the unconscious, but it emerges from it; the poet is not unaware of this intuition, on the contrary it is his most precious light and the primary rule of his virtue of art. But he is aware of it *sur le rebord de l'inconscient*, as Bergson would have said, on the edge of the unconscious.
My contention then, is that everything depends, in the issue we are discussing, on the recognition of the existence of a spiritual unconscious, or rather, preconscious. . . . There are *two kinds of unconscious*, two great domains of psychological activity screened from the grasp of consciousness: *the preconscious of the spirit* in its living springs, and *the unconscious of blood and flesh*, instincts tendencies, complexes, repressed images and desires, traumatic memories, as constituting a closed or autonomous dynamic whole. . . deaf to the intellect, and structured into a world of its own apart from the intellect; we might also say, in quite a general sense, leaving aside any particular theory, *Freudian unconscious*.[4]

Yet both of these domains at their own level and in their own ways are constituted according to what is proper to them within the irreducible order of *esse intentionale*, the former by virtue of that immateriality engendered by the dynamisms of spirit, the latter by virtue of that intermediate immateriality engendered by certain dynamic organizations of the material order itself. Yet too, by reason of that very unity of *esse* which entitatively grounds them both in the human mode of being,

these two kinds of unconscious life are at work at the same time; in concrete [existentiell] existence their respective impacts on conscious activity ordinarily interfere or intermingle in a greater or less degree; and, I think, never – except in some rare instances of supreme spiritual purification – does the spiritual unconscious operate without the other being involved, be it to a very small extent. But they are essentially distinct and thoroughly different in nature.[5]

To gain a preliminary insight into what is at stake here, "it is enough to think of the ordinary and everyday functioning of intelligence, in so far as intelligence is really in activity, and of the way in which ideas arise in our minds, and every genuine intellectual grasping, or every new discovery, is brought about; it is enough to think of the way in which our free decisions, when they are really free, are made, especially those decisions which commit

---

[4] CI, pp. 91-2: my emphasis.
[5] *Ibid.*, p. 92.

our entire life"; it is enough, in a word, to consider with care the everyday-ness of Dasein, "to realize that there exists a deep nonconscious world of activity, for the intellect and the will, from which the acts and fruits of human consciousness and the clear perceptions of the mind emerge, and that the universe of concepts, logical connections, rational discursus and rational deliberation, in which the activity of the intellect takes definite form and shape, is preceded by the hidden workings of an immense and primal preconscious life. Such a life develops in night, but in a night which is translucid and fertile. . ."[6]

Reason does not only consist of its conscious logical tools and manifestations, nor does the will consist only of its deliberate conscious determinations. Far beneath the sunlit surface thronged with explicit concepts and judgments, words and ex-pressed resolutions or movements of the will, are the sources of knowledge and creativity, of love and suprasensuous desires, hidden in the primordial translucid night of the intimate vitality of the soul. *Thus it is that we must recognize the existence of an unconscious or preconscious which pertains to the spiritual powers of the human soul and* to the inner abyss of personal freedom, and of the personal thirst and striving for knowing and seeing, grasping and expressing: a spiritual or musical unconscious *which is specifically different from the automatic or deaf unconscious.*[7]

If then we wish to enquire as to the nature of this unconscious which becomes at its summit or point the conscious self, into this "onto-conscious" self, this ontological dimension of the conscious self *as* conscious, where ought we to look for historical antecedents of the notion?

To understand this notion of *Dasein* as a presubjective, onto-conscious (*un*cons-cious) self, let us recall for a moment Heidegger's polemic against subjectivism. He engages it in two ways: in *Sein und Zeit* by the conception of *Dasein* as transcendence (Being-in-the-World); in the later works by his effort to overcome metaphysics, which, he maintains, since Descartes has been profoundly subject-ist. . . The ego, whose existence for Descartes is certified in the act of thinking, is for the first time in the history of thought conceived as a subject, something that 'lies under' every-thing else – in this case, that underlies all truth. In other words, the ego that is aware of its own existence is a 'subject' for the very same reason that it is a 'foun-dation' of truth. But if we go one step further, we see that everything that is not the thinking subject becomes something about which the subject thinks, i.e., an 'ob-ject' of thought. As a result, everything that is becomes either a subject or an ob-ject of thought. As a matter of fact, the world itself is nothing more than the sum total of the objects of thought, a sort of Collective Object. In a word, the first con-sequence of Descartes' discovery of the unshakable foundation of truth in the self-

---

[6] *Ibid.*, pp. 93-4. This text holds particular significance in correlation with the early Heidegger's observation that the procedures of scholasticism include "elements of pheno-menological intuiting, perhaps more than any other." *Die Kategorien- und Dedeutungslehre des Duns Scotus* (Doctoral dissertation of 1916), p. 11. (As cited in Spiegelberg, I, 295).

[7] CI, p. 94: my emphasis.

awareness of the thinking ego is that all reality becomes divided into subjects and objects... The marvelous mystery of presence – i.e., of Being – is forgotten.[8]

Philosophically, in short, "the notion of the psychological unconscious was made into a self-contradictory enigma by Descartes, who defined the soul by the very act of self-consciousness."[9] "Thus we must be grateful to Freud and his predecessors for having obliged philosophers to acknowledge the existence of unconscious thought and unconscious psychological activity,"[10] and more grateful still to Heidegger for having obliged philosophers to go beyond simple recognition by thematically considering this sphere according to its own irreducibly proper (spec., non-entitative) kind of Being.

But if it was principally Descartes who made the unconscious (and therewith the onto-conscious) self into an antinomy, what about philosophy prior to Descartes?

Before Descartes, the human soul was considered a substantial reality accessible in its nature only to metaphysical analysis, a spiritual entelechy informing the living body, and distinct from its operations; and this, of course made a completely different picture. *The Schoolmen were not interested in working out any theory about the unconscious life of the soul, yet their doctrines implied its existence.* What Thomas Aquinas teaches about the structure of the intellect seems to me especially significant in this regard. The question does not have to do with poetry, but, on the contrary, with abstract knowledge and the birth of abstract ideas. But for that very reason *we find there basic views about the spiritual preconscious life of the intellect,* which can be utilized later on with respect to poetry.

The intellect, as perennial philosophy sees it, is spiritual and, thus, distinct in essence from the senses. Yet, according to the Aristotelian saying, nothing is to be found in the intellect which does not come from the senses. Then it is necessary to explain how a certain spiritual content, which will be seen and expressed in an abstract concept, can be drawn from the senses, that is, the phantasms and images gathered and refined in the internal sensitive powers, and originating in sensation.[11]

In a word, what primordial power brings together pure sense and pure understanding in such a way as to render the "unity of transcendental apperception" comprehensibly possible?

It is under the pressure of this necessity that Aristotle was obliged to posit the existence of a merely active and perpetually active intellectual energy, *nous poietikos,* the intellect agent, let us say the Illuminating Intellect, which permeates the images with its pure and purely activating spiritual light and actuates or awakens the potential intelligibility which is contained in them [ontological truth as the basis for

---

[8] Richardson, "The Place of the Unconscious in Heidegger," pp. 280-82.

[9] CI, p. 104.

[10] *Ibid.*

[11] *Ibid.,* p. 96.

the possibility of ontic truth]. . . It was the work of St. Thomas to show and insist that, because the human person is an ontologically [entitatively] perfect or fully equipped agent, master of his actions, the Illuminating Intellect cannot be separate, but must be an inherent part of each individual's soul and intellectual structure, an inner spiritual light which is. . . through its pure spirituality ceaselessly in act, the primal quickening source[12]

within the being of man of that process of transcendence relative to beings which has come to be called "Dasein." The analysis is entitative, but not subjective, for the root of subjectivity is the materiality of the person, circumscribing and defining his individuality which, as *personal*, yet tends through the higher powers of the spirit to be intersubjective. The point to be here marked well is that St. Thomas was able to overcome the difficulties of Aristotle and his later Arab commentators who tended to conceive of this illuminating source of man's understanding of beings as *separate* from the individual and consequently numerically one for all men, by an analysis of *esse*, the entitative unity of beings as such, that is, by securing an understanding of *existentia ut exercita*. What parallels might be drawn between this difficulty of Arab philosophy and that of the later Heidegger, who sees Being in its difference from beings as the sole common content in the various "mittences" or cultural eras of Being, a consequence of his failure to work out with any rigor the relation of Being to (man in his) Dasein?[13] For to raise the question of the relation of Being to Dasein in a possibly soluble form presupposes that the concept of Dasein itself has been authentically and adequately worked out – and we have already seen that such an integral thematization of Dasein must itself presuppose the irreducibility and therewith validity of predicamentally metaphysical Interpretation of Dasein's ontic dimension, a presupposition which requires for justification an exact determination of the sense in which the phenomenologically reinterpreted Being-question enjoys philosophical priority. For the present context then we must be content with no more than pointing out that we encounter in an historical consideration a philosophical difficulty not altogether dissimilar to that which is encountered in an exclusively phenomenological pursuit of the meaning of Being.

Having noted that, let us continue our consideration of the *intellectus agens* as the primal, quickening source in human *esse* of the process of transcending beings to Being.

---

[12] *Ibid.*, pp. 96-7.
[13] See fn. 33 of Ch. II, p. 27 above; and the concluding pages (pp. 57-61) of Ch. IV above.

On the one hand, our intellect is fecundated by intelligible germs on which all the formation of ideas depends. And it draws from them, and produces within itself, through the most vital [and complex] process [of progressive spiritualization], its own living fruits, its concepts and ideas. But *it knows nothing either of these germs it receives within or of the very process through which it produces its concepts.* Only the concepts are known. *And even as regards the concepts, they cause the object seen in them to be known, but they themselves are not directly known* [they are literally *praecognitum tamquam ignotum*, i.e., *formaliter*]; they are not known through their essence, *they are known only through a reflective return of the intellect upon its own operations*; and this kind of reflective grasping can possibly not occur.[14]

(Thus Phenomenology, which is the methodological restriction of consideration to beings *as* appearing, must seek to determine primarily and above all – at least to the extent to which it has "become conscious of itself" – that which is constitutive of such appearing; that is, it must concern itself not with the beings but with the Being of Beings, with beings as they have entered for the researcher upon the mode of *esse intentionale*: and the first requisite for securing such a standpoint is precisely the phenomenological "turn of sight" or "reflective gaze", by virtue of which "the Being of all that which for the subject can be experienced in a different way, the *transcendent* in the broadest sense, is constituted."[15])

On the other hand, and this is the fundamental point for me, we possess in ourselves the Illuminating Intellect, a spiritual sun ceaselessly radiating, which activates everything in intelligence, and whose light causes all our ideas to arise in us, and whose energy permeates *every* operation of our mind. And *this primal source of light cannot be seen by us; it remains concealed in the unconscious of the spirit.*
Furthermore, it illuminates with its spiritual light the images from which our concepts are drawn. *And this very process of illumination is unknown to us, it takes place in the unconscious*; and often these very images, without which there is no thought, remain also unconscious or scarcely perceived in the process, at least for the most part.

Thus it is that we know (not always, to be sure!) what we are thinking, but we don't know how we are thinking. . .

I have insisted upon *these considerations* because they *deal with the intellect, with reason itself, taken in the full scope of its life within us. They enable us to see how the notion of a spiritual unconscious or preconscious is philosophically grounded. . . being one with the root activity of reason. . .* Well, if *there is in the spiritual unconscious a nonconceptual or preconceptual activity of the intellect even with regard to the birth of the concepts*, we can with greater reason assume that such a nonconceptual activity of the intellect, such a non-rational activity of reason, in the spiritual unconscious, plays an essential part in the genesis of poetry and poetic inspiration.[16]

[14] CI, p. 98: my emphasis.
[15] ". . . das Sein alles dessen, was für das Subjekt in verschiedener Weise erfahrbar ist, das *Transzendente* in weitesten Sinne, sich konstituiert. . ." ("Die Idee der Phänomenologie," p. 257).
[16] CI, pp. 98-100: my emphasis.

Let us take up these same considerations under another aspect. Let us consider "the manner in which the powers of the soul, through which the various operations of life – biological, sensitive, intellective life – are performed, emanate from the soul."[17]

At this point St. Thomas states that with respect to this order of natural priorities [with respect not to time but to nature], the more perfect powers emanate before the others, and he goes on to say (*here is the point* in which I am interested) that in this ontological [entitative] procession one power or faculty proceeds from the essence of the soul *through the medium or instrumentality of another* – which emanates beforehand (cf. *Summa theol.*, I, q. 77, a. 4, 6, & 7). For the more perfect powers are the principle or *raison d'être* of others, both as being their end and as being their 'active principle,' or the efficacious source of their existence... Hence it is that in the order of natural origin the senses exist, as it were, from the intellect, in other words, proceed from the essence of the soul through the intellect.

Consequently, we must say that imagination proceeds or flows from the essence of the soul through the intellect, and that the external senses proceed from the essence of the soul through imagination.[18]

It is by reason of man's spiritual (i.e., non-genetically or physiologically circumscribed) *esse* that human awareness is transcendent. If there is a sense in which it is proper to speak of the imagination as "transcendental" (in this perspective), it is in consequence of its emanation from the center of man's being through or "by way of" the Illuminating Intellect.

"*What matters to us is the fact that there exists a common root of all the powers of the soul, which is hidden in the spiritual unconscious, and that there is in this spiritual unconscious a root activity* in which the intellect and the imagination, as well as the powers of desire, love, and emotion, are engaged in common."[19] The powers of the soul for this reason envelop and compenetrate one another, "the universe of sense perception is in the universe of imagination, which is in the universe of intelligence" – all together constituting the single universe which exists according to what is proper to it in the mode of *esse intentionale*, and which is in virtue of this fact rightly designated the *Intentional Life of man*. And this universe, these universes within a single universe, "they are all, within the intellect, *stirred and activated by the light of the Illuminating Intellect*."[20] Fr. Richardson, in his

---

[17] *Ibid.*, p. 106.

[18] *Ibid.*, p. 107: my emphasis.

[19] *Ibid.*, p. 110.

[20] *Ibid.* See p. 109: "The life and activity of Intellect or Reason are not to be viewed only in the circle of the conceptualized externals of Reason. They are an immense dynamism emanating from the very center of the Soul and terminating in this circle of externals.

"The life and activity of Imagination are not to be viewed only in the circle of the organized externals of Imagination. They are an immense dynamism working upwards and downwards along the depths of the Soul and terminating in this circle of externals.

"general remarks" on Heidegger's Kant book, notes simply that "it is perfectly obvious that the center of transcendence, which in *Kant und das Problem der Metaphysik* goes by the name of the transcendental imagination, is what in *Sein und Zeit* is designated as There-being," Dasein.[21] He then goes on to make this significant summary:

We saw, but did not develop, the fact that the transcendental imagination is the center of the entire man. Let us reflect on what this implies. The transcendental imagination, as that center in man where transcendence comes-to-pass, is the source that gives rise to the structure which renders possible his sensate, theoretical and moral life, sc. all that characterizes him as a man. Giving rise to these three dimensions, it is their fundament, their ground, hence ontologically precedes them all and enjoys over them a certain primacy. Granting that the pure imagination is equivalent to There-being, we can understand how There-being can be profoundly "human" without being identified in unqualified fashion with man as such.[22]

In short, "if it is true that reason possesses a life both deeper and less conscious than its articulate logical life," if "reason indeed does not only articulate, connect, and infer,"[23] then "we can come to a decision concerning the possible origin of the understanding only by looking to the original essence of the understanding itself and not to a 'logic' which does not take this essence into account."[24] Thus in the Kant book, Heidegger articulates the relation between (the onto-conscious) self (transcendence) and subject (consciousness) in terms of the relation between transcendental imagination (center of transcendence) and transcendental apperception (transcendental unity of consciousness), expressed by the ego ("I think substance, accident, causality, etc."):

In presentative or 'representational' self-orientation toward ... [a being to-be-known], the "self" is carried along, 'taken outside' as it were, in the orientation.

"As to the life and activity of the External Senses, it takes place, no doubt, at the level of the intuitive data afforded by Sensation – there where the mind is in contact with the external world, all things seized upon by sense perception, all treasures of that sapid and sonorous Egypt, enter and make their way up to the central regions of the soul.

"Finally we can delimit ... the region of what I have called the Spiritual Unconscious or Preconscious [as well as] the area of the Animal or Automatic Unconscious. So the fact is represented that concepts and ideas as well as images and sense perceptions can be contained in these two obscure areas. And as for images, they can be considered in three different states. They can belong in the field of consciousness (a), or in the field of the Automatic Unconscious (b), or in the field of the Spiritual Preconscious (c). This is a point which can be remembered for some further discussion."

[21] H:TPT, p. 152.

[22] *Ibid.*, pp. 153-4.

[23] CI, p. 75.

[24] "Nur vom ursprünglichen Wesen des Verstandes her, keineswegs aber aus der dieses Wesen nichtachtenden 'Logik' kann über seinen möglichen Ursprung entschieden werden." (KM, p. 137/156).

In such an orientation as this wherein a "self" is "exteriorized", the "ego" of this self is necessarily made manifest. It is in this way that the "I present. . ." "accompanies" every act of representation. And it is not a question here of a secondary act of knowledge which takes thought as its object. The "ego" "goes along with" the pure self-orientation. Inasmuch as this "ego" is what it is only in the "I think," the essence of pure thought as well as that of the ego lies in "pure self-consciousness." This "consciousness" of the self however can only be explained by the Being of the self, not conversely, sc. where the Being of the self is explained or rendered superfluous by consciousness. [25]

And that is why what matters to us is the fact that there exists *a common root* of all the powers of the soul, which is hidden in the spiritual unconscious, and that there is in this spiritual unconscious *a root activity* in which the intellect and the imagination, as well as the powers of desire, love, and emotion, are engaged in common - because

The Being of Dasein, upon which the structural whole as such is ontologically supported, becomes accessible to us when we look all the way *through* this whole *to a single* primordially unitary phenomenon which is already in this whole in such a way that it provides the ontological foundation for each structural item in its structural possibility. [26]

And indeed in this "looking through" the basic meaning of Dasein as a structural totality gradually takes form and emerges into the light. Consider:

In the spiritual unconscious the life of the intellect is not entirely engrossed by the preparation and engendering of its instruments of rational knowledge and by the process of production of concepts and ideas. . . which winds up at the level of the conceptualized externals of reason. There is still for the intellect another kind of life, [still intentional but] which makes use of other resources and another reserve of vitality, and *which is free*, I mean free from the engendering of abstract concepts and ideas, free from the workings of rational knowledge and the disciplines of logical thought, free from the human actions to regulate and the human life to guide,

[25] "In solchem vorstellenden Sich-zuwenden-zu. . . wird das 'Sich' gleichsam in das Zuwenden-zu. . . hinausgenommen. In solchem Zuwenden-zu. . ., bzw. in dem mit ihm 'geäusserten' 'Sich', ist notwendig das 'Ich' dieses 'Sich' offenbar. In solcher Weise 'begleitet' das 'ich stelle vor' alles Vorstellen. Nicht aber handelt es sich um einen nebenbei vollzogenen Akt des auf das Denken selbst gerichteten Wissens. Das 'Ich' 'geht' im reinen Sich-Zuwenden 'mit'. Insofern es selbst nur ist, was es ist, in diesem 'ich denke', liegt das Wesen des reinen Denkens sowohl wie das des Ich im 'reinen Selbstbewusstsein'. Dieses 'Bewusstsein' des Selbst aber kann nur aus dem Sein des Selbst, nicht umgekehrt dieses aus jenem aufgehellt, bzw. durch jenes sogar überflüssig gemacht werden." (KM, p. 137-8/ 156-7). See Richardson, H:TPT, p. 156.

[26] "Zugänglich wird uns das Sein des Daseins, das ontologisch das Strukturganze als solches trägt, in einem vollen Durchblick *durch* dieses Ganze *auf ein* ursprünglich einheitliches Phänomen, das im Ganzen schon liegt, so dass es jedes Strukturmoment in seiner strukturalen Möglichkeit ontologisch fundiert." (SZ, p. 181).

and free from the laws of objective reality as to be known and acknowledged by science and discursive reason.[27]

We can see here in the first place a sense in which freedom and transcendence are but one, a sense that is in which "the original phenomenon of freedom is the disclosedness of There-being, sc. transcendence";[28] or, put otherwise, "the transcendence unto the World [Being] is freedom itself,"[29] not the derivative freedom of ontic-existentiell reflection and behavior, but the essence of freedom in its origin at the ontological-existential level of human reality, that is, in Dasein. We will see that not only freedom but truth and original time as the base of history are all one with the process that comes-to-pass as transcendence beyond beings to Being (World) through Dasein, i.e., the ontological dimension of the conscious self as conscious (the onto-conscious self), so that, in the end, if one is faithful to the principle of phenomenological research and the methodologically consequent restrictions thereto, "*only* Being 'is'; beings, properly speaking, 'are' not,"[30] and this "is" must be understood transitively!

But for the present let us confine our consideration to the problem of Dasein as a structural totality. Suppose that at this center of transcendence, i.e., in this free life of the intellect which enfolds a free life of the imagination, at the single root of the soul's powers, and in the unconscious of the spirit, suppose that here in the density of such a secretly alive sleep and such a spiritual tension, emotion intervenes (whatever this emotion may be: what matters is where it is received).

On the one hand it spreads into the entire soul, it imbues its very Being, and thus certain particular aspects in things become connatural to the soul affected in this way. On the other hand, emotion, falling into the living springs, is received in the vitality of intelligence, I mean intelligence permeated by the diffuse light of the Illuminating Intellect and virtually turned toward all the harvests of experience and memory preserved [*secundum esse intentionale*] in the soul, all the universe of fluid images, recollections, associations, feelings, and desires latent, under pressure [in this pulsing realm of *entia intentionalia*]. . . and now stirred. And it suffices for emotion disposing or inclining, as I have said, the entire soul in a certain determinate manner to be thus received in the undetermined vitality and productivity of the spirit, where it is permeated by the light of the Illuminating Intellect: then, while remaining emotion, it is made – with respect to the aspects in things which are connatural to, or *like*, the soul it imbues – into an instrument of intelligence judging through connaturality, and plays, in the process of this knowledge through *likeness* between reality and subjectivity [achieved *formaliter* and in numerical

[27] CI, pp. 110-11.
[28] Richardson, H:TPT, p. 191. See also pp. 217-81.
[29] "Der Überstieg zur Welt ist die Freiheit selbst." (WG, p. 43).
[30] Richardson, H:TPT, p. 7 fn. 12.

identity thanks to the mediating mode of *esse intentionale*], the part of a non-conceptual intrinsic determination of intelligence in its preconscious activity. By this very fact it is transferred into the state of objective intentionality; it is spiritualized, it becomes intentional [according to this most perfect of the intentional modes], that is to say, conveying, in a state of [pure] immateriality, things other than itself. It becomes for the intellect a determining means or instrumental vehicle through which the things which have impressed this emotion on the soul, and the deeper, invisible things that are contained in them or connected with them [thanks to their preservation in intentional life], and which have ineffable correspondence or coaption with the soul thus affected, and which resound in it, are grasped and known obscurely.

It is by means of such a spiritualized emotion that poetic intuition, which in itself is an intellective flash, is born in the unconscious of the spirit. In one sense it is. . . a privilege of those souls in which the margin of dreaming activity and introverted natural spirituality, unemployed for the business of human life, is particularly large. In another sense, because it emanates from a most natural capacity of the human mind, we must say that every human being is potentially capable of it: among those who do not know it, many, in fact, have repressed it or murdered it within themselves. . .

Of itself poetic intuition proceeds from the natural and supremely spontaneous [that is, free] movement of the soul which seeks itself by communicating with things in its capacity as a spirit endowed with senses and passions. . . Poetic knowledge is as natural to the spirit of man as the return of the bird to his nest; and it is the universe which, together with the spirit, makes its way back [via *esse intentionale*] to the mysterious nest of the soul [as Dasein, the *locus* of intentional life]. For the content of poetic intuition is both the reality of the things of the world and the subjectivity of the poet [both gathered up ontoconsciously through the ceaseless intentionalizing illumination of the *intellectus agens* out of their natural, entitative bounds into the suprasubjective-supraobjective sphere of *esse intentionale*], both obscurely conveyed through an intentional or spiritualized emotion. The soul is known in the experience of the world and the world is known in the experience of the soul, through a knowledge which does not know itself [i.e., a knowledge which lies anterior to the conceptualized externals of reason and the subjectivity of consciousness].

. . .In poetic intuition [trans]objective reality and subjectivity, the world and the whole of the soul, coexist [at the level of *esse intentionale*] inseparably. At that moment sense and sensation are brought back to the heart, blood to the spirit, passion to intuition. And through the vital non-conceptual actuation of the intellect all the powers of the soul are also actuated in their roots.[31]

Thus we see how it was that Heidegger came to regard poetry "as legitimate a domain for the interrogation of Being as philosophy; that henceforth the poets whom Heidegger considers authentic (. . .) have as much authority for him as the great thinkers"[32] in his efforts to re-trieve phenomenologically "the aboriginal questioning of the Being of beings with which philosophy

---

[31] CI, pp. 122-4. Cf. SZ, p. 151, as cited in fn. 52, p. 103 below.
[32] H:TPT, pp. 295-6.

began";[33] for the poet more than any other sort of man incarnates in his existence (and remember: "existence for Heidegger means to be in that relationship to Being that we have called 'comprehending'. Only this!"[34]) the Dasein in man as such, allows to resonate in his work the full range and richness of Intentional Life, according to the sentence of Novalis: "The poet is literally out of his senses – in exchange, all comes about *within him*. He is, to the letter, subject and object at the same time, soul and universe."[35] And indeed, is not the whole of Heidegger's existential conception of the "who" of Dasein compressed without overflow into Rimbaud's saying: "Je est un autre"?[36] But most significant for our proximate context is the way in which the lengthy citation above secures our Interpretive understanding of Dasein's structural totality as "essentially the process of transcendence that comes-to-pass in the profoundly unified fashion that is concern"[37] – *cura* or *Sorge*, intended in such wise that

If one takes the expression "concern" – despite the specific directive that the term has nothing to do with an ontic characteristic of man – in the sense of an ethical and ideological evaluation of "human life" rather than as the designation of the structural unity of the inherently finite transcendence of Dasein, then everything falls into confusion and no comprehension of the problematic which guides the analytic of Dasein is possible.[38]

If the reader keeps well in mind that we are not concerned with reducing Heidegger to scholastic categories but only with the possibility of locating what is proper to his thought within the perspectives of Thomistic philosophy, he will see that the sense of our Interpretation throughout this chapter is not at all reductive but intending rather to show the proportion and intrinsic analogy of Dasein to the notion of man's intentional life adequately considered.

The problem obviously is that Intentionality (*esse intentionale*), in this sense of the "ontological" dimension in man which, as ontoconscious, is

---

[33] *Ibid.*, p. 296.

[34] See H:TPT, p. 35.

[35] Novalis, *Schriften*, ed. Kluckhohn (Leipzig: Bibliographisches Institut, n.d.), Vol. III, 349.

[36] Letter of May 15, 1871, to Paul Demeny ("Lettre du Voyant"), first published by Paterne Berrichon in *La Nouvelle Revue Française*, October, 1912. (As cited in CI, p. 124 fn. 18).

[37] Richardson, H:TPT, p. 179.

[38] "Nimmt man nun aber den Ausdruck 'Sorge' – entgegen und trotz der noch ausdrücklich gegebenen Anweisung, dass es sich nicht um eine ontische Charakteristik des Menschen handelt – im Sinne einer weltanschaulich-ethischen Einschätzung des 'menschlichen Lebens' statt als Bezeichnung für die *strukturale Einheit* der in sich endlichen Transzendenz des Daseins, dann gerät alles in Verwirrung. Von der die Analytik des Daseins einzig leitenden Problematik wird dann überhaupt nichts sichtbar." (KM, p. 213/245).

Dasein, has never even been thematically, let alone adequately, considered in Thomism before. It may be conjectured that this is largely behind the dilemma (or, in certain individuals, the hostility) of scholasticism before contemporary historical, cultural, and social thought. But it is precisely the deepened insight into the ontological character (this time in the sense of *entitas*) of *esse intentionale*, and the rendering of that dimension in the mode of being human fully thematic – both thanks largely to Heidegger – that may equip scholasticism to integrate more adequately than has been possible to now the social and cultural and historical phenomena which are primary functions of human reality not in the dimension of *esse* (*sensu traditionali*) directly but in the dimension of *intelligere* (*sensu latissimo*).

"If so, this could go very far: for one might be able to find here an onto-logical ground, i.e., ground in an ontological unconscious, for such classic phenomena as illogicality, distortion, displacement, ambivalence, resistance, etc., and all that these imply."[39] After all, is it not precisely in *becoming* a conscious self, i.e., in establishing on the basis and within the bounds of existence (the biological-individual unity of man as *suppositum*) an inten-tional identity on the basis and within the bounds of awareness-possibility (the social-personal unity of man as *Dasein*), is it not, in short, through actualizing the "mineness" of Dasein that man undergoes the subtle, deep, deep influence of cultural, social, and historical determinisms? "I am thinking of the facticity of *Dasein's* thrownness into a situation of concrete possibil-ities – some bequeathed, some imposed by milieu, some chosen by *Dasein* itself."[40] "I am thinking of the fact that *Dasein* for Heidegger is not only singular but plural and therefore that its onto-conscious dimension is [in a very exact sense] not only individual but collective."[41] I am thinking, in short, of Dasein as culture-bearer, of man as culture bearing, as the histor-ical being, from which standpoint it is apparent that Dasein is the soil and foliage of what Dilthey called "the historical world." This is because the philosophically elaborated concept of Dasein opens for the first time *in principle* "the possibility that meaning and significance arise only in man and his history, not in the isolated individual but in man as an historical being."[42] For, if the process in Dasein by which it discovers beings as they are – in their Being, through their Being, and by their Being (which is exactly what is meant by transcendence) – is more fundamental than truth in the sense of

---

[39] Richardson, "The Place of the Unconscious in Heidegger," p. 289.

[40] *Ibid.*, p. 288. Cf. Maritain, DS, pp. 457-61/231-2.

[41] *Ibid.*, p. 289. One thinks here, inevitably, of Carl Jung.

[42] Wilhelm Dilthey, "Meaning and Historical Relativity," in *Pattern and Meaning in History*, ed. H. P. Rickman (New York: Harper, 1961), p. 168.

judged conformity which touches the very *esse* exercised by things independently of their manifestation, truth in the sense of the discovery by
Dasein that the being that is judged is (manifest) as it is judged to be; if,
that is to say, so far as conscious, explicit knowledge is concerned (to say
nothing of unconscious and ontoconscious knowledge) "the proper existence
things possess in order to maintain themselves outside nothingness" (in the
sense of independently of the mind *in rerum natura*) is posterior to and
dependent upon *esse intentionale* as "the existence that supervenes upon
things in their apprehension by the soul in order that they may be known,"[43]
upon *esse intentionale* as the necessary but not sufficient condition for the
accessibility of the *esse entitativum* of things to the consideration of intelligence and the decision of judgment; and if we call this process in Dasein
through which beings become open to circumspection "original truth"; then
it must be said that "original" truth, as that openness into which the truth of
knowledge (judged conformity) can only enter derivatively, is identical with
Dasein's existence: "then everything that the analysis has so far yielded concerning the structure of *Dasein* now characterizes the nature of truth,"[44]
at least so far as the origin of its possibility is concerned – because whenever
anything gets judged, truth (the disclosedness of beings thanks to *esse intentionale*) has been presupposed. Thus "Being and truth 'are' equiprimor-
dially."[45]

This permits us to understand the essentially temporal character of Being. Because

---

[43] "Il y a pour les choses deux *esse* différents, deux plans d'existence: l'existence propre
dont elles jouissent pour se tenir elles-mêmes hors de néant, et l'existence qui leur survient
dans l'appréhension de l'âme, pour être connues." (DS, p. 166/86).

[44] Richardson, "The Place of the Unconscious in Heidegger," p. 287; H:TPT, pp. 95-7.
Cf. Dondeyne, pp. 286, 285: "En d'autres mots, la problématique heideggerienne de
l'essence de la vérité pourrait s'exprimer comme suit: comment décrire, définir et nommer
ce qui rend possible en nous l'avènement de la vérité, entendu que, d'une part, pour re-
prendre le jeu de mot de Paul Claudel, la vérité est d'abord 'co-naissance' (*Seinlassen*),
avant d'être connaissance, 'être avec' avant d'être 'pensée *sur* les choses' et que, d'autre
part, si la part de l'homme est immense dans l'avènement de la vérité, à telle enseigne
qu'elle représente l'événement humain par excellence, l'homme n'en est pas pour autant
l'auteur purement et simplement mais plutôt le gardien et le prophète, encore que cette
vocation prophétique ne soit pas encore celle de la Bible, sans quoi il faudrait bien dire que
c'est Dieu même qui parle dans la parole de l'artiste et du poète et du penseur. Mais alors
Qui parle dans cette parole? Comment le nommer? Ce n'est pas une superpersonne, par
exemple le Dieu de la Bible ou de la philosophie scolastique (pour saint Thomas non plus
l'intellect agent, source première en nous de la vérité, n'est pas Dieu), et cependant, il
s'agit de ce qui est à l'origine de toute parole personelle et révélatrice. Quand on tient
compte de tout cela, il paraît déjà moins déconcertant que chez certains auteurs – dont
Heidegger – le vocabulaire philosophique traditionnel, qui le plus souvent se situe au
niveau de la considération de l'étant comme tel et en totalité, soit tenu pour insuffisant et
cède la place à un langage plutôt poétique, voire mythique."

[45] "Sein und Wahrheit 'sind' gleichursprünglich." (SZ, p. 230). See par. 44, pp. 212-230.

Being is a continual coming to beings, it is older than the time-spans (*Zeiten*) that are measured by beings such as man, people and things. But it is not older than time, for it *is* time in its origin.[46]

More importantly, perhaps, this permits us to understand through sharing "the essential experience that only in and from Dasein, as a thing to which we have entry, can any approximation to the truth of Being evolve for historical man."[47] Because "only as long as Dasein *is* (that is, only as long as an understanding of Being is ontically possible), 'is there' Being";[48] and conversely, " 'there is' truth only insofar as Dasein *is* and so long as Dasein is."[49] Moreover, the expression "for historical man" must not be left out, for the Being of Heidegger is the *locus* of human valuation and meaning without direct concern for any entitative character of beings as such, i.e., as unreferenced by the Historical World. That is why "all refutation in the field of foundational thinking is absurd,"[50] why "it is impossible to refute a genuine thinker provided that thought remain historical."[51]

Beings within-the-world generally are projected upon the world – that is, upon a whole of significance, to whose reference-relations concern, as Being-in-the-world, has been tied up in advance. When beings within-the-world are discovered along with the Being of Dasein – that is, when they have come to be comprehended – we say that they have *meaning* (*Sinn*).[52]
According to that analysis, meaning is that wherein the comprehensability of something maintains itself – even that of something which does not come into view explicitly and thematically.[53]

Accordingly, "meaning is an *existentiale* of Dasein, not a property attaching to beings, lying 'behind' them, or floating somewhere as an 'intermediate

[46] Richardson, H:TPT, p. 424.
[47] "Das im Vortrag versuchte Denken erfüllt sich in der wesentlichen Erfahrung, dass erst aus dem Da-sein, in das der Mensch eingehen kann, eine Nähe zur Wahrheit des Seins für den geschichtlichen Menschen sich vorbereitet." (WW, p. 27/333).
[48] ". . . nur solange Dasein *ist*, das heisst die ontische Möglichkeit von Seinsverständnis, 'gibt es' Sein." (SZ, p. 212).
[49] "Wahrheit 'gibt es' nur, sofern und solange Dasein ist." (SZ, p. 226). Heidegger italicizes the whole sentence.
[50] "Alles Widerlegen im Felde des wesentlichen Denkens ist töricht." (HB, p. 82/285).
[51] Richardson, H:TPT, p. 546.
[52] "Das innerweltlich Seiende überhaupt ist auf Welt hin entworfen, das heisst auf ein Ganzes von Bedeutsamkeit, in deren Verweisungsbezügen das Besorgen als In-der-Welt-sein sich im vorhinein festgemacht hat. Wenn innerweltliches Seiendes mit dem Sein des Daseins entdeckt, das heisst zu Verständnis gekommen ist, sagen wir, es hat *Sinn*." (SZ, p. 151). Cf. the passage from CI, pp. 122-4, as cited on pp. 98-99 above.
[53] "Danach ist Sinn das, worin sich die Verstehbarkeit von etwas hält, ohne dass es selbst ausdrücklich und thematisch in den Blick kommt." (SZ, p. 324). See references in fn. 55 below.

domain'."[54] For any characteristic of *esse intentionale* as such is mediary (*ad aliud*) only on an entitative accounting. Thus meaning is "between" man as knowing subject and beings as known subjects, but it is intrinsic to man in his Intentional Life, i.e., as Dasein.

Dasein only 'has' meaning, so far as the disclosedness of Being-in-the-world can be "filled in" by the beings discoverable in that disclosedness. *Hence only Dasein can be meaningful or meaningless.* That is to say, its own Being and the beings disclosed with its Being can be appropriated in understanding, or can remain relegated to non-understanding.

This Interpretation of the concept of "meaning" is one which is ontologico-existential in principle; if we adhere to it, then all entities whose kind of Being is of a character other than Dasein's must be conceived as *unmeaning*, essentially devoid of any meaning at all.[55]

And if we are inquiring about the meaning of Being, our investigation "asks about Being itself insofar as Being enters into the intelligibility of Dasein,"[56] that is to say, "the question about the meaning of the Being of any being takes as its theme the 'upon which' of that understanding of Being which underlies all ontical *Being towards* beings."[57]

---

[54] "Sinn ist ein Existenzial des Daseins, nicht eine Eigenschaft, die am Seienden haftet, 'hinter' ihm liegt oder als 'Zwischenreich' irgendwo schwebt." (SZ, p. 151). See refs. in fn. 55 below.

[55] "Sinn 'hat' nur das Dasein sofern die Erschlossenheit des In-der-Welt-seins durch das in ihr entdeckbare Seiende 'erfüllbar' ist. *Nur Dasein kann daher sinnvoll oder sinnlos sein.* Das besagt: sein eigenes Sein und das mit diesem erschlossene Seiende kann im Verständnis zugeeignet oder dem Unverständnis versagt bleiben.

"Hält man diese grundsätzlich ontologisch-existenziale Interpretation des Begriffes von 'Sinn' fest, dann muss alles Seiende von nichtdaseinsmässiger Seinsart als *unsinniges*, des Sinnes überhaupt wesenhaft bares begriffen werden. 'Unsinnig' bedeutet hier keine Wertung, sondern gibt einer ontologischen Bestimmung Ausdruck." (SZ, pp. 152). To grasp something of the implications of this existential-phenomenological conception of "meaning," certain analyses by Mortimer Adler concerning the nature and source of meanings may prove extremely helpful to the reader; in fact, many of Adler's points are simply indispensable if one wishes to grasp securely the decisive character of Maritain's distinction between the two kinds of unconscious for understanding the structure and sense of what Fr. Richardson terms the "onto-conscious self," Heidegger terms "Dasein," and we have termed the "Intentional Life of Man": see Mortimer J. Adler, *The Difference of Man and the Difference It Makes* (New York: Holt, Rinehart & Winston, 1967), pp. 175-189, esp. 185-7; and fn. 8 pp. 320-321, fn. 9 pp. 321-2, fn. 5 pp. 325-6, fn. 8 p. 326, fn. 9 p. 326, fn. 10 pp. 327-31, fn. 11 pp. 331-2, fn. 12 pp. 332-3. At the same time, it must be said with reference to the Aristotelian-Thomistic tradition which he claims to present, certain reservations must be kept in mind when reading Adler's analysis; these I have tried to indicate in the article "The Immateriality of the Intentional As Such", *The New Scholasticism*, XLII (Spring, 1968), pp. 293-306.

[56] "Und wenn wir nach dem Sinn von Sein fragen, dann ... die Untersuchung ... fragt nach ihm selbst, sofern es in die Verständlichkeit des Daseins hereinsteht." (SZ, p. 152).

[57] "Die Frage nach dem Sinn des Seins eines Seienden macht das Woraufhin des allem ontischen *Sein zu* Seiendem zugrundeliegenden Seinsverstehens zum Thema." (SZ, first edition, p. 325). See Macquarrie-Robinson translation, p. 372 fn. 1.

Thus Vycinas formulates the decisive recognition of the structural ramifications of the original Heideggerean problematic: "Investigation of *Dasein* ultimately *is* the investigation of Being";[58] for phenomenologically disengageable truth of Being lies entirely within Dasein and is therefore historical *in principle*, for Dasein is in principle *historical* man. Behold in man's intentional life integrally taken the structure and compass of the Historical World:

> *Dasein* is finite transcendence, whose ultimate meaning – i.e., whose ultimate source of unity – is time. As transcending existence, *Dasein* is always coming to Being through beings, and it is thus that Being comes continually to *Dasein*. This coming is *Dasein's* future. But Being comes to a *Dasein* that in the matter-of-fact condition of its thrownness is already existing. This condition of already-having-been is *Dasein's* past. Finally, Being as it comes to *Dasein* renders all beings (including itself) manifest as present to *Dasein*. This presence is *Dasein's* present. What gives unity (therefore ultimate meaning) to *Dasein* is this unity of future, past and present, i.e., the unity of time itself. *Dasein*, then, is essentially temporal. Because temporal, it is also historical, and this historicity is the foundation of history. And because *Dasein* is never solitary but shares transcendence with other *Daseins*, it also shares their common history.[59]

So much for our translation of the proper sense of Dasein into the notion of man's intentional life adequately considered. Suffice it to remark some final points relevant to this "Thought of Being."

This order of *esse intentionale* "constitutes unto itself a whole metaphysical order apart";[60] the moment one neglects or forgets the irreducible originality of matters affecting awareness, all genuine rapport between Heidegger and Thomistic thought becomes impossible. Since as a matter of fact most philosophers have not effectively (let alone consistently) recognized this irreducible order of *esse intentionale* over against the order of *esse naturale seu entitativum* (witness the disappearance from philosophy of the idea of intentionality after Aquinas, a notion reintroduced only with the advent of phenomenology – and even then in a very anemic condition), it is small wonder that Heidegger's thought is so perplexing and enigmatic to most, labelled everything from myth and mysticism to vain display. Finally, let us note that even in the traditional perspectives of authentic Thomism, this problem of the nature of thought taken in its full amplitude and in itself

---

[58] Vincent Vycinas, *Earth and Gods* (The Hague: Martinus Nijhoff, 1961), p. 26 fn. 3.

[59] Richardson, "The Place of the Unconscious in Heidegger," p. 287. See fn. 47 of this Chapter. As to how this perspective on the Historical World shifts with the "reversed" vantage of Heidegger II, see Chapter X of this study, and Richardson's "Heidegger and God" article, pp. 34-5.

[60] ". . . celle-ci . . . constitue à elle seule tout un ordre métaphysique à part. . ." (DS, p. 227/117).

according to what is proper to it "is the most important of all the problems of noetic, and one that can only be treated as it should by bringing into play the most delicately refined metaphysical equipment."[61] "Before tackling it," notes Maritain, St. Thomas and his greatest commentators "warn us that we must raise our minds, because we are entering quite a different order of things, *et disces elevare ingenium, aliumque rerum ordinem ingredi.* Errors, that are so frequent in this realm, arise from the fact that too often we confuse a spiritual event, like knowledge, with the material events by which our ordinary experience is nurtured."[62]

We might re-express using Heidegger's words what seems to us the same admonition:

Every formulation is open to misunderstanding. In proportion to the intrinsically manifold matter of Being and Time, all words which give it utterance (like reversal, forgottenness and mittence) are always ambiguous. Only a [commensurately] manifold thought succeeds in uttering the heart of this matter in a way that corresponds with it.

This manifold thought requires, however, not a new language but a transformed relationship to the essenc[-ing] of the old one.[63]

In any event, Dasein is what man endures in existing[64] as the field of awar-

---

[61] ". . . est le plus important de tous les problèmes de la noétique, et qui ne peut être traité comme il faut qu'en mettant en oeuvre l'outillage métaphysique le plus affiné. . ." (DS, p. 217/112).

[62] "Avant de l'aborder ils nous avertissent d'avoir à élever notre esprit, car nous entrons alors dans un autre ordre de choses, *et disces elevare ingenium, aliumque rerum ordinem ingredi*: les erreurs si fréquentes en ce domaine provenant de ce que nous confondons trop souvent un événement spirituel comme la connaissance, avec les événements matériels dont notre expérience commune est nourrie." (DS, p. 217/112). Pitirim A. Sorokin, in his *Social and Cultural Dynamics* (New York: Bedminster Press, 1937), Vol. II, esp. pp. 206-207, sec. k, suggests certain external factors which in our present culture contribute no small share to misunderstandings in this area.

[63] ". . . bleibt alles Formelhafte missverständlich. Gemäss dem in sich mehrfältigen Sachverhalt von Sein und Zeit bleiben auch alle ihn sagenden Worte wie Kehre, Vergessenheit und Geschick mehrdeutig. Nur ein mehrfältiges Denken gelangt in das entsprechende Sagen der Sache jenes Sachverhalts.

"Dieses mehrfältige Denken verlangt zwar keine neue Sprache aber ein gewandeltes Verhältnis zum Wesen der alten." (Heidegger's "Vorwort" to H:TPT, p. XXIII).

[64] See HB, pp. 71-2/279-80; also pp. 111-12/298. "All of our . . . knowledge is a process of bringing gradual distinction into our primitive concept of the *primum cognitum ens*, which is utterly confused. . . The process of bringing distinction never eliminates all confusion from [even] our intellectual knowledge, so that all our knowledge remains more or less confused." (Recall the passage from the *De veritate*, q. 4, art. 4, cited on p. 25 of this study, which disclosed the ineluctable disproportion between the knowledge expressed in an act and the object and principles of that act.) "On this basis we distinguished being-as-known-to-us, *which is always confused and hence non-being*, from real-being-which-is-distinct-in-itself . . . For our knowledge cannot be restricted to the mere knowledge of being-as-it-is-in-our-intellect since that would shut us up in non-being . . .

eness-*possibility* as such, and here we must keep in the fore an explicit advertance to the fact that this "field" always embraces far more than the factors explicit in consciousness strictly so called,[65] in such wise, to tell the truth, that its ontoconscious dynamisms enjoy the fundamental priorities of nature and time in determining its basic character as transcendent relative to beings. Never found apart from man, Dasein is nevertheless not identified with him, for the profound and – Heidegger notwithstanding – finally metaphysical reason that "intelligere (sensu latissimo) et esse (sensu traditionali) non sunt idem apud nos." Or, to express the point in other terms, "*Dasein* is different from other beings – not in its ontic but in its ontological dimension," in the dimension, that is to say, according to which man precisely is *not* a substance, but "a process of transcendence. . ."[66] Dasein is that constitutive state of man by which he stands in an original intersubjectivity, an original relationship to a World expressed in modal disclosures of Being; it is simply the There of Being thrown among beings as that being among the rest through which all (itself included) are lit up *as* beings.[67] In fine, "Dasein *is* its world existingly."[68] Being itself accordingly is the *Sein* of

"Now we must go further by observing that it is *by means* of being-as-it-is-in-our-intellect [Sein] that we know real-being-distinct-in-itself [*das Seiende* or things-in-Being]. Indeed being-as-it-is-in-our-intellect becomes mere non-being if we attempt to isolate it from real being which it makes known . . . Therefore, the confusion of being-as-it-is-in-our-intellect cannot terminate thought in an ultimate manner . . . *Being-as-it-is-in-our-intellect is unthinkable except as an intermediate term distinguished from the real being which renders being-in-our-intellect itself thinkable and thought possible.* Being-as-it-is-in-our-intellect must not only be distinguished against real being in order to be thinkable, it must be considered as virtually containing real being. For it is only as virtually containing real being that it is distinguishable from real being. *For we have no other contact with real being except from within being-as-it-is-in-our-intellect* . . . In short, inasmuch as our intellectual knowledge is knowledge of real being distinct from itself, it is intentional being, *intentionally* identical with real being. Because it is merely intentionally identical with real being, it must participate in real being, and it is therefore passive towards its object." (Ralph A. Powell, *Truth or Absolute Nothing*, River Forest, Ill.: The Aquinas Library, 1952, pp. 35-6: my emphases). Man in short is passive to Being, Dasein is what man undergoes in existing: "Das Nichten west im Sein selbst und keineswegs im Dasein des Menschen, insofern dieses als Subjektivität des ego cogito gedacht wird. Das Dasein nichtet keineswegs, insofern der Mensch als Subjekt die Nichtung im Sinne der Abweisung vollzieht, sondern das Da-sein nichtet, insofern es als das Wesen, worin der Mensch ek-sistiert, selbst zum Wesen des Seins gehört. Das Sein nichtet – als das Sein . . . Das Nichtende im Sein ist das Wesen dessen, was ich das Nichts nenne. Darum, weil es das Sein denkt, denkt das Denken das Nichts." (HB, p. 113-4/299).

[65] Cf. Vycinas, p. 32.

[66] Richardson, "The Place of the Unconscious in Heidegger," p. 280. Cf. H:TPT, pp. 97-103.

[67] Richardson, H:TPT, p. 409.

[68] "*Worinnen* das existierende Dasein *sich* versteht, das *ist* mit seiner faktischen Existenz 'da'. Das Worinnen des primären Selbstverständnisses hat die Seinsart des Daseins. Dieses *ist* existierend seine Welt." (SZ, p. 364).

Bewusstsein and *Selbstbewusstsein*, that is, it is the onto-conscious self.[69] As the ontological dimension of the conscious self as conscious, therefore, it is the original process of knowing in which the known shines forth,[70] by which beings emerge into non-concealment; and this non-concealment is the genuine meaning of truth as an original possibility.[71]

Being functions as the mediation between beings, establishing among them their mutual relationship, and they, since they are mediated by Being, may be called "mediate." But Being, the Open itself, as source of this mediation, is itself not mediated, sc. rendered present by reason of another. It is the "im-mediate." The point seems to be a double one: that Being, as the source of presence by which beings are present to each other and to There-being, is absolutely ultimate and needs no further mediation between itself and the beings which it renders present (it is the immediate mediation between them); that it is because Being is the im-mediate that it is inaccessible.[72]

The subject-object dichotomy occurs it is true "within" Dasein as field-of-awareness-possibility, but only because Dasein itself, as the There of Being, is phenomenologically prior to the heterogeneity of representational 'intentions': "all 'outside' is 'inside' in respect to Dasein."[73] Thus Fr. Richardson comments: "The known is differentiated from the knowing self by and through the knowing which simultaneously is, at least implicitly, a Self-knowing. This differentiating belongs to the very nature of Awareness, *whose own unity makes it from another point of view no differentiating at all.*" And Heidegger "adds": "As this difference that is no difference, Awareness is in its essence ambiguous [for both the self and the other as 'objects' are modalizations of *ens intentionale*, which itself wells from a hidden spring]. This ambiguous condition is the essence of representation" – therefore of present-ative thought (an essence which accordingly must be thought beyond and through).[74] That this interpretatorily confirmative citation cannot be dismissed as misleading (since, in context, it purports to interpret Hegel in Heidegger's terms precisely as in the mode of non-foundational or "presentational" thinking) is clear from the statement by Fr. Richardson we have already had occasion to cite: "*Dasein* as a self that is *not a* (conscious) *subject* is very Heideggerean. It is one of the important themes of *Sein und Zeit*, but to call it simply 'non-subjective' is more misleading than to call

---

[69] See WM:In, p. 16/215.
[70] See Richardson, H:TPT, p. 345.
[71] See *ibid.*, p. 373.
[72] *Ibid.*, p. 424. Cf. DS, p. 224/115; John of St. Thomas, *Cur. Phil.*, I, 693a 45-694a 46.
[73] Vycinas, p. 33.
[74] H:TPT, pp. 346ff.: my emphasis. "Das Bewusstsein ist in sich ein Unterscheiden, das keines ist. Das Bewusstsein ist als dieser Unterschied, der keiner ist, in seinem Wesen zweideutig. Dieses Zweideutige ist das Wesen des Vorstellens." (HW, p. 153).

it 'pre-subjective,' for it is a self that can *become* conscious as an ego."[75]

We can go no further in our apprehension of the original Heideggerian problematic unless we re-view at this point the requirements of the Being-question itself, in order to open therewith for evaluation the nature of its philosophical priority. We have already been compelled to note obliquely (e.g., pp. 39-40, 42, 45, 51ff., 55, 56, 58-60, 93-94) that the notion of Dasein as the "ontological" dimension of a profoundly unified being (namely, man) which has qua being (*Seiende*) an ontic dimension as well, establishes foundational problematic exigencies which the phenomenological research-mode is not sufficient to meet; and we have had occasion to suggest specifically that this insufficiency consisted in the fact that Phenomenology, restricted in principle to an ontologico-existential analysis, is unable to thematically incorporate into its researches the ontic dimension of Dasein *as* ontic – for that would require in principle an entitative-predicamental analysis on Heidegger's own accounting.[76] We were able to suggest in this way that the characterization of Dasein as the being whose ontic excellence "consists in the fact that it *is* ontologically"[77] has *already presupposed* the thematic validity of a metaphysically predicamental consideration – not to be sure in terms of substance-accident ontology, but potency and act are not said to so divide being that whatsoever exists is a substance or an accident, but simply in such wise that whatever exercises existence is either *Actus Purus* or necessarily composed as to its primordial and intrinsic principles of actual determinations and potential limitations.

We are now in a position to vindicate this suggestion through a consideration of the priority retained by the philosophical guide-question as Phenomenology (re)interprets it .We have already seen that Dasein provided for the early Heidegger the necessary point of departure for any authentic determination of the sense of Being. Accordingly, it is within Dasein that the priority as such of the (phenomenological) *Seinsfrage* comes initially into view and receives determination. We will see that the very character of its priority is a function of Dasein's ontic-ontological structure. (It is indeed for this very reason that "the overall argument of *Sein und Zeit* ultimately rests on the distinction between the ontic and the ontological."[78]) If therefore it

---

[75] "The Place of the Unconscious in Heidegger," p. 280.

[76] See Chapter VI of the present study, esp. pp. 57-61.

[77] "Die ontische Auszeichnung des Daseins liegt darin, dass es ontologisch *ist*." (SZ, p. 12).

[78] See Powell, "The Late Heidegger's Omission of the Ontic-Ontological Structure of Dasein," pp. 16-18. This essay has since been published in a slightly edited or revised form, in *Heidegger and the Path of Thinking*, ed. by John Sallis (Pittsburgh: Duquesne University Press, 1970), pp. 116-137. In the printed version, the cited remark basically appears

can be shown that the ontic-ontological distinction is an application of an understanding of Being secured in terms of act and potency, then it will follow immediately that the phenomenological characterization of an ontic-ontological structure of Dasein presupposes a metaphysical Interpretation, and presupposes it in such a way that it is possible to retain the determinate shape and rigor of the early Heidegger's thought (therefore the original possibilities of the original problematic) only if this presupposition be in the end justified. (Coincidentally, such a showing would collate very well with what has been our guiding theme throughout, namely, the primary correspondence of the *ontisch-ontologisch* distinction with the *entitativum-intentionale* distinction of Thomism.)

on pp. 131-2. In subsequent references to this essay, after giving the unpublished page reference, I will add: (Cf. p. ooo of printed version).

CHAPTER VIII

THE PRESUPPOSITIONED PRIORITY OF THE BEING-QUESTION

"Now the problem of truth is essentially the problem of transcendence. For ontic truth (the manifestation of beings in their Being) is rendered possible by ontological truth (the unveiledness of the Being of beings). These two types of truth presuppose, then, the distinction between Being and beings (the ontological difference), but how is such a distinction possible except by reason of a being, immersed among the rest, so constituted that, ontological as well as ontic, it can comprehend, sc. disclose or project, the Being of beings, including itself, and thus pass beyond beings to their Being? This, however, is the prerogative of There-being, for There-being is transcendence. If we are to understand ground, we must explore the nature of transcendence. . . . By the same token, we can see that if we define There-being as "existence," this characterizes man [as human] on a different and deeper level than that whereon the word *existentia* in the tradition found its meaning, sc. as opposed (whether really or rationally) to essence. Would it not be possible, then, that the entire problematic of Heidegger, placed as it is on a different level [and, we might add, developed according to a different methodological conception altogether proportioned to this new and distinct level], might leave intact the traditional questions concerning essence-existence, substance-accident, etc. . . .?"
William J. Richardson, *Heidegger: Through Phenomenology to Thought*, pp. 164 & 154, respectively.

For the philosophy of Martin Heidegger, that which must be brought into the Open, "ever since the philosophical awakening with Brentano, is the Being of beings in its difference from beings,"[1] and indeed in its difference from what may be said about beings precisely as such. Once he felt he had the powerful probe of Phenomenology well under his mastery, he at last felt himself in a position to bring the pressure of reflection to bear on this ques-

---

[1] Richardson, "Heidegger and God," p. 32; H:TPT, p. 631.

tion in such a way as to force the elusive determination to reveal itself, to become visible, to enter into the Open. *Sein und Zeit* opened the inquiry into the "disclosure of Being," which means as we have seen "the unlocking of what forgetfulness of Being," i.e., the traditional interpretation of the Being-question as the question of beings (*res existentes*) as such, "closes and hides."[2]

Accordingly, *Sein und Zeit* opens with the preliminary clarifications required for the re-interpretation of the question of Being. Certain presuppositions and prejudices are exposed as clouding the question over, first as regards the "soil" from which the basic ontological concepts of philosophy have developed; and then as regards whether the various categories have been demonstrated in a manner that is appropriate and complete.[3]

This at once reveals the need for an explicit restatement of the question of Being in reference to a threefold ambiguity in the traditional manner of posing the problem:

1. First is the ambiguity concerning *the unity of Being as over against the multiplicity of 'categories' applicable to things* – i.e., the problem of the categorial interconnections, which the doctrine of analogy comes to terms with but cannot clarify in principle: "An understanding of Being is already included in conceiving anything which one apprehends in beings."[4]

2. Next there is the ambiguity regarding *the meaning of Being*, which emerges from the fact that 'Being' cannot be derived from higher concepts by definition, nor can it be presented through lower ones – i.e., it can neither be conceived as an entity (being), nor even acquire such a character as to have the term *Seiende* applied to it.[5]

3. *There is also the enigmatic character of Being as the a-priori of human comportment*: since an understanding of Being is employed whenever one cognizes anything or makes an assertion, this understanding permeates and makes possible man's comportment towards entities.[6]

In each of these ways it seems to Heidegger " 'Being' has been presupposed in all ontology up till now, but not as a *concept* at one's disposal – not as the sort of thing we are seeking. This 'presupposing' of Being has rather the character of taking a look at it beforehand, so that in the light of it beings

---

[2] "Die Grundfrage der Vorlesung ist anderer Art als die Leitfrage der Metaphysik. Die Vorlesung frägt im Ausgang von 'Sein und Zeit' nach der 'Erschlossenheit von Sein' (Sein und Zeit S. 21f. und 37f.). Erschlossenheit besagt: Aufgeschlossenheit dessen, was die Vergessenheit des Seins verschliesst und verbirgt." (EM, p. 15/19).

[3] SZ, pp. 2-3.

[4] *Ibid.*, p. 3.

[5] *Ibid.*, p. 4.

[6] *Ibid.*

presented to us get provisionally articulated in their Being."[7] In accordance with its proper nature, "metaphysical thinking does, of course, inquire about the being which is the source and originator of this light; but the light itself is considered sufficiently illuminated as soon as we recognize that we look through it whenever we look at beings."[8] It is precisely the nature of the light (of Being) itself which philosophy has till now left unthematized.

The problem of Being then is exactly how to render this light itself and as such thematic, for it is in that way that the triple ambiguity of the metaphysical Being-question may be overcome. How re-place the question so as to eliminate this ambiguity virtually? The way is to frame the question phenomenologically rather than metaphysically. For any determination of the meaning of Being as such requires that an adequate phenomenal base be assured, and that means that, if Being itself is to be understood, we must start with a *phenomenological* and not with an ordinary phenomenon (what exactly is at stake in this distinction we take up in the next chapter) and keep the lines of analysis secured at each step by phenomenological phenomena subsequently uncovered (hermeneutically) as linked necessarily with the point of departure. There can be no break in the series of (phenomenological) determinations, something which can be assured in principle only by a closed hermeneutical, i.e., phenomenological,[9] situation established from the very first. Man must be changed into his Dasein to acheive this last assurance, and, that accomplished, the continuity of determination will continue to be assured if the phenomenological researcher keeps always to the *Da des Seins* which has "mine-ness' as its second (after existence) fundamental characteristic: for "the Being of beings is comprehensible – and in this lies the innermost finitude of transcendence – only if Dasein by virtue of its very nature constrains itself within the Nothing," i.e., keeps within the compass of

[7] "Das Sein wird zwar in aller bisherigen Ontologie 'vorausgesetzt', aber nicht als verfügbarer *Begriff* –, nicht als das, als welches es Gesuchtes ist. Das 'Voraussetzen' des Seins hat den Charakter der vorgängigen Hinblicknahme auf Sein, so zwar, dass aus dem Hinblick darauf das vorgegebene Seiende in seinem Sein vorläufig artikuliert wird." (SZ, p. 8).

[8] ". . . fragt das metaphysische Denken allerdings nach der seienden Quelle und nach einem Urheber des Lichtes. Dieses selbst gilt dadurch als erhellt genug, dass es jeder Hinsicht auf das Seiende die Durchsicht gewährt." (WM: In, p. 7/207).

[9] "Assistant to Husserl until invited to Marburg in 1923, the young Heidegger gave his first loyalty to phenomenology and sought simply to think the essence of phenomenology in its origins, so as to give to it a rightful place in the philosophical tradition of the West. This probing into origins was from the very beginning the sense of re-trieve. . . At any rate, . . . 'hermeneutic' (the process of letting-be-manifest) and *phainesthai* (that which manifests itself), plus *legein* (to let-be-manifest), rejoined each other to such an extent that 'hermeneutic' and 'phenomeno-logy' became for Heidegger but one. If 'hermeneutic' retains a nuance of its own, this is the connotation of language." (Richardson, H:TPT, p. 631).

that event "which underlies all finding oneself in the midst of beings already on hand."[10] The clarification in principle of this event will be achieved through the radicalization of that essential tendency-of-Being which belongs to Dasein centrally, namely, the pre-ontological comprehension of Being, and the question of this radicalization is the question of Being itself.[11]

All this simply recounts what we have already investigated in great detail. It is our present concern to show how this notion of Dasein as the avenue to the meaning of Being overcomes virtually the triple ambiguity residual to the Being-question set up in terms of *ens quod est extra animam*.

The second ambiguity, that regarding the meaning of Being, cannot be overcome by a substance-accident ontology since substance can be handled with the logical tools of genus and species, whereas the ambiguity regarding the meaning of Being results precisely from the inapplicability of the concept

[10] "Das Sein des Seienden ist aber überhaupt nur verstehbar – und darin liegt die tiefste Endlichkeit der Transzendenz – wenn das Dasein im Grunde seines Wesens sich in das Nichts hineinhält. Dieses Sichhineinhalten in das Nichts ist . . . ein Geschehen, das allem Sichbefinden inmitten des schon Seienden zugrundeliegt. . ." (KM, pp. 214-5/246). See Chapter III, esp. p. 38, of this present study.

[11] SZ, p. 15. The horizon within which this radicalization must be effected so that Being should be laid bare (i.e., rendered comprehensible) in its own ultimate unity, is the horizon of Time. Indeed, queries Fr. Richardson, "how can we speak of Being in a human way except in terms of time?" (H:TPT, p. 379). Yet it has taken sustained phenomenological analysis to disclose in anything like an adequate manner the decisive connection between *time* and the '*I think*'. The issue is central to any attempt at fully working out Heidegger's sense of the Being-question, but we can do no more than indicate the orientation of the temporality problematic toward the term of investigation: "Wenn Sein aus der Zeit begriffen werden soll und die verschiedenen Modi und Derivate von Sein in ihren Modifikationen und Derivationen in der Tat aus dem Hinblick auf Zeit verständlich werden, dann ist damit das Sein selbst – nicht etwa nur Seiendes als 'in der Zeit' Seiendes, in seinem 'zeitlichen' Charakter sichtbar gemacht." (SZ, p. 18).

Thus Heidegger designates "die ursprüngliche Sinnbestimmtheit des Seins und seiner Charaktere und Modi aus der Zeit" as the *Temporal determinateness (temporale Bestimmtheit)* of comprehensible unifications; and this notion is to be developed in such wise that "die spezifische Seinsart der bisherigen Ontologie, die Geschicke ihres Fragens, Findens und Versagens als daseinsmässig Notwendiges zur Einsicht kommt." (SZ, p. 19). "On sait que cette structure extatique du *Dasein*, qui ouvre un espace de rencontre, c'est, pour Heidegger, le temps." (Dondeyne, p. 271). See pp. 160-61 in Chapter X of this present study.

For the purposes of our re-trieve, as will be apparent from the reason given below (see fn. 11 of Chapter X), there is no need to go into the notion of temporality as elaborated in *Sein und Zeit*. We only note then in passing the insight inseparable from the problematic of Heidegger from the first, namely, that the intentional life of man (Dasein) is historical and temporal in its very nature as disclosive awareness (see pp. 160-61 above; also useful in this connection is Edmund Husserl's *The Phenomenology of Internal Time-Consciousness*, ed. M. Heidegger, trans. James S. Churchill, Bloomington, Ind.: Indiana University Press, 1964); and that the Being-question itself is one of proces, a 'lighting process': "dann muss jedes entwerfende Offenhalten der Wahrheit des Seins als Verstehen von Sein in die Zeit als den möglichen Horizont des Seinsverständnisses hinaussehen. (Vgl. S. u. Z. pars. 31-4 u. 68)" (WM:In, p. 18/217).

of definition as presented in traditional logic (*definitio fit per genus proximum et differentiam specificam*) to Being. (But see the *caveat* entered in Ch. II, fn. 20 above, and the text of this Ch. at fn. 59 below.) The ontological dimension of Dasein according to which it is not a substance but a process of transcendence relative to beings ("substances" and "things" generally) responds to this ambiguity, for no more than Being itself can the *Da des Seins* as such be defined in entitative, substantive terms.

The third ambiguity, the enigmatic character of Being as the a-priori of human comportment, gives the question of Being, in addition to its ontological priority, an ontic priority to which the ontic distinctiveness of Dasein responds. Even as a being among other beings, Dasein stands out not by reason of a "specifying difference" (*rationale*), but solely by reason of its preoccupation with Being: what is decisive for man is not the nature of things in their proper existence apart from human projects, but their historical meaning (*Geschicke des Seins*) as it emerges out of the *Differenz*. (It will be noted then that the ontic uniqueness of Dasein is not an ontic uniqueness *qua* ontic, but a uniqueness recognizable as ontic only in consequence of the inseparability of the ontic and ontological dimensions in existing Dasein. This already suggests the extent to which phenomenological research can come to terms with the onticity of Dasein.)

The first mentioned ambiguity, the ambiguity eventuating from the unity of Being as over against the multiplicity of categories applicable to beings, is met by the priority of Dasein thanks to which, as the unity of the ontic and ontological dimensions in finite transcendence to Being, it provides the necessary condition (ontico-ontological) for the possibility of any categorial ontologies in the first place.

Thus the phenomenological Being-question is seen to have a threefold priority corresponding to the threefold ambiguity of its metaphysical counterpart, and these priorties are grounded by distinct dimensions which are one in the transcending Dasein which they structure. Let us examine each of these priorities in turn, for together they constitute in the unity of Dasein *the* priority of the Being-question so interpreted as to penetrate directly the residual ambiguities of traditional philosophizing.

First of all, the question has an *ontological* priority. By this is meant that an interrogation of the nature and ground of Dasein's awareness of things-in-Being ought to go before any inquiry into the things themselves in terms of their causal relationships. Heidegger thus considers it a *basic insight* that

while the different epistemological directions which have been pursued have not gone so very far off epistemologically, their neglect of any existential analytic of Dasein has kept them from obtaining any basis for a well secured phenomenal problematic. Nor is such a *basis* to be obtained by subsequently making phenomenological corrections on the concepts of subject and consciousness. Such a procedure would give no guarantee that the inappropriate *formulation of the question* would not continue to stand.[12]

We may put this fundamental insight into more traditional terms by saying that both epistemology and Metaphysics as traditionally developed fail to provide "a preliminary ontological analytic of the subjectivity of the subject,"[13] i.e., of the intentional life of man: "an ontology with Dasein as its theme" alone takes as the principal object of inquiring concern the *ens* of *esse intentionale*:

The question of Being aims therefore at ascertaining the a-priori conditions not only for the possibility of the sciences which examine beings as entities of such and such a type, and, in so doing, already operate with a comprehension of Being, but also for the possibility of those ontologies themselves which are prior to the ontical sciences and which provide their foundations.[14]

Here we encounter again the profound reason behind Heidegger's substitution of Dasein for Husserl's pure consciousness, a substitution demanded (this will become fully transparent in the next chapter) by the very nature of Phenomenology as Heidegger conceives it, and one which led to the ultimate break between the two thinkers.[15] We see here as well the basis for Heidegger's important remark that the problem of the Being of Dasein as the focus for the question of the meaning of Being itself lies in some sense prior to any consideration of essence-existence as the basic structure of beings in terms of *esse proprium*:[16] the existential analytic of Dasein according to the phenomenological method aims at the very basis of the possibility of reason,

---

[12] "Es bedarf vielmehr der grundsätzlichen Einsicht, dass die verschiedenen erkenntnistheoretischen Richtungen nicht so sehr als erkenntnis-theoretische fehlgehen, sondern auf Grund des Versäumnisses der existenzialen Analytik des Daseins überhaupt gar nicht erst den Boden für eine phänomenal gesicherte Problematik gewinnen. Dieser *Boden* ist auch nicht zu gewinnen durch nachträgliche phänomenologische Verbesserungen des Subjekts- und Bewusstseinsbegriffes. Dadurch ist nicht gewährleistet, dass die unangemessene *Fragestellung* nicht doch bestehen bleibt." (SZ, p. 207).

[13] ". . . wird gezeigt, warum Kant die Einsicht in die Problematik der Temporalität versagt bleiben musste. Ein zweifaches hat diese Einsicht verhindert: einmal das Versäumnis der Seinsfrage überhaupt und im Zusammenhang damit das Fehlen einer thematischen Ontologie des Daseins, Kantisch gesprochen, einer vorgängigen ontologischen Analytik der Subjektivität des Subjekts." (SZ, p. 24).

[14] "Die Seinsfrage zielt daher auf eine apriorische Bedingung der Möglichkeit nicht nur der Wissenschaften, die Seiendes als so und so Seiendes durchforschen und sich dabei je schon in einem Seinsverständnis bewegen, sondern auf die Bedingung der Möglichkeit der von den ontischen Wissenschaften liegenden und sie fundierenden Ontologien selbst." (SZ, p. 11).

[15] Cf. also Spiegelberg, I, pp. 301-3.

[16] HB, pp. 68-9/278, esp. 72-3/280, 74-5/281, 110-11/298, 114-5/300.

ratio, "wherein the essence of man preserves the source that determines him" as the "There", the "Comprehendor of Being".[17] And similarly, one feels the thrust of Fr. Richardson's penetrating question: "Would it not be possible, then, that the entire problematic of Heidegger, placed as it is on a different level," and developed according to a methodological conception which constrains it at that level, "might leave intact the traditional questions concerning essence-existence, substance-accident, etc.?"[18] (And yet we will see how the very real thrust of this question is deflected from its mark when Fr. Richardson adds ". . .and if it succeeds, simply serve to lay the indispensable ground(work) for them?")

The question of Being then holds in philosophy the "ontological" primacy. "But this objectively scientific priority is not the only one."[19] The fact that Being cannot be (phenomenologically) explained through beings and that Reality (but not the Real) is possible only in the understanding, or better (because this "understanding" is generally preconceptual) comprehending, of Being, imposes on us the ontological analysis of consciousness, i.e., an inquiry into the Being of consciousness, of the *res cogitans* itself, as the task inevitably prior to the disclosure of Being as such.[20] And with the recognition of this task we are brought into confrontation with the *ontical* priority of the Being-question.

The ontical priority of the question of Being rests on the fact that Dasein itself insofar as it is an entity, enjoys a special distinctiveness as compared with beings whose character of Being is other than that of Dasein. "Dasein is ontically distinctive in that it *is* ontological,"[21] i.e., present to itself in terms of (some measure of) comprehensibility: "it is peculiar to this being that with and through its Being, this Being is disclosed to it,"[22] "that there is some way in which Dasein understands itself in its Being, and that to some degree it does so explicitly."[23]

The ontical priority of the Being-question derives from man's awareness

---

[17] "Die so verstandene Ek-sistenz ist nicht nur der Grund der Möglichkeit der Vernunft, ratio, sondern die Ek-sistenz ist das, worin das Wesen des Menschen die Herkunft seiner Bestimmung wahrt." (HB, p. 67/277). Cf. SZ, pp. 33-4; ID, pp. 43-4/41 and 54/50.

[18] H:TPT, p. 154. See also pp. 35, 173, 176, 202ff., 206, 233, 320 fn. 27, 386, 390, 531 fn. 5. And cf. Heidegger's remark cited in fn. 11 of Ch. IV.

[19] "Aber dieser sachlich-wissenschaftliche Vorrang ist nicht der einzige." (SZ, p. 11).

[20] Cf. SZ, pp. 207-8.

[21] "Die ontische Auszeichnung des Daseins liegt darin, dass es ontologisch *ist*." (SZ, p. 12).

[22] "Diesem Seienden eignet, dass mit und durch sein Sein dieses ihm selbst erschlossen ist." (SZ, p. 12).

[23] "Dasein versteht sich in irgendeiner Weise und Ausdrücklichkeit in seinem Sein." (SZ, p. 12).

not of himself, but of intentional life (Dasein) as something with its own comprehensibility, distinguishable in principle from physical individuality and personal subjectivity, his "onticity" (and in general from the onticity of things in the world): *intelligere et esse non sunt idem apud nos*. And this partial transparency of the self to the self becomes a phenomenological phenomenon to the extent that it means that "Dasein, in its Being, has a relationship towards that Being" which relationship itself is one of Being.[24] (Latent here is the entire structure of concern – *Sorge* or *cura* – wherein Dasein's Being is disclosed as "the sole authentic 'for-the-sake-of-which'."[25])

"That kind of Being towards which Dasein can comport itself in one way or another, and always does comport itself somehow, we call '*existence*'."[26] The question of existence is accordingly one of Dasein's ontical affairs, and concealed therein is the meaning of Being itself. "Thus, what matters in the determination of the humanity of man as ex-sistence is not that man is the essential, but that Being is the essential as the dimension of the ecstatic of ex-sistence."[27] As a matter of fact, "the existential nature of man is the reason why man can represent beings as such, and why he can be conscious of them";[28] but the point is that this differentiation between consciousness and beings, subject(ivity) and object(ivity), is only rendered possible by virtue of the fact that man *already* exists as Dasein, dwells from the first in *esse intentionale*.[29] That is why, within the phenomenological analysis of Dasein, "the personal, no less than the objective, misses and obstructs at the same time all that is essentially ex-sistence in its historical Being."[30]

Dasein always understands itself in terms of its existence – in terms of a possibility of itself: to be itself or not itself. Dasein has either chosen these possibilities itself, or got itself into them, or grown up in them already. Only the particular Dasein

---

[24] "Das Dasein ist ein Seiendes, das nicht nur unter anderem Seienden vorkommt. Es ist vielmehr dadurch ontisch ausgezeichnet, dass es diesem Seienden in seinem Sein *um* dieses Sein selbst geht. Zu dieser Seinsverfassung des Daseins gehört aber dann, dass es in seinem Sein zu diesem Sein ein Seinsverhältnis hat." (SZ, p. 12).

[25] "Der angezeigte Zusammenhang, der von der Struktur der Bewandtnis zum Sein des Daseins selbst führt als dem eigentlichen und einzigen Worum-willen. . ." (SZ, p. 84).

[26] "Das Sein selbst, zu dem das Dasein sich so oder so verhalten kann und immer irgendwie verhält, nennen wir *Existenz*." (SZ, p. 12).

[27] "So kommt es denn bei der Bestimmung der Menschlichkeit des Menschen als der Ek-sistenz darauf an, dass nicht der Mensch das Wesentliche ist, sondern das Sein als die Dimension des Ekstatischen der Ek-sistenz." (HB, p. 79/283).

[28] "Das existenziale Wesen des Menschen ist der Grund dafür, dass der Mensch Seiendes als ein solches vorstellen und vom Vorgestellten ein Bewusstsein haben kann." (WM:In, p. 16/214).

[29] See Powell, "The *An Sit* of Knowledge," in *Truth or Absolute Nothing*," pp. 24-9.

[30] "Allein das Personhafte verfehlt und verbaut zugleich das Wesende der seinsgeschichtlichen Ek-sistenz nicht weniger als das Gegenständliche." (HB, p. 71/279).

decides its existence, whether it does so by taking hold or by neglecting. The question of existence never gets straightened out except through existing itself. The understanding of oneself which leads *along this way* we call *"existentiell"*. The question of existence is one of Dasein's ontical 'affairs'. This does not require that the ontological structure of existence should be theoretically transparent. The question about that structure aims at the analysis of what constitutes existence. The context of such structures we call *"existentiality"*. Its analytic has the character of an understanding which is not existentiell, but rather *existential*.[31]

In this way Dasein's ontical constitution (from which side alone Dasein has "particularity") delineates in advance the task of an existential analytic of Dasein (which essentially consists in the application of the phenomenological method to the problem of the kind of Being which is proper to *Dasein* as *Da des Seins*), as regards both its possibility and its necessity.

So far as existence is the determining character of Dasein, the ontological analytic of this entity always requires that existentiality be considered beforehand. By "existentiality" we understand that state of Being that is constitutive for those beings that exist. But in the idea of such a constitutive state of Being, the idea of Being is already included. And thus even the possibility of carrying through the analytic of Dasein depends on working out beforehand the question about the meaning of Being in general.[32]

This last remark does not mean that we are trapped in a hopelessly circular analytic, a *circulus vitiosus*. Rather, it means that the question of Being, as the primary guiding task of the philosophical enterprise in the phenomenological mode strictly delimits the possibility of any ontology which takes its orientation from things-in-Being rather than Being as such ("in itself"). The ontology of Dasein becomes possible in the first instance only to the extent that the line of inquiry which leads to the meaning of Being *passes through*

---

[31] "Das Dasein versteht sich selbst immer aus seiner Existenz, einer Möglichkeit seiner selbst, es selbst oder nicht es selbst zu sein. Diese Möglichkeiten hat das Dasein entweder selbst gewählt oder es ist in sie hineingeraten oder je schon darin aufgewachsen. Die Existenz wird in der Weise des Ergreifens oder Versäumens nur vom jeweiligen Dasein selbst entschieden. Die Frage der Existenz ist immer nur durch das Existieren selbst ins Reine zu bringen. Das *hierbei* führende Verständnis seiner selbst nennen wir das *existenzielle*. Die Frage der Existenz ist eine ontische 'Angelegenheit' des Daseins. Es bedarf hierzu nicht der theoretischen Durchsichtigkeit der ontologischen Struktur der Existenz. Die Frage nach dieser zielt auf die Auseinanderlegung dessen, was Existenz konstituiert. Den Zusammenhang dieser Strukturen nennen wir die *Existenzialität*. Deren Analytik hat den Charakter nicht eines existenziellen, sondern *existenzialen* Verstehens." (SZ, p. 12).

[32] "Sofern nun aber Existenz das Dasein bestimmt, bedarf die ontologische Analytik dieses Seienden je schon immer einer vorgängigen Hinblicknahme auf Existenzialität. Diese verstehen wir aber als Seinsverfassung des Seienden, das existiert. In der Idee einer solchen Seinsverfassung liegt aber schon die Idee von Sein. Und so hängt auch die Möglichkeit einer Durchführung der Analytik des Daseins an der vorgängigen Ausarbeitung der Frage nach dem Sinn von Sein überhaupt." (SZ, p. 13). See also fn. 11 in Ch. IV above.

the Being of Dasein starting from the Being of beings (even as traditional ontology becomes possible only to the extent that the line of inquiry which leads to the meaning of *ousia* as *substantia* passes through the Being of beings starting from the Being of Dasein); but once this line has been secured, it becomes possible in the disclosed light of Being as such to make visible even those articulations of Dasein's existential constitution which are established by reason of the Being of entities.[33] The peculiar character of this reciprocating basis underlying the possibility for both foundational and metaphysical thought (but according to a certain order of mutual irreducibility) can be seen in this passage from *Sein und Zeit*:

Sciences are ways of Being [i.e., modes of comprehensible orientation] in which Dasein comports itself towards beings which it need not be itself. But to Dasein, Being is something that belongs essentially. Thus Dasein's understanding of Being pertains with equal primordiality both to an understanding of something like a 'world', and to the understanding of the Being of those beings which become accessible within the world. [This indeed we have seen to be an expression of the phenomenological content of St. Thomas' "anima est quodammodo omnia."] So whenever an ontology takes for its theme beings whose character of Being is other than that of Dasein, it has its own foundation and motivation in Dasein's own ontical structure, in which a pre-ontological comprehension of Being is comprised as a definite characteristic.[34]

"Therefore *fundamental ontology*, from which alone all other ontologies can take their rise, must be sought in the existential analytic of Dasein," and this only inasmuch as this analytic is guided and determined beforehand by the sense of Being as such.[35]

It would be difficult to find a better example of the change in meaning which seemingly traditional terms commonly undergo when employed to give expression to Heidegger's phenomenological thought concerning Being: "At first sight the questioning seems to remain within the sphere of beings as such, yet at the very first sentence it strives to depart from this sphere in order to consider and inquire into another realm."[36] "Fundamental ontol-

---

[33] Cf. SZ, pp. 17 and 15-16, 20-22, 58-9, 168-9, *inter alia*.

[34] "Wissenschaften sind Seinsweisen des Daseins, in denen es sich auch zu Seiendem verhält, das es nicht selbst zu sein braucht. Zum Dasein gehört aber wesenhaft: Sein in einer Welt. Das dem Dasein zugehörige Seinsverständnis betrifft daher gleichursprünglich das Verstehen von so etwas wie 'Welt' und Verstehen des Seins des Seienden, das innerhalb der Welt zugänglich wird. Die Ontologien, die Seiendes von nicht daseinsmässigem Seincharakter zum Thema haben, sind demnach in der ontischen Struktur des Daseins selbst fundiert und motiviert, die die Bestimmtheit eines vorontologischen Seinsverständnisses in sich begreift." (SZ, p. 13).

[35] "Daher muss die *Fundamentalontologie*, aus der alle andern erst entspringen können, in der *existenzialen Analytik des Daseins* gesucht werden." (SZ, p. 13).

[36] "Wählt man für die Behandlung der 'Seinsfrage' im unbestimmten Sinne den Titel

ogy" seeks to understand the *ens* of *esse intentionale*; "all other ontologies", i.e., all metaphysical inquiries, seek to understand the *ens* of *esse naturae*: both employ the words "What does it mean 'to be'?" yet the intention of each passes through these words in exactly opposite (not opposed) directions! The inquiry of Metaphysics takes rise from an analytic of Dasein in a very limited and special sense, specifically, to the extent that the properly metaphysical analytic "presupposes, as taken for granted by common sense or as scientifically confirmed by the criticism of knowledge, what in general terms we may call the objective *or rather transobjective* validity of understanding and knowledge" understood as the intelligible content of total experience, i.e., of Intentional Life taken in its amplitude and not in either the Husserlian sense or the sense of what the classical thinkers call "reason" – *Vernunft*.[37] How incorporation of Heidegger's central insight modifies this "traditional" perspective we shall consider in our final chapter; but the point here is that the "existential analytic" as capable of giving rise to Metaphysics is (we shall see) something which no phenomenological research which keeps rigorously to its research-principle can in the end decide one way or the other – without in that decision ceasing to be pure Phenomenology. Dawning realization of this point defines perhaps the largest interval between the "early" and the "later" Heidegger, who can say: "Such thinking, which recalls the truth of Being, is no longer satisfied with mere metaphysics, to be sure; but it does not oppose and think against metaphysics either."[38] One rightly sees in the very first question about Being which opened the way of Heidegger's inquiry and which that inquiry has pursued relentlessly ever since a basis for the reflective comment of Fr. Richardson: "The question, then, about the sense of Heidegger ultimately may reduce itself to this: what does it mean to *think*?"[39] But to see therein as well a basis for suspecting that a Heideggerean thought may, "if it succeeds, simply serve to lay the indispensable ground(work) for the traditional questions concerning essence-existence, substance-accident, etc.," is to fail to assess adequately the phenomenological research-principle, "*zu den Sachen selbst!*" But for the present this is a digression.

'Metaphysik', dann bleibt die Überschrift dieser Vorlesung zweideutig. Denn es sieht zunächst so aus, als hielte sich das Fragen im Gesichtskreis des Seienden als solchen, während es mit dem ersten Satz schon aus diesem Bezirk wegstrebt, um einen anderen Bereich fragenderweise in den Blick zu bringen." (EM, p. 15/19). See fn. II in Ch. IV above.

[37] See Jacques Maritain, *A Preface to Metaphysics* (New York: Mentor Omega, 1962), pp. 58ff.

[38] "Ein Denken, das an die Wahrheit des Seins denkt, begnügt sich zwar nicht mehr mit der Metaphysik; aber es denkt auch nicht gegen die Metaphysik." (WM:In, p. 9/209).

[39] Richardson, H:TPT, p. 16.

To summarize our immediate context: the ontic and ontological priority
of Dasein coincide in existence, as Heidegger intends the term; and the
awareness of its ecstatic or intentional character as such (*esse intentionale*) is
what is constitutive for the possibility of Dasein's understanding of existence
(whether *Angst* is the most likely and appropriate affective tonality for
arriving at this awareness does not immediately affect the issue), therefore
establishes a third priority (ontological, ontic, ontico-ontological) of Dasein
as the *locus* for disengaging the sense of Being: "Dasein names that which
should first of all be experienced, and subsequently thought of, as a place –
namely, the location of the truth of Being."[40] "*Dasein*, then, will be the
phenomenon *par excellence*,"[41] i.e., the hermeneutically closed phenomenological phenomenon.

Dasein – that being among all other beings endowed with a privileged comprehension of the Being-process, where 'comprehension' must be understood in its
most radical sense: not as abstract knowledge or intellectual perception, but as a
seizure (*-prehendere*) of Being along with (*cum-*) its own self – a radical, preconceptual, prephilosophical openness to Being that constitutes the very structure of
Dasein as a being.[42]

Heidegger rightly points out that what he has phenomenologically characterized as the ontico-ontological priority of Dasein was realized quite early,
though it was left unthematized. And he rightly sees his preliminary notion
of Dasein as intrinsically related to St. Thomas' treatment of the transcen-
dentals, to the point of stating explicitly that "phenomenological truth (the
disclosedness of Being) is *veritas transcendentalis*," and "Being is the *transcendens* pure and simple."[43] Suffice it to note here that his limited acquaintance with the thought of St. Thomas becomes plain in his identification
therein of the pre-phenomenological formulation of Dasein: "This distinctive
being, the *ens quod natum est convenire cum omni ente*, is the soul (*anima*)."[44]
For such an identification bypasses entirely the *esse intentionale* of the *cum*,
and we have already seen that it is not according to its natural being (*esse*

---

[40] "Vielmehr ist mit 'Dasein' solches genannt, was erst einmal als Stelle, nämlich als die
Ortschaft der Wahrheit des Seins erfahren und dann entsprechend gedacht werden soll."
(WM:In, p. 14/213).

[41] Richardson, "Heidegger and God," p. 33.

[42] William J. Richardson, "Heidegger and Theology," *Theological Studies* (March,
1965), 92. Cf. Powell, *Truth or Absolute Nothing*, pp. 24-9; John of St. Thomas, *Cursus
Phil.*, II, q. 1, art. 3.

[43] "Phänomenologische Wahrheit (Erschlossenheit von Sein) ist veritas transcendentalis." (SZ, p. 38). Heidegger italicizes the entire sentence. "Sein ist das transcendens
schlechthin." (SZ, p. 38). Heidegger italicizes this entire sentence.

[44] "Dieses ausgezeichnete Seiende, das ens, quod natum est convenire cum omni ente,
ist die Seele (anima)." (SZ, p. 14).

entitativum) that St. Thomas regards the soul as "quodammodo omnia," but rather according to the intentional life irreducibly distinct from the soul (man's ontic dimension) *in what is proper to it* (man's ontological dimension) even though it is as "mine" necessarily based on that *natum est convenire* specifying the entitative character of the soul as such (the inseparability in the Dasein of man of the ontological from the ontic which it structures so far as meaningfulness is involved in existentiell comportment). What it is important to keep clearly in mind here is that Heidegger places his investigation entirely in the context of Being as known prior to the categories (we will examine this starting point for itself only after we have adequately clarified Heidegger's methodological conception in the next chapter).[45] And for this reason it is prior to all metaphysical considerations which thematize beings as such, i.e., in terms of intrinsic (that is, entitative) necessities of structure.[46]

Yet the priority of the Being-question is grounded for both methodological and research reasons in the ontic-ontological structure of Dasein; and the central ambiguity of traditional philosophizing, that surrounding the meaning of Being, is to be penetrated by the phenomenological (or "existential") analytic of Dasein. For "the roots of the existential analytic, on its part, are ultimately *existentiell*, that is, *ontical*."[47] Let us meditate the statement, for we are less concerned in this chapter with the priority of the phenomenological *Seinsfrage* as Heidegger construes it (the intent of the exposition to now) than with what that priority can be shown to presuppose.

The key element entailed in the priority and formal structure of the Being-question as *Sein und Zeit* presents it is the co-presentation of the There of Being, Dasein, as a profoundly unified whole comprised of two really distinct dimensions, one, an ontic dimension, according to which it is a "particular" Dasein and has as its second most fundamental characteristic "mineness"; and another dimension, an ontological one, according to which this whole is ecstatic, literally "standing outside" itself, that is, beyond its onticity, according to which it is (constitutively) *In- und Mitsein* and has as

---

[45] SZ, p. 3. "In der Einleitung zu 'S. u. Z.' (S. 38). steht einfach und klar und sogar im Sperrdruck: 'Sein ist das transzendens schlechthin.' . . . Die einleitende Bestimmung 'Sein ist das transzendens schlechthin' nimmt die Weise, wie sich das Wesen des Seins bisher dem Menschen lichtete, in einen einfachen Satz zusammen. Diese rückblickende Bestimmung des Wesens des Seins aus der Lichtung des Seienden als eines solchen bleibt für den vordenkenden Ansatz der Frage nach der Wahrheit des Seins unumgänglich. So bezeugt das Denken sein geschickliches Wesen." (HB, p. 83/285).

[46] See HB, pp. 56-8/272-3 and 71/279. As we shall mention in the next chapter, Being as known prior to the categories is prior to all act-potency analysis, since the categories are the fundamentally diverse modes of act-potency composition.

[47] "Die existenziale Analytik ihrerseits aber ist letztlich *existenziell*, d. h. *ontisch* verwurzelt." (SZ, p. 13).

its most fundamental characteristic "existence". On this issue the best Heideggerean scholars speak with one accord. Fr. Richardson summarizes the
situation this way:

> We are examining [throughout *Sein und Zeit*] the ontological structure of There-
> being, whose essence lies in existence. Let the analysis be called, then, "existentiAL."
> But the term must be understood. Since existence for Heidegger is that structure
> by which There-being, thrown among beings, comprehends their Being, only that is
> existentiAL which pertains to There-being's comprehension of the Being-structure
> of beings, hence to the primordial constitution of There-being itself. The term per-
> tains to existence in its ontological dimension.
>   It is to be distinguished carefully from what is to be called "existentiELL." For
> existence, as a finite comprehension, is thrown among beings and remains always
> fallen among them with the need of achieving transcendence only through comport-
> ment with beings. Hence, if by reason of its Being-comprehension There-being
> exists in an ontological dimension, then by reason of its finitude it exists simultane-
> ously in an ontic dimension as well, sc. in continual engagement with beings,
> whether this engagement be imposed upon There-being by circumstances, the
> result of unconscious adaptation to milieu, or the result of a free choice. This
> dimension of existence and all that pertains to it is called "existentiELL," and is
> synonymous with "ontic."
>   It is worth while insisting on the fact that although existential and existentiell in
> There-being are distinct, they are not separate. They are different dimensions of a
> unique and profoundly unified phenomenon: finite transcendence. The function
> of the existential analysis as a re-collection of forgotten transcendence will be to
> discern the existential dimension which structures everydayness. It must respect the
> unity of the phenomenon that it analyses. The existential analysis must be rooted
> in the existentiell, sc. unless it discerns the existential within the existentiell, it re-
> mains groundless. One begins to see more clearly what the phenomenology of
> There-being as a process of transcendence will imply. It must be itself brought to
> achievement in some existentiell (ontic) comportment through which There-being
> recollects the existential dimension of its self. [48]

Now, the question we wish to pose is precisely this: Where does the notion
of distinct dimensions maintained within an absolute unity derive from?
Granting that the existential analysis must *respect the unity* of the phenomenon that it analyses, is the notion of distinct dimensions that are identical
an originally and properly and purely phenomenological conception? We
must discern whence the *Daseinsanalyse* derives its idea of wholeness.

     Fr. Richardson suggests that "for a lucid exposé of the unity of existential-
existentiell (ontic-ontological)," we should consult the text of Walter
Biemel. [49] Turning to this reference, we find that Biemel is responding to
Sartre's criticism wherein it is maintained that for Heidegger it is (metho-

---

[48] H.TPT, pp. 49-50.
[49] H:TPT, p. 50 fn. 65.

dologically) impossible to pass from the ontological level to the ontic level, an impossibility that "bursts forth when we meet the problem of the Other."[50] Biemel's reply is forthright.

That objection comes from a misunderstanding of the sense accorded by Heidegger to the term "ontological". The ontological level is not at all a level entirely separated from the ontic, it is a dimension that includes the essential structures of the concrete (ontic) real.[51]

The two levels – if this expression be allowed – necessarily hold together; the ontological is ontological only in the measure that it refers to an ontic existence (what Sartre calls the concrete). That is what what Heidegger explicitly writes: "The existential analytic (that is, ontological investigation of the Being of Dasein) is in final analysis rooted in the *existentiell*, that is to say, in the ontic."[52]

Precisely because finite transcendence is at bottom (*im Grunde*) a unified totality, Dasein "need not withdraw from the ontic" in order to achieve authenticity, i.e., recall Being from its forgottenness; "it need only recall the ontological."[53] Existing in both dimensions simultaneously as the process of transcendence, the ontic dimension is the *terminus a quo* of the transcendence while the ontological dimension (World, Being) is the *terminus ad quem*.[54] As a coming-to-pass that dynamically continues, therefore an occurrence which is always in the process of being achieved, Dasein, "constituted by ontological comprehension, is essentially not a thing but a happening, and this happening *is* transcendence (better: transcending)."[55] In this way "the ontological dimension, though structurally prior to the ontic, is not disclosed until after some instrumental complex has been discovered on the ontic level. Conversely, insofar as There-being *is*, sc. exists in its ontological dimension, it is already oriented to a 'World' of beings in its ontic dimension."[56] In short, "both the World of There-being's ontological dimension

---

[50] Jean-Paul Sartre, *Being and Nothingness*, trans. by Hazel E. Barnes (New York: The Philosophical Library, 1956), pp. 248-9.

[51] "Cette objection provient d'une méprise sur le sens accordé par Heidegger au terme 'ontologique'. Le plan ontologique n'est nullement un plan tout à fait séparé de l'ontique, c'est le plan qui comprend les structures essentielles du réel (ontique) concret (. . .)." – Walter Biemel, *Le Concept de Monde chez Heidegger* (Paris: Vrin, 1950), p. 88.

[52] "Les deux plans – si cette expression est permise – tiennent nécessairement ensemble, l'ontologique n'est ontologique que dans la mesure où il se réfère à une existence ontique (ce que Sartre appelle le concret). C'est ce que Heidegger écrit explicitement: 'L'analytique existentiale (à savoir la recherche ontologique de l'être du *Dasein*) est en fin de compte enracinée dans l'*existentiel*, c'est-à-dire dans l'*ontique*.' " (*Ibid.*, p. 89; SZ, p. 13 – as cited in fn. 47 *supra*).

[53] Richardson, H:TPT, p. 71.

[54] *Ibid.*, p. 58.

[55] *Ibid.*, p. 37.

[56] *Ibid.*, pp. 57-8.

which is disclosed [*erschlossen*], and 'World' of its ontic dimension which is discovered [*entdeckt*], are revealed together."[57] Biemel concludes:

If we wish to challenge the foundation of the Heideggerian analysis of Dasein, we cannot therefore do it by declaring that passage from the ontological to the ontic level is impossible: in fact, Heidegger starts from the ontic, and the ontological is nothing other than an explication of what is envelopped in the ontic, in other words, of the root of its possibility.

As soon as one has understood the nature of the relation which unites the ontological to the ontic, and their fundamental inseparability, the problem of their conjunction obviously no longer arises, because it is radically impossible to disjoin them at all.[58]

It would be difficult to express the unity of Dasein's ontico-ontological *Seinsverfassung* more unequivocally. But if the understanding of these two eminent Heideggerean scholars is accurate on this matter (and we think it is), it brings us before a scandalous situation. On this point the observations of Ralph Powell can neither be discredited nor ignored:

Distinct dimensions that are identical constitute what was always called an act-potency composition. For such dimensions are co-principles that are distinct but which cannot exist separately. (Hegel in his *Enzyklopädie der philosophischen Wissenschaften*, Glockner edition, Vol. 6, takes up matter and form – pp. 78-9 – before he considers substance – pp. 88ff. The scholastics disputed about correlative inseparables and mutual causality of material and formal cause without explicitly mentioning substance. For a history of the opinions of the principal schools, cf. John of St. Thomas, *Cursus Philosophicus Thomisticus*, Turin: Reiser edition, 1933, Vol. II, pp. 223-226 and 233-4.) For, the last question to be answered by an act-potency analysis of beings is: how do the alleged components form an *unum per se*? And the answer must be: because the distinct dimensions cannot exist apart.

Perhaps the reader will balk at this conclusion because act-potency philosophy is a philosophy of substance, whereas Dasein is not a substance, not even in *Sein und Zeit* which still allows the existence of substances [among some of the beings whose character of Being is] other than [that of] Dasein (e.g., the reference on p. 88 to "...Seiendes dessen Sein den Character reiner Substantialität hat.") Historically, this is a well founded objection. But *intrinsically, act-potency composition is not principally concerned with substance but rather with identifying a certain type of*

---

[57] *Ibid.*, p. 58. "... we reserve the word 'disclosed' to translate *erschlossen*, a term that always pertains to There-being, and 'discovered,' or, when occasion permits, 'un-covered,' to translate *entdeckt*, sc. a term that pertains always to beings other than There-being." (Richardson, H:TPT, p. 55 fn. 78).

[58] "Si nous voulons contester le bien-fondé de l'analyse heideggerienne du *Dasein*, nous ne pourrons donc le faire en déclarant impossible le passage du plan ontologique au plan ontique: en fait, Heidegger part de l'ontique, et l'ontologique n'est rien d'autre qu'une explication de ce qui est enveloppé dans l'ontique, autrement dit, de la racine de sa possibilité." (Biemel, p. 90). "Dès que l'on a compris la nature de la relation qui unit l'ontologique à l'ontique, et leur foncière inséparabilité, le problème de leur réunion ne se pose évidemment plus puisqu'il est radicalement impossible de les désunir." (Biemel, p. 91).

whole, namely, a whole with distinct dimensions which are inseparable. Thus the difference of magnitude involved in a nerve impulse and the molecular events which underlie it exemplify what act-potency philosophy claims are diverse dimensions that are identical. The macroscopic events of the nerve impulse follow their own laws and structures: the molecular events follow another system of laws and structure at the microscopic level. But both levels constitute one identical reality, since the nerve impulse occurs only through the molecular event: yet the two levels of magnitude are distinct. These inseparable but distinct dimensions would be act-potency components according to act-potency philosophy. *No question of substance need be raised in order to raise and adjudicate this general claim.* For substance is only one alleged distinct inseparable dimension [with regard specifically to accidents] among others.

Hence Dasein's not being a substance does not remove the act-potency character of its ontic-ontological structure in Sein und Zeit. But such act-potency composition is metaphysical according to the late Heidegger, whereas his thought is [then claimed to be] a step backwards out of metaphysics (back step, i.e., *Schritt zurück,* a phrase frequently used by Heidegger. Richardson translates it: step in reverse). Whether consciously or not, any backward step [really and entirely] out of metaphysics had to take him out of the ontic-ontological structure of Dasein in *Sein und Zeit:* in any case, that structure is missing in the late Heidegger.[59]

It must be said that Biemel's reply to Sartre's objection begs a more fundamental question than it answers. The entire basis for this assertion will not be established until we have arrived in the next chapter at an explicit determination of the limitations intrinsic to the phenomenological research-mode. But the above text already makes it clear that it is not enough to simply affirm and respect the infrangible unity of the ontic and ontological dimensions in existing Dasein, and then proceed to explicate the structure of existence phenomenologically. Why not? Because the notion of Dasein's always unified *Seinsverfassung* of distinct dimensions has presupposed an Interpretation grounded in the fundamental categories of Metaphysics. But we can add along this same line of critique that the ontic dimension *as such* does not constitute a phenomenological phenomenon; it is discerned only by reason of its necessary connection with the properly phenomenological phenomenon of Dasein's existence. Dasein's ontico-ontological *Seinsverfassung* is certainly the material object of the existential analytic, but it is the ontological dimension which specifies the *Daseinsanalyse* as its formal concern. That is why, even in affirming from a phenomenological standpoint the ontic-existentiell roots of the existential analytic, Heidegger does so only insofar as the ontic-existentiell dimension of Dasein is *terminus a quo* for the process of illuminating transcendence which is his proper theme. There is

---

[59] "The Late Heidegger's Omission of the Ontic-Ontological Structure of Dasein," pp. 2-3: my emphasis. (Cf. pp. 117-118 of printed version).

small need to point out that *where* research begins is not a decisive consideration unless one specifies as well *how* it departs from its starting point, that is,
what *guides* the departure. In the case of research into the Being of Dasein
as the avenue to Being as such, the roots are ultimately ontical simply in
consequence of the particularity of the Dasein who undertakes the analytic,
that is, in consequence of Dasein's fundamental characteristic of "mineness"
which is secondary and ipso facto subordinated to "existence". "Only if the
inquiry of philosophical research is itself seized upon in an existentiell
manner as a possibility of the Being of each existing Dasein, does it become
at all possible to disclose the existentiality of existence and to undertake an
adequately founded ontological problematic";[60] but we have seen in countless ways already that, for Heidegger, to keep to or concentrate on this facet
of Dasein under which it is a personal conscious self "misses and obstructs
at the same time all that is essentially ex-sistence," that is, all that is formal
to the problematic of *Sein und Zeit*.[61] We may say in sum that no more than
the ontological-existential dimension of Dasein can be treated in what is
proper to it according to categorial analysis (*praedicamenta*) can the ontic-
existentiell dimension be treated in what is proper to *it* according to existential analysis (*existentialia*): what enters into an analytic in only a secondary
way, however integrally, can only be treated in a secondary way within the
horizon of that analytic:

All *explicata* to which the analytic of Dasein gives rise are obtained by considering
Dasein's existence-structure. Because Dasein's characters of Being are defined in
terms of existentiality, we call them "existentialia". These are to be sharply distinguished from what we call "categories" [*praedicamenta*] – characteristics of
Being for beings whose character is not that of Dasein.[62]

"Dasein is essentially," that is, ontologically, "not a Being-present-at-
hand";[63] but even Dasein itself inasmuch as it is the constitutive state of a
being is present-at-hand "in" the world (of nature), "or, more exactly, *can
with some right and within certain limits be taken* as merely present-at-hand

---

[60] "Nur wenn das philosophisch-forschende Fragen selbst als Seinsmöglichkeit des je
existierenden Daseins existenziell ergriffen ist, besteht die Möglichkeit einer Erschliessung
der Existenzialität der Existenz und damit die Möglichkeit der Inangriffnahme einer zureichend fundierten ontologischen Problematik überhaupt." (SZ, pp. 13-14).

[61] "... das Personhafte verfehlt und verbaut zugleich das Wesende der seinsgeschichtlichen Ek-sistenz nicht weniger als das Gegenständliche." (HB, p. 71/279).

[62] "Alle Explikate, die der Analytik des Daseins entspringen, sind gewonnen im Hinblick auf seine Existenzstruktur. Weil sie sich aus der Existenzialität bestimmen, nennen
wir die Seinscharaktere des Daseins *Existenzialien*. Sie sind scharf zu trennen von den
Seinsbestimmungen des nicht daseinsmässigen Seienden, die wir *Kategorien* nennen." (SZ,
p. 44).

[63] "... das wesenhaft kein Vorhandensein ist. . ." (SZ, p. 104).

(*Vorhandenes*)."[64] It is certainly not in terms of its ontological dimension that Dasein can with any right be taken as a mere entity "present-at-hand" since to do this one must completely disregard the existential state of Being-in.[65] Therefore neither can Dasein be taken as *vorhanden* existentielly, that is, in terms of comportment strictly considered, since in all comportment the Being of Dasein is finally at issue. How then? All that retains candidacy are Dasein's ontic structural elements, or more exactly, some facets of Dasein's ontic dimension. That is why "*sometimes* the couplet *ontic-ontological* is used for Heidegger's analysing of Dasein; but *usually* the couplet *existentiell-existential* is used for phases of his analysing, so that the couplet ontic-ontological is reserved for a diversity of elements uncovered in Dasein by the analysing."[66] Man in his *Dasein* (the phenomenological phenomenon) is not something present-at-hand, therefore must be Interpreted existentially; but *man* in his Dasein (the ordinary or "formal" phenomenon) is present-at-hand, therefore must be Interpreted categorially or "predicamentally." If therefore we were to take Sartre's criticism to mean that Heideggerean Phenomenology cannot pass from the ontological level to the ontical level in such wise as to treat that ontic dimension directly as such in terms of its own proper character as elementally structural for Dasein as in man, i.e., Dasein as "particular" and "mine", – in such wise, briefly, as to treat the ontic dimension in terms of its fundamentally (rather than secondary) proper character of Being, then Biemel's response to that criticism must be judged inadequate.

One being, disclosed in its Being as simultaneously ontological and ontic: if we take each in its proper character of comprehensibility, these two dimensions "require different kinds of primary interrogation respectively," for although the former characterizes Dasein formally as a "*who*" (in the non-personal sense of existence), the latter, in some respects at least, characterizes Dasein materially as a "*what*" (presence-at-hand in the broadest sense). Mutually irreducible if both are considered in a formal sense (and notice that the ontic dimension is never thematized formally in *Sein und Zeit* for what we shall see are altogether fundamental methodological

---

[64] ". . . auch Seiendes, das nicht weltlos ist, z. B. das Dasein selbst, 'in' der Welt vorhanden ist, genauer gesprochen: mit einem gewissen Recht in gewissen Grenzen als nur Vorhandenes *aufgefasst* werden *kann* . . . Mit dieser möglichen Auffassung des 'Daseins' als eines Vorhandenen und nur noch Vorhandenen darf aber nicht eine dem Dasein *eigene* Weise von 'Vorhandenheit' zusammengeworfen werden." (SZ, p. 55).

[65] "Hierzu ist ein völliges Absehen von, bzw. Nichtsehen der existenzialen Verfassung des In-Seins notwendig." (SZ, p. 55).

[66] Powell, "The Late Heidegger's Omission of the Ontic-Ontological Structure of Dasein," p. 1. (See p. 116 of printed version).

reasons), neither dimension can be entirely explained by reference to the other, any more than a categorial analysis can adequately subsume and replace an existential one or vice versa.[67] Everywhere Heidegger I makes this distinction and affirmation; nowhere does he take it seriously enough to follow out its implications. Yet he does advert to it explicitly in important passages of the Kant book which openly link "the unique totality of the possibility of experience as ground of contingent real experience to the traditional metaphysical distinction between the possible and the actual";[68] and similarly in *Sein und Zeit*, the ontological possibility of experience as a whole is presented as the ground of ontic contingent experience – or more exactly, the unique totality of possible experience in authentic Dasein (which alone can be a whole) is stated by Heidegger to be the ontological condition of the possibility and the ground of the historicity of Dasein as such (structurally, whether "authentic" or not, since authenticity is after all but an existentiell modalization of everyday Dasein's possibilities), while the historicity of Dasein is ontic inasmuch as it springs from an "existenzielle Verstehen".[69] To deny in short the derivation of the ontic-ontological distinction from the same traditional metaphysical distinction which the analyses of the Kant book acknowledge would require a stepping back from the rigorously structured problematic of *Sein und Zeit*, and the abandonment therewith of any way or hope of clarifying foundationally the properly metaphysical *Seinsfrage* which survives all the attempts to phenomenologically reinterpret it, the later (unlike the early) Heidegger allows, as "the basis of philosophy" – ". . .das Erste der Philosophie."[70]

And there is more. In *Sein und Zeit*, only authentic Dasein can be a whole. We are now in a position, having discerned the remote analytic origin of Dasein's distinct dimensions as such, to discern the derivation in the *Daseinsanalyse* of the idea of Dasein's wholeness, i.e., its structural unity. For if, as we shall directly show, the notion of (actually or possibly authentic) Dasein's wholeness were founded on an analysis drawn from the *Vorhandenen*, from the very *locus* of the idea of substantiality, the merely present-at-hand entities whose character of Being is not only other than that of Dasein, but even un-

---

[67] "Existenzialien und Kategorien sind die beiden Grundmöglichkeiten von Seinscharakteren. Das ihnen entsprechende Seiende fordert eine je verschiedene Weise des primären Befragens: Seiendes ist ein *Wer* (Existenz) oder ein *Was* (Vorhandenseit im weitesten Sinne)." (SZ, p. 45). See the citation in fn. 39 of Ch. IV above from p. 186b3-16 of John of St. Thomas' *Cursus Philosophicus*, Vol. III.

[68] Powell, "The Late Heidegger's Omission of the Ontic-Ontological Structure of Dasein," p. 19. (Cf. p. 134 of printed version).

[69] SZ, p. 383.

[70] WM:In, p. 9/209.

related in its proper character to the purposeful pattern of Dasein's concern – if this were so, all the less can the *Daseinsanalyse* as such establish, in its radicalization that will lay bare the sense of Being, the notion of a *unified* whole of distinct dimensions: it will needs respect the unity of the phenomenon, but since the very notion of a unitary or "whole" phenomenon rests in the first instance on an analogy with the beings, phenomenological research proves constitutionally dependent on whatever philosophical analysis can establish of itself and directly the sense of correlative dimensions within a single whole, namely, the act-potency analysis of Metaphysics.

Now "Heidegger clearly shows at the outset of Part II of *Sein und Zeit* that the method of this part is taken from *Seienden* other than Dasein, i.e. from *Vorhandenen*."[71] For the problem of Dasein's wholeness arises in the first place only because the *Daseinsanalyse*, proceeding as it does in the mode of Phenomenology, must respect what belongs to any such investigation (*jede Auslegung*), that is, any phenomenological Interpretation;[72] and it is precisely the method of *jede Auslegung* which demands of primordial ontological (i.e., phenomenological) *Interpretation* that it get the thematic *Seiende* as a whole. If Heidegger had really stepped out of or below act-potency Metaphysics, in such wise that its validity was not at least granted beforehand by the phenomenological research-mode, then Dasein's capacity for wholeness could not legitimately have been drawn from the wholeness of *Vorhandenen*, because that implicates *at least* presuppositionally thinking Dasein (and therewith Being) by analogy to the beings – and yet how within the structural exigencies of the *Sein und Zeit* problematic can this implication be suppressed, since the very problem of Dasein's (ontological) wholeness arose to begin with only by virtue of that method to be employed in interpretation (*Interpretation*) of any kind of *Seiende*:

Hence it is not mere traditional phraseology that leads *Sein und Zeit* to analyse Dasein in the ontic-ontological categories dependent upon traditional act-potency metaphysics. The very method that leads to it is derived from *Seienden* of any *Seinsart*, i.e., *Vorhandenen*, and then applied to the particular *Seinsart* counterdistinguished against the generality of *Seinsart*, applied namely to Dasein.[73]

Let us summarize. The formal structure and priority of the Being-question as it is raised in *Sein und Zeit* are grounded in the ontic distinctiveness of Dasein

[71] Powell, "The Late Heidegger's Omission of the Ontic-Ontological Structure of Dasein," p. 21. (Cf. p. 135 of printed version.)

[72] See SZ, p. 232.

[73] Powell, "The Late Heidegger's Omission of the Ontic-Ontological Structure of Dasein," p. 21f. (Cf. p. 173f. of printed version) Heidegger seems to allude to this fault in the basic structure of SZ when he recalls its incongruous intention ("ungemässe Absicht") respecting science and research (see HB, p. 110/297-8).

according to which it *is* ontologically. Fundamental ontology is concerned directly with only the character of Being proper to Dasein's existence as Dasein, i.e., as existing. Although it takes its departure in an existentiell modification of Dasein, it does so only to explicate the ontological structure of all ontical Being towards. . . without any consideration for its ontic nature as such, i.e., as prior to or independent of Dasein's referential dependence upon the onticity of "natural" entities in general. For this reason, the characterization of Dasein's structure as ontic-ontological must needs presuppose the validity of a Metaphysical Interpretation of Dasein's ontic presence-at-hand as such in act-potency terms. Only with this presupposition are the problematic exigencies of the "prior task" for determining the meaning of Being respected *in toto*. Far from laying the foundations for Metaphysics, Phenomenology turns out in the end to depend on Metaphysics for *its* foundations, that is, if it is to secure any meaning that is not purely and totally historical in principle[74] or, what amounts to the same thing, if it is not to fall into reverse inauthenticity by forgetting the ontic dimension of Dasein by virtue of which it has the particularity of mineness as its second most fundamental characteristic.[75] The exact nature of this presupposing remains to be determined; but since it is one with the sense in which the phenomenological Being-question enjoys a philosophical priority, the finality of our re-trieve demands that we secure in principle our understanding of Dasein's establishment as the necessary phenomenal basis for pursuing the Being-question; and this is the same as requiring that we work toward an understanding of Heidegger's basic conception of Phenomenology. In accomplishing that, we will come to see (Richardson and Biemel notwithstanding) a decisive sense in which, as Sartre contends, the philosophical inadequacy of Heidegger's stance "bursts forth when we meet the problem of the Other," provided that we understand by this "other" a transobjective subject, a *subjectum capax essendi* possessed of *its own* possibilities of Being "independent of the fate of Being-meaning."[76] We will say: Heidegger is

---

[74] *Ibid.*, pp. 22-3. (Cited on p. 169 at fn. 47 of Ch. X below.)

[75] See Chapter IV of this present study, pp. 48 and esp. 52.

[76] Powell, "Has Heidegger Destroyed Metaphysics?", p. 59. "Heidegger defines metaphysics as the intellectual grasp of subjects in the forgottenness of Being. Since Being is the fate of Being-meaning, the definition reduces to: 'an intellectual grasp of subjects as independent of fate.' This can serve as a working definition for us as we ask the question whether Heidegger's phenomenological thought leaves such a metaphysics possible." (p. 58).

"When Heidegger says Dasein is not a subject he does not thereby foreclose all study of subjects. On the contrary, Heidegger's fundamental experience finds various subjects, and each one differs in a unique way. Subjects differ by *falling out of the light of Being*: 'Plants and animals are never in the light of Being' (HB, 70/279). 'They hang worldless in their

separated from Aristotle and Aquinas phenomenologically by the gulf between the conditions or mode of thought (in the full and proper sense of *ens quod est intra animam non vero sicut accidens in subjecto sed secundum esse intentionale*) and the conditions or mode of the thing (as transobjective subject – *ens quod est extra animam et independens ab ea per esse entitativum proprium*).

We will come to see too why the *Daseinsanalyse* structuring fundamental ontology is incapable in principle of vindicating or grounding the act-potency *praedicamenta* which it has presupposed, and bound up with that insight is the fate of Heidegger's claim that Phenomenology provides the only genuine philosophical method. We will say: Heidegger is separated from Aristotle and Aquinas metaphysically by the chasm of act-potency.

Finally, an understanding of Phenomenology as the medium of the re-interpreted Being-question will complete the programmatic sequence of our re-trieve, for it will ground methodologically, that is (so far as Heideggerean thought is concerned), in principle, all the issues and contentions that have been raised in the course of our study. It will put us in a position, thanks to the intensive critiques of Ralph Powell (the bulk of which remain unpublished), to adjudicate the nature of Heidegger's celebrated "reversal" (*Kehre*), and therewith the difference in continuity between Heidegger I and II.

environment' (*ibid.*). World, of course, is Being-meaning. But man, in so far as he is a rational animal and is still fundamentally an animal (cf. HB. p. 66/277), also hangs 'worldless' in his environment and never enters into the light of Being. This simply means that *subjects as subjects are independent of the fate of Being-meaning. . .*

"Given Heidegger's criteria, metaphysics seems to have withstood its attempted destruction." (P. 59).

CHAPTER IX

PHENOMENOLOGY: THE MEDIUM OF THE BEING-QUESTION

> "Im Horizont der Kantischen Problematik kann das, was phänomenologisch unter Phänomen begriffen wird, vorbehaltlich anderer Unterschiede, so illustriert werden, dass wir sagen: was in den Erscheinungen, dem vulgär verstandenen Phänomen je vorgängig und mitgängig, obzwar unthematisch, sich schon zeigt, kann thematisch zum Sichzeigen gebracht werden und dieses Sich-so-an-ihm-selbst-zeigende ("Formen der Anschauung") sind Phänomene der Phänomenologie."
> Martin Heidegger, *Sein und Zeit*, p. 31.

In the course of our study to now we have had to remark repeatedly the importance of the phenomenological attitude in the development of Heidegger's thought of Being. It is time for us to precise this attitude especially as adopted by the so-called early Heidegger.

"With the question of the meaning of Being," writes Heidegger, "our investigation comes up against the fundamental question of philosophy. *This is one that must be treated phenomenologically.*"[1] The statement is a strong one. It indicates that heretofore the fundamental question of philosophy has never admitted of accurate formulation, because heretofore failure to methodologically settle the philosophical task has made it impossible to delineate in a recognizable and proper sense a sphere or domain or area of possible investigation which would be at once open to philosophical investigation and closed in principle to the research-modes of endlessly multiplying and diversifying positive sciences guided by formal aspects of things (*Seiende*), by object-domains. In a word, the preliminary clarification of Being as the Problem Area constantly attended to by philosophy becomes possible for the first time, according to Heidegger, with a mature understanding of the nature of phenomenological research.

---

[1] "Mit der leitenden Frage nach dem Sinn des Seins steht die Untersuchung bei der Fundamentalfrage der Philosophie überhaupt. Die Behandlungsart dieser Frage ist die *phänomenologische*." (SZ, p. 27).

How is this so? Because only phenomenology is able, as it were, to precise and isolate beings in their Being, and thereby (with the aid of hermeneutic) Being as such as a thematic subject of possible investigation, rather than take its primary orientation from beings through their Being as is the case (in principle) for all other research-modes.

"The universe of beings is the sphere from which the positive sciences of nature, history, space secure at any given time their domain of objects. Directed straight to beings, they take over in its totality the analysis of all that is."[2] Directed straight to the beings: such for Heidegger is the defining characteristic, the hallmark, of "positive science"; and consequently the research-mode proper to all positive science as such with intrinsic methodological necessity "leaves untouched the question which concerns all [positive science] in the same way, namely, the question of the meaning of the Being of their domains of Being."[3]

The phenomenological research-mode, by contrast, touches only on the meaning of the Being of all the various positive sciences' (methodologically constituted and delimited[4]) domains of Being. "What is the pervasive, simple, unified determination of Being that permeates all of its multiple

[2] "Das All des Seienden ist das Feld, aus dem die positiven Wissenschaften von Natur, Geschichte, Raum jeweils ihre Gegenstandsgebiete gewinnen. Geradehin auf das Seiende gerichtet, übernehmen sie in ihrer Gesamtheit die Erforschung alles dessen, was ist." ("Die Idee der Phänomenologie," p. 256).

[3] "Denn sie ist selbst positive Wissenschaft und lässt nach der Forschungsart positiver Wissenschaften überhaupt die sie alle in gleicher Weise betreffende Frage nach dem Seinssinn ihrer Seinsgebiete unberührt." (Ibid., p. 257)

Since the object and method even of phenomenological psychology are restricted "to the fundamental structures of the exact 'being' of positivity according to all of its kinds and grades," it is clear in the first place that mere psychology "is in principle not in the position to establish the foundations for philosophy," and that consequently the "regression to conscious awareness" that will occupy the 'controlling' or central position for a laying of philosophy's foundations "extends back beyond the domain of the pure psychic" – and that means into the spiritual preconscious distinguished by Maritain: "Fragestellung, methodische Forschung und Lösung folgen der prinzipiellen Gliederung des geradehin 'Seienden' der Positivität nach allen seinen Arten und Stufen. Aber ist diese selbe Aufgabe nicht schon seit Locke von der Psychologie übernommen? Fordert eine radikale Grundlegung der Philosophie anderes als nur eine methodisch konsequent auf innere Erfahrung sich einschränkende Psychologie der reinen Bewusstseinssubjektivität? Jedoch die grundsätzliche Besinnung auf den Gegenstand und die Methode einer reinen Psychologie kann vor Augen legen, dass sie grundsätzlich ausser Stande ist, die Fundamente beizustellen für die Philosophie als Wissenschaft. Denn sie ist selbst positive Wissenschaft und lässt nach der Forschungsart positiver Wissenschaften überhaupt die sie alle in gleicher Weise betreffende Frage nach dem Seinssinn ihrer Seinsgebiete unberührt. Der Rückgang auf das Bewusstsein, den alle Philosophie mit wechselnder Sicherheit und Klarheit sucht, erstreckt sich daher über das Gebiet des rein Psychischen zurück in das Feld der reinen Subjektivität." (P. 257).

[4] See SZ, pp. 8-10, 27-8, 303, 324, 361-3, 50 fn. 1.

meanings?. . . . Whence does Being as such (not merely beings as beings) receive its determination?"[5] The precision of the dichotomy brings the issue into sharp focus for the (historically) first time: the research-mode of positive science as such is directed straight to the beings, and so in principle leaves untouched the question which concerns all positive science in the same way, namely, the question of the sense of the Being of their domains of Being; while the research-mode of phenomenology as such, or, what amounts to the same thing, of ontology as such (for, Heidegger will say, "only as phenomenology is ontology possible"[6]), is directed straight to the Being of beings and so in principle leaves untouched the questions which concern the beings within the various domains (physical, chemical, physiological, psychological, sociological, etc.) of Being, the "object domains" secured at any given time by the progress of positive science.

Thus "the expression 'phenomenology' signifies primarily a *methodological conception*. This expression does not characterize the what of the objects of philosophical research as subject-matter, but rather the *how* of that research."[7] "Thus the term 'phenomenology' expresses a maxim which can be formulated as 'To the things themselves'!"[8] Phenomenology is that research-mode which enables us by a reflective turn of sight to precise the question of the "existence" of beings *as* appearing from any question of their existence as possessed quite independently of the experience by which they are disclosed, the acquaintance in which they are discovered, the grasping in which their nature is ascertained;[9] and, having made that precision, Phenomenology is guided in its research not by that which is constitutive of such appearing as an actual event, not, that is to say, with an intentional assessment of the content of consciousness actual or possible in this or that respect at this or that time (this was Husserl's mistake) – no, phenomenological research which is fully aware of itself is guided by that which is constitutive of the prior possibility of becoming aware of beings, not in terms of any productivity of the mind, but of the very appearing of beings in the realm of explicit

[5] "Welches ist die alle mannigfachen Bedeutungen durchherrschende einfache, einheitliche Bestimmung von Sein? . . . Woher empfängt das Sein als solches (nicht nur das Seiende als Seiendes) seine Bestimmung?" (Heidegger's "Vorwort" to H:TPT, p. XI).

[6] "Ontologie ist nur als Phänomenologie möglich." (SZ, p. 35). Heidegger italicizes this sentence. See also SZ, p. 38.

[7] "Der Ausdruck 'Phänomenologie' bedeutet primär einen *Methodenbegriff*. Er charakterisiert nicht das sachhaltige Was der Gegenstände der philosophischen Forschung, sondern das *Wie* dieser." (SZ, p. 27).

[8] "Der Titel 'Phänomenologie' drückt eine Maxime aus, die also formuliert werden kann: 'zu den Sachen selbst!'. . ." (SZ, p. 27).

[9] Cf. SZ, p. 183; Richardson, "Heidegger and God", p. 30; and "Die Idee der Phänomenologie," pp. 260-61.

conscious awareness, therefore by beings in their Being "beyond the domain of the pure psychic."[10]

The idea is dominating and decisive for the nature of philosophizing in a rigorous mode as Heidegger conceives it. From the very outset of the philosophical project, reflexivity, clearly recognized as such, must be taken as primary. That sphere toward which the phenomenological stance alone is directly and immediately oriented is the very Problem Area which, under the title of Being, "all philosophy searches for with varying sureness and clarity."[11] From reflexion philosophy sets out to perceive, a-priori, what is immediate; and therefore the conviction is taken over (i.e., the assumption is made) that reflexion can, by turning back upon direct operations and their objects (which are grasped first in the mind's "natural attitude" of spontaneity), fashion for itself in and through the latter an "object" that would be grasped beforehand (not temporally, to be sure) and grasped more immediately. The reflective stance phenomenologically defined, the mind's "second movement" rather than its "first (and spontaneous) movement," is for Heidegger the starting point of philosophy as a whole.[12]

Thus, in 1927, in a draft article composed after the completion of *Sein und Zeit* and at Husserl's request, Heidegger gave this characterization of what seemed to him to be Phenomenology's decisive philosophical role:

The clarification in principle of the necessity for regression to conscious awareness [not indeed as the preclusive sphere of philosophical research (this would end in psychologism), but as the point of departure for that research, i.e., its adequate phenomenal basis], the radical and explicit determination of the way or path and of the procedural steps of this retrogression, the fundamental circumscription and systematic exploration of the sphere of pure subjectivity [which extends back beyond the pure psychic, i.e., the intentionality of consciousness as a subjective state or determination,[13] and, as equally accessible, according to what is proper to it, in intersubjective experience and self-experience,[14] must let alone, 'abstract from,'

---

[10] ". . . erstreckt sich daher über das Gebiet des rein Psychischen zurück. . ." ("Die Idee der Phänomenologie," p. 257).

[11] "Der Rückgang auf das Bewusstsein. . . alle Philosophie mit wechselnder Sicherheit und Klarheit sucht. . ." (*Ibid.*)

[12] "Aber Erschliessung des Apriori ist nicht 'aprioristische' Konstruktion. Durch *E. Husserl* haben wir wieder den Sinn aller echten philosophischen 'Empirie' nicht nur verstehen, sondern auch das hierfür notwendige Werkzeug handhaben gelernt. Der 'Apriorismus' ist die Methode jeder wissenschaftlichen Philosophie, die sich selbst versteht. Weil er nichts mit Konstruktion zu tun hat, verlangt die Apriorforschung die rechte Bereitung des phänomenalen Bodens." (SZ, p. 50 fn. 1). See Macquarrie-Robinson translation, p. 490 n. x. Also Maritain, DS, ch. 3, esp. pars. 1-4.

[13] "Der Rückgang auf das Bewusstsein. . . erstreckt sich daher über das Gebiet des rein Psychischen zurück. . ." ("Die Idee der Phänomenologie," p. 257).

[14] "Das Ganze eines Erlebniszusammenhangs, eines seelischen Lebens existiert jeweils im Sinne eines selbst (Ich) und als dieses lebt es faktisch in Gemeinschaft mit Anderen.

all pure psychic facticity which presents itself chiefly as a de facto individual coherence:[15] and, finally] which is opened up along this way back: such is what constitutes Phenomenology. The final clarification of the philosophical Being-question and the systematic reduction or "cutting back" to the methodologically settled philosophical task overcomes the vague generality and vacuity of traditional philosophizing.[16]

We have already seen sufficient to our purpose Heidegger's reason for replacing "pure" or "unalloyed" consciousness, the *Cogito*, with the Intentional Life of Man taken in its full amplitude:[17] as long as we restrict our-

Das rein Psychische wird daher zugänglich sowohl in der Selbsterfahrung als in der intersubjektiven Erfahrung fremden Seelenlebens." (*Ibid.*, pp. 258-9: my italics). ". . . muss die reduktive Einstellung auf das reine Psychische (*ibid.*, pp. 261-2)," "das heisst zu den *Phänomenon* (*ibid.*, p. 261)," "das sich zünachst als individuell faktischer Erlebniszusammenhang gibt, absehen von aller psychischen Faktizität." (*Ibid.*, p. 262). "Sofern die Reduktion in dem gekennzeichneten Sinne lediglich den Zugang zu dem je eigenen Seelenleben vermittelt, heisst sie *egologische*. Weil jedoch jedes Selbst mit anderen in Einfühlungszusammenhang steht und dieser sich in intersubjektiven Erlebnissen konstituiert, bedarf es einer notwendigen Erweiterung der egologischen Reduktion durch die *intersubjektive*. . . Was sich hier in einer besonderen Evidenzgestalt bewährt, ist *Mitdasein* eines konsequent und mit immer neuem Bestimmungsgehalt indizierten konkreten anderen Selbst. . . Die Durchführung der phänomenologischen Reduktion in meinem wirklichen und möglichen in Geltung Setzen 'fremden' Seelenlebens in der Evidenzform einstimmiger Einfühlung ist die intersubjektive Reduktion." (*Ibid.*, pp. 262-3).

In short, the intersubjective is *equiprimordial* with the subjective (pp. 262, 263) in the sense that the latter is never given apart from the former, *although insofar as relation to corporality is comported* (i.e., with an eye to the ontic) the intersubjective is given in a different way – "Andererseits aber ist dieses fremde Selbst nicht originaliter da wie das je eigene in seiner originalen Beziehung auf *seine* Körperlichkeit." (pp. 262-3).

[15] "Die Idee der Phänomenologie," pp. 261-2. See immediately preceding footnote.
[16] "Die grundsätzliche Klärung der Notwendigkeit des Rückgangs auf das Bewusstsein, die radikale und ausdrückliche Bestimmung des Weges und der Schrittgesetze dieses Rückgangs, die prinzipielle Umgrenzung und systematische Durchforschung des auf diesem Rückgang sich erschliessenden Feldes der reinen Subjektivität heisst Phänomenologie. Die letzte Klärung des philosophischen Seinsproblems und die methodische Zurückführung auf wissenschaftlich erledigende philosophische Arbeit überwinden die undefinierte Allgemeinheit und Leere des traditionellen Philosophierens." (*Ibid.*, pp. 256-7). Thus we anticipated above (Chapter V, esp. p. 77) and are demonstrating in this present Chapter that phenomenological research as Heidegger conceives it in principle can properly consider man only in his *vita intentionalis* (which "extends beyond" all *vita psychica sensu traditionali*), preclusive of all entitative considerations whether anterior or even concomitant to this intentional life: ". . . abgesehen ist von allen seelischen Funktionen im Sinne der Organisation der Leiblichkeit, das heisst vom Psychophysischen." ("Die Idee der Phänomenologie," p. 258). See fn. 48 of Chapter V in this present study.
And this methodological isolation of the adequately considered intentional life of man, i.e., taken at its source as well as in its proper integrity, will be the sense of Dasein as the necessary phenomenal basis for (phenomenological) ontology.
[17] See Chapters V, VI, and VII of this study. Also SZ, pp. 65-6 and 130, then 95, 116, 201, 206-7 as supplementation of the QED. See also WM:In, p. 16/214-5 (as cited in fn. 7 of Chapter VI in this study); and cf., for what it is worth, Spiegelberg's interesting discussion, I, 302-4.

selves to the level of consciousness we cannot engage the properly ontological problematic, the question of Being, adequately. We may only add here the remark that Heidegger's reference to the "essence" of Dasein as transcendence in the sense of going beyond what is explicitly manifest at any given moment is little more than the "phenomenologicalization," the transposition into the perspectives of phenomenological research, of the pre-phenomenological insight which Scheler reports as that which made the breakthrough to Phenomenology in Husserl's *Logische Untersuchungen* initially possible, namely, the insight that "what was given to our intuition was originally much richer in content than what could be accounted for by sensuous elements, by their derivatives, and by logical patterns of unification."[18]

Let us pass on however, without further aside, to limn the basic understanding of Phenomenology secured by Heidegger in the methodological chapter of the "Introduction" to *Sein und Zeit*, as the medium for determining the "sense," i.e., the ultimate unifying intelligibility (or perhaps simply, "comprehensibility"), of the Being-question. We have already seen the format of the preliminary conception:

The term "phenomenology" is quite different in its meaning from expressions such as "theology" and the like. Those terms designate the objects of their respective sciences according to the subject-matter which they comprise at the time (in ihrer jeweiligen Sachhaltigkeit). 'Phenomenology' neither designates the object of its researches, nor characterizes the subject matter thus comprised. The word merely informs us of the "*how*" with which *what* is to be treated in this science gets exhibited and handled.[19]

"Thus our treatise does not subscribe to a 'standpoint' or represent any special 'direction'; for Phenomenology is nothing of either sort, nor can it become so as long as it understands itself."[20] "Being, as the basic theme of philosophy, is no class or genus of beings; yet it pertains to every being. Its 'universality' is to be sought higher up," without regard to the object-

[18] Philipp Withok, ed., *Deutsches Leben der Gegenwart* (Berlin: Wegweiser Verlag, 1922, pp. 197-8, as cited in Spiegelberg, I, p. 229. Cf. Ernest W. Ranly, *Scheler's Phenomenology of Community* (The Hague: Martinus Nijhoff, 1966), pp. 3-4. See St. Thomas Aquinas, *Summa*, I, q. 84, art. 6 ad 1; *In II Phys.*, lect. 4, n. 175.

[19] "Der Titel Phänomenologie ist demnach hinsichtlich seines Sinn ein anderer als die Bezeichnungen Theologie u. dgl. Diese nennen die Gegenstände der betreffenden Wissenschaft in ihrer jeweiligen Sachhaltigkeit. 'Phänomenologie' nennt weder den Gegenstand ihrer Forschungen, noch charakterisiert der Titel deren Sachhaltigkeit. Das Wort gibt nur Aufschluss über das *Wie* der Aufweisung und Behandlungsart dessen, *was* in dieser Wissenschaft abgehandelt werden soll." (SZ, pp. 34-5).

[20] "Damit verschreibt sich diese Abhandlung weder einem 'Standpunkt', noch einer 'Richtung', weil Phänomenologie keines von beiden ist und nie werden kann solange sie sich selbst versteht." (SZ, p. 27).

categories into which positive science would distribute entities (*Seiende*) for one or another research purpose.[21] "Phenomenology is our way of access to. . . the theme. . . and it is our way of giving it demonstrative precision."[22]

In these terms, as we have seen in some detail, it is clear that Phenomenology is not a "method" in the accustomed sense of a mode of investigation specifically related to a certain region of objects at a certain conceptual level, i.e., under one of several possible formal aspects. No, it prescribes rather the gaze which must obtain through the entire range of cognitive vision insofar as it is philosophically mature. In this sense, Phenomenology is no "respector of objects". The term "phenomenon" therefore will not mean the same thing in phenomenological research that it does in any other kinds of research:

It is very clear that for Heidegger the function of phenomenology is the process of letting that be manifest (revealed) whose nature it is to become manifest (revealed) – in other words, to let beings be revealed in their Being, their non-concealment, their truth. But if it is the very nature of beings that they be revealed, why do they need any help from phenomenology? Because the revelation in them is so finite, so limited by a "not" (let us call it "negativity"), that the Being-dimension of them is concealed as much as it is revealed, with the result that "first of all and for the most part" they seem to be what they are not.[23]

In the research-mode of positivity, objects seem first of all and for the most part to stand before the researcher directly, with no mediary of their presence, in the full independence of their natural being, without any prior dependence on the *ens* of *esse intentionale* in order to be known. Things after all *do seem* to stand before us proximally (*zünachst*) in the proper existence they possess in order to maintain themselves *in rerum natura* (and it is precisely those conditions of independence which positive science seeks to uncover and dominate), whereas they are present to us proximally, in the first place, not in that entitative mode at all, but rather in that mode of existence, *esse intentionale*, which supervenes upon them (first preconsciously – indeed, with preconscious *priority*) in their apprehension by the soul in order that they be knowable. Heidegger puts it this way: "When one designates Things as the beings that are 'proximally given', one goes ontologically astray, even though ontically one has something else in mind. What one really has in mind remains undetermined," for in addressing the beings which we encounter "as 'Things' (*res*), we have tacitly anticipated their

---

[21] "Das Sein als Grundthema der Philosophie ist keine Gattung eines Seienden, und doch betrifft es jedes Seiende. Seine 'Universalität' ist höher zu suchen." (SZ, p. 38).

[22] "Phänomenologie ist Zugangsart zu dem und die ausweisende Bestimmungsart dessen, was Thema der Ontologie werden soll." (SZ, p. 35).

[23] Richardson, "The Place of the Unconscious in Heidegger," p. 284.

ontological character."[24] The phenomenological task becomes the task of constraining entities or "beings" we encounter to "show themselves with the kind of access which genuinely belongs to them."[25] "Objects," 'things of nature,' enter into the depths of Intentional Life before they can possibly emerge according to specified differentiations at the level of circumspection and positivity generally (i.e., as beings). And the conditions that attach to *esse naturale* are not the same as those that attach to *esse intentionale*, which is the genuine ontological condition of beings *as* appearing. Why does that which is truly "proximal" recede to the background in our comportment with beings? And how bring to light the disparity between the conditions attaching to these two distinct states, and so bring to the fore that which is truly primary so far as awareness-possibility is concerned, rather than that which *seems* to be? How restrain ourselves in principle, i.e., methodologically, from naively and unwittingly crossing the gulf which separates beings in their Being from beings as beings, and so render thematic Being as such, in and for itself, rather than for beings? Obviously, if we are to methodologically settle the philosophical task, it is the distinctive phenomenological notion of phenomenon that we must work toward. Here the lines of consideration are tightly (*streng*) drawn. Etymologically, the term "Phenomenology" has two components, "phenomenon" and "logos." By characterizing the sense of these two components and proceeding from there to establish the meaning of the name in which these two are joined, we can best bring the idea of phenomenological phenomenon into the open.

The proper concept of *phenomenon* designates a distinctive way in which something can be encountered, namely, as *that which shows itself in itself*, the manifest. *Semblance* (or "seeming") is the privative modification of a phenomenon. *Appearance*, on the other hand, in full contrast to phenomenon, is what does not show itself in itself, but by means of something else: this term designates a reference-relationship within some being. It means that something which does not show itself in itself "announces" its presence nonetheless by the medium of something which does show itself, e.g., a "symptom." Yet even here, the reference-relationship which is in a being itself "is such that what *does the referring* (or the announcing) can fulfill its

[24] "Mit der Nennung von Dingen als dem 'zunächst gegebenen' Seienden geht man ontologisch fehl, obzwar man ontisch etwas anderes meint. Was man eigentlich meint, bleibt unbestimmt." (SZ, p. 68). "Denn in diesem Ansprechen des Seienden als 'Ding' (res) liegt eine unausdrücklich vorgreifende ontologische Charakteristik." (SZ, pp. 67-8).

[25] "Weil Phänomen im phänomenologischen Verstande immer nur das ist, was Sein ausmacht, Sein aber je Sein von Seiendem ist, bedarf es für das Absehen auf eine Freilegung des Seins zuvor einer rechten Beibringung des Seienden selbst. Dieses muss sich gleichfalls in der ihm genuin zugehörigen Zugangsart zeigen." (SZ, p. 37).

possible function only if it shows itself in itself and is thus a 'phenomenon'."[26]

Thus both appearance and semblance are founded upon the phenomenon, but in different ways (*secundum rationes diversas*): the former is a *carentia*; the latter, a *privatio*. The distinction is capital, because "all indications, presentations, symptoms, and symbols have the basic formal structure of appearing, even though they differ among themselves."[26] In fine: all appearances are dependent on phenomena as the totality of what can be "brought to light" so as to become "visible" in itself; but phenomena themselves are *never* appearances.[28]

A *phainomenon* is that which of its own accord manifests itself. Whatever may be the senses accorded to this word – and the history of philosophy enumerates many of them – they all finally come down to one principal meaning: somewhere or other there is some kind of self-manifestation. It is only in terms of the latter that we can, or must, subsequently construct the eventual distinction between that which does the manifesting and that which is manifested. Here we find in all rigor the *Sache selbst* of Husserl. But this point, common to both, is doubtless the only one. For Heidegger separates himself from Husserl in the commentary that he makes on *logos*, as also in the determination of the *phainomena* which he assigns as the object of phenomenology.[29]

Let us turn our attention then to the achievement of a root understanding of *logos*. "We say that the basic signification of *logos* is 'discourse' ":[30] all other translations, such as "reason," "judgment," "concept," "definition," "ground," "relationship," must be derivatively referred to this basic designation.[31]

Discourse for our purpose must itself be taken in its fundamental mode: to make manifest what one is "talking about" in one's discourse. The expressions of discourse (*logos*) thus let something be seen (*phainesthai*), either for some one who is discoursing (the *medium*), as is the case in monologue; or for a number of persons who are talking among themselves – the case of dialogue. "In discourse [*logos* in the basic mode of *apophansis*, or simply

[26] "*Phänomen* – das Sich-an-ihm-selbst-zeigen – bedeutet eine augezeichnete Begegnisart von etwas. *Erscheinung* dagegen meint einen seienden Verweisungsbezug im Seienden selbst, so zwar, dass das *Verweisende* (Meldende) seiner möglichen Funktion nur genügen kann, wenn es sich an ihm selbst zeigt, 'Phänomen' ist." (SZ, p. 31).

[27] "Alle Indikationen, Darstellungen, Symptome und Symbole haben die angeführte formale Grundstruktur des Erscheinens, wenngleich sie unter sich noch verschieden sind." (SZ, p. 29).

[28] See SZ, p. 30.

[29] De Waelhens, p. 478.

[30] "Wenn wir sagen, die Grundbedeutung von *logos* ist Rede, dann wird diese wörtliche Übersetzung erst vollgültig aus der Bestimmung dessen, was Rede selbst besagt." (SZ,p. 32). Cf. De Waelhens, p. 478.

[31] E.g., cf. SZ, p. 34.

'apophantical discourse'], so far as it is genuine, *what* is said is drawn *from* what the talk is about, so that discursive communication in what it says, makes manifest what it is talking about, and thus makes it accessible to the other party."[32] This mode of making manifest in the sense of letting something be seen (in itself) by pointing it out is the fundamental mode of discourse which as we have said is the one of present interest to us.

"Here everything depends on our steering clear of any conception of truth which is construed in the sense of 'agreement',"[33] formal, clear, definite notes of beings. We are here at a point prior to judgment: *logos* as *apophansis* is precisely the kind of thing that cannot be regarded phenomenologically as the primary *locus* of truth, and this precisely because and insofar as it implies a measure of *judicium*.[34] The phenomenological enterprise

---

[32] "In der Rede (*apophansis*) soll, wofern sie echt ist, das, *was* geredet ist, *aus* dem worüber geredet wird, geschöpft sein, so dass die redende Mitteilung in ihrem Gesagten das, worüber sie redet, offenbar und so dem anderen zugänglich macht. Das ist die Struktur des *logos* als *apophansis*." (SZ, p. 32).

[33] "Auch liegt alles daran, sich von einem konstruierten Wahrheitsbegriff im Sinne einer 'Übereinstimmung' freizuhalten." (SZ, p. 33).

[34] Here let us make an interesting textual juxtaposition.

HEIDEGGER: "Im konkreten Vollzug hat das Reden (Sehenlassen) den Charakter des Sprechens, der stimmlichen Verlautbarung ... in der je etwas gesichtet ist.

"Und *weil* die Funktion des *logos* als *apophansis* im aufweisenden Sehenlassen von etwas liegt, kann der *logos* die Strukturform der *sunthesis* haben. Synthesis sagt hier nicht Verbinden und Verknüpfen von Vorstellungen, Hantieren mit psychischen Vorkommnissen, bezüglich welcher Verbindungen dann das 'Problem' entstehen soll, wie sie als Inneres mit dem Physischen draussen übereinstimmen. Das *sun* hat hier rein apophantische Bedeutung und besagt: etwas in seinem *Beisammen* mit etwas, etwas *als* etwas sehen lassen.

"Und wiederum, weil der *logos* ein Sehenlassen ist, *deshalb* kann er wahr oder falsch sein. Auch liegt alles daran, sich von einem konstruierten Wahrheitsbegriff im Sinne einer 'Übereinstimmung' freizuhalten. Diese Idee ist keinesfalls die primäre im Begriff der *aletheia*...

"Weil aber... der *logos* ein bestimmter Modus des Sehenlassens ist, darf der *logos* gerade *nicht* als der primäre 'Ort' der Wahrheit angesprochen werden...

"Was nicht mehr die Vollzugsform des reinen Sehenlassens hat, sondern je im Aufweisen auf ein anderes rekurriert und so je etwas *als* etwas sehen lässt, das übernimmt mit dieser Synthesisstruktur die Möglichkeit des Verdeckens. Die 'Urteilswahrheit' aber ist nur der Gegenfall zu diesem Verdecken – d. h. ein *mehrfach fundiertes* Phänomen von Wahrheit. Realismus und Idealismus verfehlen den Sinn des griechischen Wahrheitsbegriffes, aus dem heraus man überhaupt nur die Möglichkeit von so etwas wie einer 'Ideenlehre' als philosophischer *Erkenntnis* verstehen kann, mit gleicher Gründlichkeit." (SZ, pp. 32-4).

MARITAIN: "L'expression *verbe mental* ne s'applique pas seulement au concept tel que nous l'avons considéré jusqu'à présent [as pure and direct beholding, i.e. *medium quo formaliter*], mais aussi à des ouvrages complexes formés par l'intellect, comme la définition et la division (qui concernent la première opération de l'esprit) et l'énonciation (qui concerne la seconde).

"Il y a dans la définition et dans la division une complexité qui est notre oeuvre propre; ... Le verbe mental en question manifeste ce que *je pense* (composition ou séparation) des

properly understood and undertaken constrains all verity at the level of original manifestation or "revealment" simply considered:

If, as has become quite customary nowadays, one defines 'truth' as something that 'really' pertains to judgment. . . the Greek conception of truth has been misunderstood. *Aisthesis*, the sheer sensory perception of something, is 'true' in the Greek sense, and indeed more primordially than the *logos* which we have been discussing. Just as seeing aims at colors, any *aisthesis* aims at its *idia* (those entities which are genuinely accessible only *through* it and *for* it); and to that extent this perception is always true. This means that seeing always discovers colors, and hearing always discovers sounds. Pure *noein* is the perception of the simplest determinate ways of Being which beings as such may possess, and it perceives them just by looking at them. This *noein* is what is 'true' in the purest and most primordial sense; that is to say, it merely discovers, and it does so in such a way that it can never cover up. This *noein* can never cover up; it can never be false; it can at worst remain a *non-perceiving, agnoein*, not sufficing for straightforward and appropriate access.[35]

When this last occurs, phenomenological research enters a certain impasse because semblance can maintain itself as long as our Interpretation is unable to grasp the basic comprehensibility of a phenomenon in its primary form.

With this much said, we are prepared to assign a *preliminary, formal meaning* to the kind of research which calls itself "phenomenology." In accord with the maxim, "To the things themselves," Phenomenology means the noetic discipline which lets that which shows itself be seen from itself in the very way in which it shows itself from itself. "To have a science 'of' phenomena means to grasp its objects *in such a way* that everything about

choses (rendues objets d'intellection en acte dans mes concepts du sujet et du prédicat).
"Si saint Thomas, lorsqu'il parle du verbe mental et de sa distinction d'avec la chose, met ordinairement en cause la définition et l'énonciation plutôt que le simple concept, c'est justement qu'ici il y a quelque chose qui nous appartient tout à fait en propre, – la composition mentale, – qui rend cette distinction plus manifeste que ne le fait la simple différence d'état ou d'*esse* entre concept et objet." (DS, pp. 786-7/395-6).
[35] "Wenn man, wie es heute durchgängig üblich geworden ist, Wahrheit als das bestimmt, was 'eigentlich' dem Urteil zukommt, und sich mit dieser These überdies auf *Aristoteles* beruft, dann ist sowohl diese Berufung ohne Recht, als vor allem der griechische Wahrheitsbegriff missverstanden. 'Wahr' ist im griechischen Sinne und zwar ursprünglicher als der genannte *logos* die *aisthesis*, das schlichte, sinnliche Vernehmen von etwas. Sofern eine *aisthesis* je auf ihre *idia* zielt, das je genuin nur gerade *durch* sie und *für* sie zugängliche Seiende, z. B. das Sehen auf die Farben, dann ist das Vernehmen immer wahr. Das besagt: Sehen entdeckt immer Farben, Hören entdeckt immer Töne. Im reinsten und ursprünglichsten Sinne 'wahr' – d. h. nur entdeckend, so dass es nie verdecken kann, ist das reine *noein*, das schlicht hinsehende Vernehmen der einfachsten Seinsbestimmungen des Seienden als solchen. Dieses *noein* kann nie verdecken, nie falsch sein, es kann allenfalls ein *Unvernehmen* bleiben, *agnoein*, für den schlichten, angemessenen Zugang nicht zureichen." (SZ, p. 33).

them which is up for discussion must be treated by exhibiting it directly and demonstrating it directly."[36]

"The signification of 'phenomenon'," Heidegger observes, "as conceived both formally and in the ordinary manner, is such that any exhibiting of a being as it shows itself in itself, may be called 'phenomenology' with formal justification."[37] If however "the formal conception or phenomenon is to be deformalized into the [properly] phenomenological one," it must be understood as signifying something which lies hidden or in concealment, but which belongs to what is proximally and for the most part manifest, and belongs to it in such a way as to constitute its meaning or sense (ultimate basis of comprehensible unity) and therefore its ground (though not in the derivative sense of *ratio formalis constitutiva*).

A case in point: *Dasein* itself in its normal everyday condition appears to be what it is not, namely a being in all respects like the rest, simply because it is. The task of a phenomenological analysis of *Dasein*, then, is to penetrate through what *Dasein* "first of all and for the most part" seems-to-be on the existentiell level of everyday intercourse and let it appear as what it is, existential as well as existentiell. The whole phenomenological analysis of *Dasein* is therefore an "existential" analysis, which slowly discerns what it means to say that (*Sein und Zeit*, p. 32)" . . . the ontic excellence of *Dasein* consists in the fact that it is ontologically."[38]

This may seem rather puzzling at first. Yet we should note that what Heidegger terms the purely "formal" meaning of phenomenology actually expresses nothing more than the underlying principle of any kind of serious research whatsoever, including the research of positivity. If therefore one regards the matter in this light, little if any justification appears for regarding the formal notion of phenomenology as entitling a special and distinct branch of research – which is precisely Heidegger's point! If after setting forth the proper conception of phenomenon we leave indefinite what with respect to beings we consider as "phenomena" and leave it open whether

---

[36] "Wissenschaft 'von' den Phänomenen besagt: eine *solche* Erfassung ihrer Gegenstände, dass alles, was über sie zur Erörterung steht, in direkter Aufweisung und direkter Ausweisung abgehandelt werden muss." (SZ, p. 35).

[37] "Formal berechtigt die Bedeutung des formalen und vulgären Phänomenbegriffes dazu, jede Aufweisung von Seiendem, so wie es sich an ihm selbst zeigt, Phänomenologie zu nennen." (SZ, p. 35).

[38] Richardson, "The Place of the Unconscious in Heidegger," p. 284. "Sachhaltig genommen ist die Phänomenologie die Wissenschaft vom Sein des Seienden – Ontologie. In der gegebenen Erläuterung der Aufgaben der Ontologie entsprang die Notwendigkeit einer Fundamentalontologie, die das ontologisch-ontisch ausgezeichnete Seiende zum Thema hat, das Dasein, so zwar, dass sie sich vor das Kardinal-problem, die Frage nach dem Sinn von Sein überhaupt, bringt." (SZ, p. 37). "Der Nachweis der ontisch-ontologischen Auszeichnung der Seinsfrage gründet in der vorläufigen Anzeige des ontisch-ontologischen Vorrangs des Daseins." (SZ, p. 14).

what shows itself is a being or rather some characteristic which a being may have in its Being, then we have not grasped the whole meaning of the phenomenological method, let alone the proper nature of phenomenological thought.

Having renounced, as we have already said, the primacy of the *cogito* as theoretical consciousness in order to transform intentionality à la Husserl into concern [see pp. 97-100], Heidegger could not stop at describing the tasks of phenomenology in such a way as to reduce them to an elucidation of the relationships of *consciousness* to the world. Phenomenology will elucidate what in originating fashion *makes* be seen that which manifests itself, that, indeed, which for this reason is hidden in, covered over by, what manifests itself, i.e., its Being.[39]

The phenomena which Phenomenology seeks to disclose in short are those (disclosive) facets of Reality[40] behind which there is essentially nothing else. "When one designates Things as the beings that are 'proximally given', one goes ontologically astray. . . What one really has in mind remains undetermined."[41] And only because the phenomena in this sense are proximally and for the most part *not* given, because what is to become a phenomenon can (and usually does) remain hidden – only for this reason is there both justification and need for Phenomenology as a distinct mode of research.

In the phenomenological conception of "phenomenon" what one has in mind as that which shows itself is the Being of beings, its meaning, its modifications and derivatives. And this showing-itself is not just any showing-itself, nor is it some such thing as appearing. Least of all can the Being of beings ever be anything such that 'behind it' stands something else 'which does not appear.'[42]

With this a number of things become clear. First of all we can understand why Heidegger was able to make little progress in determining the sense of the Being-question before he had familiarized himself with the techniques of

[39] De Waelhens, p. 479.
[40] Man as leading Intentional Life = Dasein. "Independent" beings as entered upon (see WG, p. 39, as cited on p. 174 of this study) or participating that Intentional Life in the mode of "thing", i.e., at the level of specified differentiations = Reality. Obviously the two are reconciled and coincide in the notion of Dasein as *being* its world 'existingly' (SZ, p. 364). See SZ, p. 212.
[41] "Mit der Nennung von Dingen als dem 'zünachst gegebenen' Seienden geht man ontologisch fehl. . . Was man eigentlich meint, bleibt unbestimmt." (SZ, p. 68).
[42] "Der phänomenologische Begriff von Phänomen meint als das Sichzeigende das Sein des Seienden, seinen Sinn, seine Modifikationen und Derivate. Und das Sichzeigen ist kein beliebiges noch gar so etwas wie Erscheinen. Das Sein des Seienden kann am wenigsten je so etwas sein, 'dahinter' noch etwas steht, 'was nicht erscheint'.
" 'Hinter' den Phänomenen der Phänomenologie steht wesenhaft nichts anderes, wohl aber kann das, was Phänomen werden soll, verborgen sein. Und gerade deshalb, weil die Phänomene zunächst und zumeist *nicht* gegeben sind, bedarf es der Phänomenologie." (SZ, pp. 35-6).

phenomenological research to the point where the principle of that research became adequately transparent:

Now that we have delimited our preliminary conception of Phenomenology, the terms *"phenomenal"* and *"phenomenological"* can also be fixed in their signification. That which is given and explicable in the way the phenomenon is encountered is called "phenomenal"; this is what we have in mind when we talk about "phenomenal structures." Everything which belongs to the species of exhibiting and explicating and which goes to make up the way of conceiving demanded by this research, is called "phenomenological."[43]

Thus Fr. Richardson wrote me: "I agree of course with your insistence on the phenomenal character of Dasein and would insist, besides, on the phenomenal character of Being."[44]

We can also understand why, despite the fact that he deliberately discards the term "phenomenology" in later writings,[45] Heidegger never abandons the phenomenological attitude; for "the whole interrogation of Being and beings is conditioned by the initial experience of the phenomenologist: that a being is that which appears, *is* a being for him only insofar [and] as it appears."[46] As the whole weight of Fr. Richardson's scholarship demonstrates, "Heidegger's perspective from beginning to end remains phenomenological."[47]

In like manner, we can now appreciate Heidegger's claim that all Phenomenology which has become fully transparent to itself stands in the service of the question about the Being of entities as things-in-Being, in full contrast to the research modes of positives science which are guided only by the "things" as such according to the positivity of all their kinds and grades. Covered-up-ness is the counter-concept to "phenomenon":

Yet that which remains *hidden* in an egregious sense, or which relapses and gets *covered up* again, or which shows itself only "in disguise," is not just this being or that, but rather the *Being* of beings, as our previous observations have shown. This Being can be covered up so extensively that it becomes forgotten and no question

[43] "Auf dem Boden des umgrenzten Vorbegriffes der Phänomenologie können nun auch die Termini *'phänomenal'* und *'phänomenologisch'* in ihrer Bedeutung fixiert werden. *'Phänomenal'* wird genannt, was in der Begegnisart des Phänomens gegeben und explizierbar ist; daher die Rede von phänomenalen Strukturen. 'Phänomenologisch' heisst all das, was zur Art der Aufweisung und Explikation gehört und was die in dieser Forschung geforderte Begrifflichkeit ausmacht." (SZ, p. 37).
[44] Letter of August 1, 1966.
[45] Concerning this striking elimination of both the title and terminology in the later writings, Heidegger himself in *Unterwegs zur Sprache* (Pfüllingen: Neske, 1959), p. 121, testifies: "Es geschah nicht, wie viele meinen, um die Bedeutung der Phänomenologie zu verleugnen, sondern um meinen Denkweg im Namenlosen zu lassen."
[46] Richardson, "Heidegger and God," p. 23.
[47] H:TPT, p. 627.

arises about it or about its meaning. Thus that which demands that it become a phenomenon, and which demands this in a distinctive sense and in terms of its ownmost content as a thing, is what Phenomenology has taken into its grasp thematically as its object [viz., Being as such].[48]

We can understand too why man as Dasein stands central to the initially constituted phenomenological *Seinsfrage* as the (phenomenological) phenomenon *par excellence* – because "the Dasein in man characterizes him as that being who, placed in the midst of beings, comports himself to them as such," which comportment "determines man in his Being" as a "who" rather than simply a "what" – though a referentially dependent and so historically constituted "who" (which is why Dasein cannot be defined fundamentally in terms of any selfhood) – "and makes him essentially different from all other beings which are manifest to him."[49] Taking its origin in the re-collection that all commerce with beings – even when it seems to concern only the latter – presupposes the transcending of Dasein to Being (World),

the construction proper to fundamental ontology is distinguished by the fact that it lays bare the internal possibility of that which holds sway over Dasein. This dominating element is not only that which is most familiar to Dasein but is also that which is most indeterminate and self-evident. This construction can be understood as an effort on the part of Dasein to grasp in itself the primordial metaphysical fact which consists in this, that the most finite in its finitude is known without being understood.

The finitude of Dasein – the comprehension of Being – *lies in* forgottenness.

This forgottenness is nothing accidental and temporary but is constantly and necessarily renewed. All construction relevant to fundamental ontology, construction which strives toward the disclosure of the internal possibility of the comprehension of Being, must in its act of projection wrest from forgottenness that which it thus apprehends. The basic fundamental-ontological act of the metaphysics [*lege*: existential analytic] of Dasein is, therefore, a re-collecting.

But true recollection must always interiorize what is recollected, i.e., let it come closer and closer in its most intrinsic possibility. This signifies, relative to the development of a fundamental ontology, that this recollection must let itself be guided constantly, uniquely, and effectively by the question of Being in order thus

[48] "Was aber in einem ausnehmenden Sinne *verborgen* bleibt oder wieder in die *Verdeckung* zurückfällt oder nur '*verstellt*' sich zeigt, ist nicht dieses oder jenes Seiende, sondern, wie die voranstehenden Betrachtungen gezeigt haben, das *Sein* des Seienden. Es kann so weitgehend verdeckt sein, dass es vergessen wird und die Frage nach ihm und seinem Sinn ausbleibt. Was demnach in einem ausgezeichneten Sinne, aus seinem eigensten Sachgehalt her fordert, Phänomen zu werden, hat die Phänomenologie als Gegenstand thematisch in den 'Griff' genommen." (SZ, p. 35). See Heidegger's "Vorwort" to H:TPT, p. XV.

[49] "Das Dasein im Menschen bestimmt diesen als jenes Seiende, das, inmitten von Seiendem seiend, zu diesem als einem solchen sich verhält und als dieses Verhalten zu Seiendem wesenhaft anders in seinem eigenen Sein bestimmt wird denn alles übrige im Dasein offenbare Seiende." (KM, p. 211/242).

to keep the existential analytic of Dasein, the development of which is the responsibility of fundamental ontology, on the right path.[50]

Finally, we can understand Heidegger's enigmatic attestation (the decisiveness of rightly understanding which is immediately consequent upon the very manner in which the priority and formal structure of the Being-question is established in *Sein und Zeit*) that "in the disclosure and explication of Being, beings are in every case our preliminary and accompanying theme; but our real theme is Being."[51] This is nothing more than a restatement of the inner nature of properly conceived phenomenological research: since phenomena, as understood phenomenologically, are never anything but what goes to make up Being, while Being yields itself (phenomenally, because within Dasein) as in every case the Being of some being, we must first bring forward the beings themselves – and this in the mode of phenomena, i.e., in terms of awareness ("revealment" as such, therefore independently of any question as to which of the positive science domains they belong as "objects") – if it is our aim that Being should be eventually laid bare in its own ultimate unity.

That is why the phenomenologically ontological analytic "takes its departure from the *traditional conception of truth*," *adaequatio intellectus et rei*, "and attempts to lay bare the ontological foundations of that conception."[52] From first to last the problematic receives its specification from the distinct and mutually irreducible conditions that attach to the state of *esse intentionale* in fundamental contradistinction to *esse entitativum*, and more

[50] "Die fundamentalontologische Konstruktion hat ihr Auszeichnendes darin, dass sie die innere Möglichkeit von etwas freilegen soll, was gerade als das Bekannteste alles Dasein durchherrscht, aber gleichwohl unbestimmt und sogar allzu selbstverständlich ist. Diese Konstruktion kann als der im Dasein selbst erwachsende Angriff des Daseins auf das metaphysische Urfaktum in ihm verstanden werden, welches Faktum darin besteht, dass das Endlichste in seiner Endlichkeit zwar bekannt, aber gleichwohl nicht begriffen ist.
"Die Endlichkeit des Daseins – das Seinsverständnis – *liegt in der Vergessenheit.*
"Diese ist keine zufällige und zeitweilige, sondern sie bildet sich notwendig und ständig. Alle fundamentalontologische Konstruktion, die auf die Enthüllung der inneren Möglichkeit des Seinsverständnisses zielt, muss im Entwerfen das in den Entwurf Genommene der Vergessenheit entreissen.
"Der fundamentalontologische Grundakt der Metaphysik des Daseins als der Grundlegung der Metaphysik ist daher 'Wiedererinnerung'.
"Echte Erinnerung muss aber jederzeit das Erinnerte verinnerlichen, d. h. es sich mehr und mehr in seiner innersten Möglichkeit wieder entgegenkommen lassen. Mit Bezug auf die Durchführung einer Fundamentalontologie bedeutet das: sie legt ihre Hauptanstrengung darauf, die einzige und ständige Führung von seiten der Seinsfrage ungeschmälert wirksam werden zu lassen, um so die ihr aufgegebene existenziale Analytik des Daseins in der rechten Bahn zu halten." (KM, pp. 210-11).
[51] "In der Erschliessung und Explikation des Seins ist das Seiende jeweils das Vor- und Mitthematische, im eigentlichen Thema steht das Sein." (SZ, p. 67).
[52] "Die Analyse geht vom *traditionellen Wahrheitsbegriff* aus und versucht dessen ontologische Fundamente freizulegen." (SZ, p. 214).

proximately from the development of a methodological conception that would suffice to restrain the researcher from crossing the gulf which separates these two ontologically fundamental states. Thus to say something about beings as entities, i.e., as subjects actually or possibly ordered to *esse*, would require a throwing off of the restrictions constitutive of the full phenomenological stance, a failure "to keep to the problem of Nothing as the problem of Being itself." Once the pure conception of the phenomenological research-principle has been achieved, there is no need to do away with transobjective subjects by an artificial *epoche* or "suspension of belief," for the "givenness" of "things" ("beings of nature") "quite independently of the experience by which they are disclosed, the acquaintance in which they are discovered, and the grasping in which their nature is ascertained"[53] simply does not constitute a formal element of the existential analytic, does not enter directly into the question of Being as such, for the excellent reason that Being itself phenomenologically approached " 'is' only in the comprehension of those beings to whose Being something like a comprehension of Being belongs."[54]

If the traditional ontological problematic is characterized (rightly) as being foundationally and finally oriented (grounded and guided) by the question of "ens quod est *extra* animam," then Heidegger's "fundamental ontological" problematic is reversely concerned (*Schritt zurück*) directly and immediately by "ens quod est *intra* animam." That is why he discerns the ontic level of Dasein only as departural for and in certain ways (spec., insofar as value and meaning are at issue) structurable by the ontological dimension. That is why the philosophical inadequacy of his thought does indeed "burst forth" when we meet the problem of the other. That is why Heidegger would write to Fr. Richardson concerning the titling of the latter's study:

Now if in the title of your book, *From Phenomenology to Thought*, you understand "Phenomenology" in the sense just described as a philosophical position of Husserl, then the title is to the point, insofar as the Being-question as posed by me is something completely different from that position. The title is fully justified, if the term "Thought" is shorn of that ambiguity which allows it to cover on the one hand metaphysical thought (the thinking of the Being of beings) and on the other the Being-question, sc. the thinking of Being as such (the revealed-ness of Being).

If, however, we understand "Phenomenology" as the [process of] allowing the

---

[53] See SZ, p. 183. See text cited in the immediately following footnote, and fn. 11 of Ch. IV above.

[54] "Seiendes *ist* unabhängig von Erfahrung, Kenntnis und Erfassen, wodurch es erschlossen, entdeckt und bestimmt wird. Sein aber 'ist' nur im Verstehen des Seienden, zu dessen Sein so etwas wie Seinsverständnis gehört." (SZ, p. 183).

most proper concern of thought to show itself, then the title should read "Through Phenomenology to the Thinking of Being." This possessive [*of* Being], then, says that Being as such (Beon) shows itself simultaneously as that which is to-be-thought and as that which has want of a thought corresponding to it.[55]

Throughout the entire way of Heidegger's philosophizing the original stance remains determining and constant; Heideggerian Thought of Being took its departure within phenomenological perspectives and strictly keeps to the hermeneutic possibilities virtual therein, i.e., from a certain "reflective turn of sight" carefully characterized and understood.

The youthful Heidegger expected in this way to "overcome," sc. ground, Metaphysics, whereas the aging Heidegger begins to perceive, fitfully, to be sure, and without consistency,[56] that the ground- *as well as and no less than* the guide-question of Metaphysics properly conceived lay in another direc-

[55] "Verstehen Sie nun im Titel Ihres Werkes 'Der Weg von der Phänomenologie zum Seinsdenken' die 'Phänomenologie' in dem zuletzt gekennzeichneten Sinne einer philosophih ischen Position Husserls, dann trifft der Titel die Sache, insofern die von mir gestellte Seinsfrage etwas ganz anderes ist als jene Position. Der Titel ist vollends berechtigt, wenn der Name 'Seinsdenken' aus der Zweideutigkeit herausgenommen wird, nach der er so- wohl das Denken der Metaphysik – das Denken des Seins des Seienden – als auch die Seinsfrage im Sinne des Denkens des Seins als solchen (die Offenbarkeit des Seins) nennt.

"Verstehen wir aber die 'Phänomenologie' als das Sichzeigenlassen der eigensten Sache des Denkens, dann müsste der Titel lauten: 'Ein Weg *durch* die Phänomenologie in das Denken des Seins'. Dieser Genitiv sagt dann, dass das Sein als Solches (das Seyn) sich zugleich als jenes zu Denkende zeigt, was ein ihm entsprechendes Denken braucht." (Heidegger's "Vorwort" to H:TPT, pp. XV-XVII).

[56] Cf. Powell, "Has Heidegger Destroyed Metaphysics?", p. 52. "Heidegger's later thought is ambiguous on the question of metaphysics. On the one hand, he implies that he has destroyed metaphysics or testifies that others have already destroyed it; but on the other hand he can say that metaphysical thinking can still say something correct. On the side of the destruction of metaphysics, Heidegger says that metaphysics is a logic (ID): patently then metaphysics cannot be a knowledge of the Real. Moreover, he asserts that he has destroyed the domination of logic in philosophy (WM). Again, he says that no meta- physical system can refute another metaphysical system, so that for example the mutually incompatible metaphysical systems of Hegel, Marx and Nietzsche are beyond all refutation (HB, p. 82/184): hence metaphysics as a transhistorically valid science disappears. Finally, the later Heidegger characterizes his thought as the thought of Being, whereas metaphysics is characterized by him as forgottenness of Being: and his thought seeks to overcome the forgottenness of Being characteristic of metaphysics (SF; WM:In). But on the other hand, the later Heidegger characterizes metaphysics by its conception of man as a rational animal set off against other animals and living beings. And he admits that metaphysics can con- stantly say correct things ("stets Richtiges") about man in this manner (HB, pp. 66/277, 64/276, 75/281, 89/288; Richardson, H:TPT, p. 38; *et alibi*). How these two aspects of Heidegger's attitude towards metaphysics can be reconciled is the puzzle we shall seek to solve. For it is not immediately clear how metaphysics could be a mere logic and a purely historical phenomenon, and yet constantly make correct assertions about man as among its characteristic objects." (We have taken this passage from Powell's original manuscript, "Has Heidegger Destroyed Metaphysics or Has He Cleared Its Foundations – or Neither?", which varies somewhat from the text printed in *Listening*.)

tion entirely than that open to a purely phenomenological research; so that, while a phenomenologically defined step back out of Metaphysics was entirely possible, a reverse back-step is precluded by the inner restrictions of any Phenomenology purely conceived. In final assessment, the Being-question as Heidegger frames it, the phenomenological question of Being, raises in the larger context of *esse intentionale* the old and acrimonious dispute of neo-scholasticism: does Metaphysics precede Critica or the reverse? – only after Heidegger the "critique of knowledge" will have to be taken in the more genuine and fundamental sense of a determination of the sense of the *Sein* of *Bewusstsein* and *Selbstbewusstsein*. No small part of Heidegger's value to the continuing dialogue of philosophers is to have shown once again the impossibility of a purely reflexive basis for Metaphysics. We shall say a word on this question of the relation of Heidegger's work to Metaphysics, however, in an Appendix. First it is necessary for us to justify our Interpretation of the original Heideggerean problematic, which is now essentially complete, by showing that our reading is able to compass the full way traversed by Heidegger's thought.

On the basis of our own study, what may we say of the shift from Heidegger I to Heidegger II? Marjorie Grene draws the contrast in these terms: "The analysis of human being as Being-in-a-world had shape and direction; beside it the search for Being itself is 'verschwommen': formless and blurred."[57] And no student of Heidegger can take exception to this as an overall impression. Yet what Miss Grene denies and entirely fails to grasp is that, as Fr. Richardson points out, "the transformation of Heidegger I into Heidegger II is born out of a necessity imposed by the original experience of Being as *finite* (negative),"[58] i.e., of Being as the "No-thing" which as such underlies all finding oneself in the midst of "things" already on hand – "given": "For the shift of focus from There-being to Being (which, as far as we can see, characterizes the decisive difference between the two periods) was demanded by the exigencies of the hermeneutic analysis itself, as soon as it became clear that the primacy in the Being-process belongs to Being itself," as soon as Heidegger began to appreciate "the full import of what it means for concealment somehow to precede non-concealment in the coming to pass of *a-letheia*."[59]

Still, in the end, Fr. Richardson's understanding is not a great deal more satisfactory than Miss Grene's misunderstanding. The true character of

[57] Marjorie Grene, *Martin Heidegger* (New York: Hillary House, 1957), pp. 124-5.
[58] H:TPT, p. 624.
[59] *Ibid.*

Heidegger's reversal *begins* to emerge in De Waelhens' assessment of Fr. Richardson's position, however:

> We cannot help but agree with Richardson, then, when he writes that with the *Introduction to Metaphysics* the accent is shifted in There-being from the There to Being: "The accent is different, for now Being maintains the primacy over There" (p. 296). But perhaps this formula disposes of the essential difficulty with a stroke of legerdemain: can man understand himself if he is defined as the lot and prey of Being? And is not the shifting of position (*glissement*) that has taken place since *Sein und Zeit* more in the nature of a sliding toward an unspeakable abyss than a consolidation of his original stand?[60]

With his first question De Waelhens suggests what has already become clear for us: the twofold ambiguity which cripples the phenomenological thought of Being, namely, the ambiguity of the relationship of Dasein to man on the one side and of the relationship of Dasein to Being on the other, can be penetrated only on condition that the ontic dimension of Dasein be kept within the problematic and moreover be directly treated in what is immediately proper to it as well as indirectly in the existential-ontological analytic which uncovers the unsuspected ambit of existentiell comportment so far as it is structured "meaningfully." But we have seen that such an interrogation formally and not just materially constituted could only proceed predicamentally in the metaphysical sense, for it would require an analytic of Dasein *insofern Seiende*, i.e., *secundum esse entitativum* – something which existential-ontological (i.e., phenomenological) analysis precludes in principle. In this way, we were able to demonstrate the still more fundamental fact that the phenomenological characterization of Dasein's structural unity as ontic-ontological had already presupposed, however covertly, the validity of the very metaphysical Interpretation which the phenomenologically re-interpreted *Seinsfrage* simply taken lay prior to the possibility – let alone the simple acceptance – of.

This placed Heidegger in a dilemma. Either he could abandon the purity of his methodological conception long enough to explicitate the act-potency structural distinctions delimiting the (ontological) region within which his problematic would then proceed to establish and elaborate itself; or he could keep to the phenomenologically defined reflexive stance and "purify" the sphere accessible therefrom by eliminating all the derivative act-potency distinctions which gave that sphere structure by initially referencing and entitatively grounding it. (No doubt the problem did not present itself to Heidegger in this direct form; but that is a matter quite distinct from any facile contention that these terms misstate the root issue.) On this latter

[60] *Art. cit.*, pp. 496-7.

alternative – and this brings us to De Waelhens' second question – "sliding toward an unspeakable abyss" would not necessarily be something opposed to "a consolidation of his original stand." Does not Heidegger himself expressly point out, in the "Letter on Humanism," that the greatest difficulty in his thought relative to traditional philosophy "does not consist in being immersed in exceptionally profound thought or in constructing complex concepts, but rather lies concealed in the step backward that permits thought to enter into an experiential questioning and to let drop the accustomed opinions of philosophy"?[61] In any event, "it behooves us, in considering the variations of the later Heidegger, to notice what he let drop; for no doubt his later thought let drop elements that gave more determinate shape to his earlier thought."[62]

This is the question we would like to reflect on now, without pursuing as such a systematic study of the writings of "Heidegger II," since in any case – and whatever may be the exceptional import of those writings – we have already at hand the elements necessary for such a reflection. Thus our Interpretation and re-trieve of the original Heideggerean problematic is open to philosophic check in this way: beginning within Heidegger's proper matrix, namely, Being as known prior to the categories, and freeing ourselves by analytical adhesion thereto from the traditional philosophic structures founded on discernment of potency and act compositions (i.e., categorial analysis), we should – independently of any text – be able to think ourselves into the world of the late Heidegger, where there is "neither a connection of cause to effect, nor the transcendental-horizontal relation," and which "can be thought of neither as ontic nor as ontological. . .," but only in terms of "determining and regioning with respect to man."[63] If that can be achieved in the direct fashion we propose, we think that the main lines of our understanding of Heidegger must indeed be accepted as marking out the bounds of the questioning in *Sein und Zeit*, characterizing in so doing the relation in

[61] "Weil in diesem Denken etwas Einfaches zu denken ist, deshalb fällt es dem als Philosophie überlieferten Vorstellen so schwer. Allein das Schwierige besteht nicht darin, einem besonderen Tiefsinn nachzuhängen und verwickelte Begriffe zu bilden, sondern es verbirgt sich in dem Schritt-zurück, der das Denken in ein erfahrendes Fragen eingehen und das gewohnte Meinen der Philosophie fallen lässt." (HB, p. 91/289).
[62] Powell, "The Late Heidegger's Omission of the Ontic-Ontological Structure of Dasein," p. 13. (Cf. p. 126 of printed version).
[63] ". . . weder ein kausaler Wirkungszusammenhang noch das transzendental-horizontale Verhältnis, mithin auch weder ontisch noch ontologisch." – Martin Heidegger, *Gelassenheit* (Pfullingen: Neske, 1959), p. 55. Cf. English translation by John M. Anderson and E. Hans Freund titled *Discourse on Thinking* (New York: Harper & Row, 1966), pp. 76-7. Hereafter referred to as G: German reference will be followed by / and corresponding reference in the Anderson-Freund translation.

which Heidegger's thinking stands to the tradition of Western philosophy. We shall have to agree in our own accounting with Fr. Richardson's conclusion that "the Heidegger of the early years was victimized by the very metaphysics he was trying to overcome,"[64] though for very different reasons; for we shall have to wonder if the "victimization" did not work the other way as well.

[64] H:TPT, p. 625.

CHAPTER X

FROM THE EARLY TO THE LATER HEIDEGGER

> "Das Denken der Kehre *ist* eine Wendung in meinem
> Denken. Aber diese Wendung erfolgt nicht auf grund
> einer Änderung des Standpunktes oder gar der Preisgabe
> der Fragstellung in "Sein und Zeit". Das Denken der
> Kehre ergibt sich daraus, dass ich bei der zu denkenden
> Sache "Sein und Zeit" geblieben bin, d.h. nach der Hin-
> sicht gefragt habe, die schon in "Sein und Zeit" (S. 39)
> unter dem Titel "Zeit und Sein" angezeigt wurde. . . . Die
> Kehre spielt im Sachverhalt selbst. Sie ist weder von mir
> erfunden, noch betrifft sie nur mein Denken. Bis heute
> wurde mir kein Versuch bekannt, der diesem Sachverhalt
> nachgedacht und ihn kritisch erörtert hat. Statt des
> boden- und endlosen Geredes über die "Kehre" wäre es
> ratsamer und fruchtbar, sich erst einmal auf den genann-
> ten Sachverhalt einzulassen."
> M. Heidegger, "Vorwort" to Fr. Richardon's *Heidegger:
> Through Phenomenology to Thought*, pp. XVII and XIX,
> respectively.

What motivated the change from Heidegger I to Heidegger II? In order to introduce this question, the point of departure for Heidegger's thought must
be considered; but let us consider it now putting aside for the moment the
exclusively phenomenological way of approach which converts it directly
into a *Da des Seins*.

Heidegger begins his first "Introduction" to *Sein und Zeit* by placing his
researches in the context of Being as known prior to the categories.[1] And two
decades later in the "Letter on Humanism" he asserts that thought must
start out from that point.[2] Let us introduce our question then by examining
"Being as known prior to the categories." The sense of this requires plainly
that we must make the effort to think out of the tradition out of which Heidegger himself thought.

[1] SZ, p. 3.
[2] HB, p. 83/285.

In that first chapter of *Sein und Zeit*, and before taking up the method and design of his own investigation, Heidegger mentions the study of Being prior to the categories as treated by the Thomists, Scotists, and Hegelians. But in those traditions, Being as prior to the categories is prior to all act-potency analysis, since the categories were expressly worked out as the fundamental diverse modes of act-potency composition. And in the "Letter on Humanism," Heidegger himself expressly acknowledges that act and potency provide the fundamental categories of that very metaphysical mode of analysing to which his thinking (as phenomenological) is prior.[3]

Now without raising the question of adequate and preclusive methodological conceptions at all (that is, without going on to the second introductory chapter of *Sein und Zeit*), it can be said that prescinding from act-potency analysis implies the removal of a whole series of structures contained in the traditional philosophical presentation of the nature of the Real, "Reality". Substances and a world of substances (a world of nature intelligibly structured by fundamental unities bound together through interaction) disappear, because the very notion of substance is one of potency correlative to accidental act. *Per se* causes of whatever genus disappear, since these are principles relative to act-potency modifications or transitions. Certitude (an issue much more fundamental than clarity) disappears because its roots are in knowledge through causes. Intellect, sense, and psychological faculties generally disappear, because they are all distinguished in the first place as accidental powers of a particular kind of substance. The difference between *ens naturale* and *ens intentionale* disappears because *esse intentionale* is distinguished to begin with in order to understand the influence exercised over spatial and temporal distances despite the substantial gap entitatively isolating the *animal rationale* type substance (and indeed substances, particularly living substances, generally) from other substances that are

---

[3] "Unsere Wörter 'möglich' und 'Möglichkeit' werden freilich unter der Herrschaft der 'Logik' und 'Metaphysik' nur gedacht im Unterschied zu 'Wirklichkeit', das heisst aus einer bestimmten – der metaphysischen – Interpretation des Seins als actus und potentia, welche Unterscheidung identifiziert wird mit der von existentia und essentia." (HB, p. 57/273). "Das, was der Mensch ist, das heisst in der überlieferten Sprache der Metaphysik das 'Wesen' des Menschen, beruht in seiner Ek-sistenz. Aber die so bedachte Ek-sistenz ist nicht identisch mit dem überlieferten Begriff der existentia, was Wirklichkeit bedeutet im Unterschied zu essentia als der Möglichkeit. In 'Sein und Zeit' (S. 42) steht gesperrt der Satz: 'Das, "Wesen" des Daseins liegt in seiner Existenz'. Hier handelt es sich aber nicht um eine Entgegensetzung von existentia und essentia, weil überhaupt noch nicht diese beiden metaphysischen Bestimmungen des Seins, geschweige denn ihr Verhältnis, in Frage stehen. Der Satz enthält noch weniger eine allgemeine Aussage über das Dasein, insofern diese im 18. Jahrhundert für das Wort 'Gegenstand' aufgekommene Benennung den metaphysischen Begriff der Wirklichkeit des Wirklichen ausdrücken soll." (HB, pp. 68-9/298).

recognized as constituting an environmental world – an interdependent many of which each is one. Note that all this neither affirms nor denies the validity of act-potency analysis, but merely remarks that all these traditional "ontological structures" presuppose the validity of that analysis. By freeing oneself from the presupposition of valid, i.e., transhistorical, act-potency Interpretations (capacity-perfection, ground-grounded, etc.), one prescinds from the structures such Interpretation discerns.

Now it is the last removal, the merger of the *intentionalia* and *entitativa*, that is cardinal for understanding the penetration of the Real available prior to the categories. Thanks to the removal of this distinction, mythical or poetic creatures, ideological structures like Democracy, Fascism, or Communism, social institutions like Fatherland or family – all these lay equal claim to the title "being" (*Seiende*) with men, animals, plants, or minerals.

Moreover, thanks to the removal of the distinction between *ens naturale* and *ens intentionale*, man himself disappears not only as a substance (all substances disappear), but insofar as he is a subject of experiences, whether individual or collective. For the notion of a subject, whether conscious, subconscious, or unconscious presupposes the distinction of *esse intentionale* from *esse entitativum*. As a consequence of the removal of subjects, all discussion of human action or of morality becomes unfeasible:

> Thinking that seeks for the truth of Being and thereby determines the essential abode of man from Being is neither ethics nor ontology. . . such thinking is neither theoretical nor practical. It occurs before such a differentiation. . . At each epoch of history one thing only is important to it: that it be in accord with its matter.[4]

Now here is why this last blurring is the decisive one. In the "Einleitung" to *Was ist Metaphysik*, Heidegger tells us that "the first way from metaphysics to the ecstatic existential nature of man," i.e., to the *Da des Seins*, "must lead through the metaphysical conception of human selfhood";[5] and he refers us to paragraphs 63 and 64 of *Sein und Zeit*. These paragraphs are a critique of Kant's failure to disengage his problematic from the substantiality of the *res cogitans*, despite having begun with a genuinely phenomenological starting point, specifically, the *Ich Denke*. And in his essay on *Kants These Über Das Sein*, Heidegger explains that Kant's relapse into the

---

[4] "Das Denken, das nach der Wahrheit des Seins fragt und dabei den Wesensaufenthalt des Menschen vom Sein her und auf dieses hin bestimmt, ist weder Ethik noch Ontologie . . . dieses Denken ist weder theoretisch noch praktisch. Es ereignet sich vor dieser Unterscheidung. . . Der Sache des Denkens gehört je geschichtlich nur eine, die ihrer Sachheit gemässe Sage." (HB, pp. 110-11/298).

[5] ". . . der erste Weg, der von der Metaphysik zum ekstatisch-existenzialen Wesen des Menschen hinleitet, durch die metaphysische Bestimmung des Selbstseins des Menschen hindurchführen." (WM:In, p. 16/215).

substantial *res cogitans* eventuated from Kant's speaking concerning the subject with its experience in terms of the traditional metaphysics of *possibilitas* and *actus*.[6] In short, the first road out of Metaphysics into the existential nature of man as *Da des Seins* (Dasein) is through a step backward (*Schritt züruck*) out of the act-potency concept of man as subject with (of) experiences. We could therefore test for ourselves this road indicated by (the later) Heidegger by removing the *actualitas-possibilitas* relation between the *Ich Denke* and "its" experience, and seeing if this would indeed convert the metaphysical concept of the (substantial) self-being of man into Dasein (Dasein *sans* the ontic-ontological *Seinsverfassung* is exactly what the later Heidegger designates "the ecstatic existential" or "historical" nature of man).

Now the removal of the *actualitas-possibilitas* distinction between *Ich Denke* and experience is nothing other than a specification of the removal of the distinction between *ens naturale* and *ens intentionale*, as can be seen immediately from its primary consequences: the self-being of man with all its different modalizations (intellect, will, emotion, phantasy) disappear insofar as they are "really" distinct from the experiences man undergoes, while with the same stroke the *Seienden* cease likewise to be distinct from the total experience of man in history; so that pagan gods and poetic creations take their place among *das Seiende*; and no *Seiende als solche* bears a distinctly intelligible structure for the very good reason that no intellect remains to which it would be correlate. The *Seienden* have thus become entirely historical (temporal) and fateful, for they *are* the "content" of the historical "experience" of the "subjects" of awareness *from which they have lost all distinction*. This leaves the beings fateful as well as historical, because beings form the context of the World where one fundamental meaning (*Sein*), that is, one fundamental way of viewing and distinguishing experience, channels all future expectancy. As many as are these fundamental meanings that dominate the interpretations of the Real as Reality, so many are the "mittences" of Being (*Geschicke des Seins*), illustrated in the incompatible metaphysical systems, each concealing more than it unveils of the mystery of Being, since their common root is the *Differenz* which cannot be spoken save perhaps by a "sagenden Nichtsagend."[7]

Thus it is not the phenomenologist as phenomenologist who can say that "beings *are* quite independently of the experience by which they are disclosed, the acquaintance in which they are discovered, and the grasping in

---

[6] Martin Heidegger, *Kants These Über Das Sein* (Frankfurt: Klostermann, 1963).
[7] See ID, pp. 67/62 and 72/66.

which their nature is ascertained,"[8] for to say that is to already have acknowledged a stepping across the gulf separating the conditions or mode of thought (*esse intentionale*)from the conditions or mode of the thing (*esse entitativum*), an eminently metaphysical acknowledgment and step! If the phenomenologist is to speak as and only as phenomenologist, if he is to make no concession even in passing to lines of thought which necessarily lead outside his methodologically delimited region, then:

. . .*only* Being "is"; beings properly speaking "are" not. The essential is to recognize the difference. (See HB, p. 80). In 1957, Heidegger will accept the formula "Being *is*," provided that "is" be understood transitively.[9]

If the reader has been puzzled up to now as to how we could claim in this study to have retrieved integrally the original Heideggerian problematic without making any particular issue the while of the question of Time (*Zeit*), he now has the reason. In translating Dasein as Intentional Life, the problem of Time in the There of Being has *already been incorporated* "if instead of 'Time' we substitute: the lighting-up of the self-concealing [that is proper to] the process of coming-to-presence" as Heidegger recommends[10] – even though it remains, as is also the case for Heidegger,[11] to work out this notion in an explicit and thematic way; for if we live most obviously in "fallenness" and find a difficulty in representing to ourselves a process which does not consist in producing anything but simply, being of an order superior to the entitative, remains and finds its completion in being itself, nevertheless, the actuality or "Being" of thought – like the factors of significance which find a place only there – has a life, *is* life *par excellence*, in whose depths the intentional presence of images and sensations and memories and longings constitute Time within the soul itself remaining distinct the while from that same soul (*anima*) so far as natural being is concerned.[12]

But the beings themselves, *das Seiende*, become part of *Zeit* and *Sein* (that is, historical and fateful) in the Heideggerian problematic only because the thought of the *Ich denke* has become indistinct from *das Sein* in such wise that Thought and Being are the same,[13] that existence (*Existenz, Ek-sistenz*)

---

[8] "Seiendes *ist* unabhängig von Erfahrung, Kenntnis und Erfassen, wodurch es erschlossen, entdeckt und bestimmt wird." (SZ, p. 183).

[9] Richardson, H:TPT, p. 7 fn. 12.

[10] "Setzen wir statt 'Zeit': Lichtung des Sichverbergens von Anwesen, dann bestimmt sich Sein aus dem Entwurfbereich von Zeit." (Heidegger's "Vorwort" to H:TPT, p. XXI).

[11] "Die in 'Sein und Zeit' gekennzeichnete ekstatisch-horizontale Zeitlichkeit ist keineswegs schon das der Seinsfrage entsprechende gesuchte Eigenste der Zeit." (*Ibid.*, p. XIII).

[12] Cf. Jacques Maritain, *Theonas*, trans. by F. J. Sheed (New York: Sheed & Ward, 1933), pp. 11 and 71. St. Thomas Aquinas, *In IV Phys.*, lect. 17. Also John of St. Thomas, *Cursus Phil.*, I P., q. 18, art. 12. See also fn. 11 of Chapter VIII *supra*.

[13] *Was Heisst Denken* (Tübingen: Niemeyer, 1954), p. 74.

as the "essence" of man which thought fulfills is one with Being,[14] so that thought *is* the thinker's existence,[15] willing nothing and causing nothing,[16] freighted with the history of Being: so that, in short, man's essence, the *humanus* of *homo humanus*, is a *seinsgeschichtliches Wesen*.

In all these ways the removal of the distinction of *ens naturale* from *ens intentionale* implies that "beings" will be presented to subjectless man (in whom we may recognize the *Da* of Dasein) as a historically determined totality, for the transepochally valid *unit* of being of course disappeared along with substances and subjects: here the "real" (what Heidegger distinguishes as "Reality") may be a single substance in one Being-epoch (Spinoza) or an indeterminate multitude of sub-atomic particles in another (modern physics), a system of tools of gods and men (Homer), etc. In the absence of substances and subjects we have no inter-epochal or "intermittent" standard for recognizing which unit *should* or even *could in principle* be recognized as "fundamentally natural" and so wear the title "being" in the primary sense which Metaphysics seeks. The units recognized in any one culture are idiosyncratic to that particular epoch in the sense that there is no phenomenological justification for diverse epochs discerning the same unit as "being," in the metaphysical sense, obviously, of *substantia*; for even if several historical "groups" should happen to be found agreeing in large measure as to the nature of the fundamental natural units (neo- and paleo-Thomists, for example), this must be understood in virtue of their common tradition, in virtue of a shared and single mittence of Being.

Thus if on the one hand these culture-bound units of "being" appear only as gathered together (*logos*) in Dasein, on the other hand non-substantial, subjectless Dasein cannot be plurified save as a *There* of diverse gatherings-into-unity of beings in the light of Being emitted out of the power of the Difference as the *Singulare Tantum*, the sole phenomenologically discernable "intermittent" or transepochal matter-of-thought. "What the Light 'in itself' or the projecting There 'in itself' might be, independently of the process in which they cooperate, is simply not Heidegger's problem, presumably because neither one nor the other in that case would be a *phainom-*

---

[14] HB, pp. 53/270-71 and 67/277. *Zur Seinsfrage* (Frankfurt: Klosterman, 1956) as appearing in *The Question of Being* (New Haven, Conn.: College & University Press, 1958), a bi-lingual edition with translation and introduction by Jean T. Wilde and William Kluback, p. 76. Hereafter this work will be referred to as SF. Since the English translation of this particular work is printed with the German facing, we will give only the single page reference to the German text as it appears in the Wilde-Kluback edition.

[15] G, p. 70/87.

[16] *Ibid.*, 55/77 and 58-9/78-9.

enon,"[17] i.e., neither would lie along an unwavering line of phenomenological vision. That is why the diverse gatherings-into-unity of beings and diverse Daseins are co-definitive. For example, the Chinese Dasein of the Han is defined by the gathering-into-unity that occurred or "was granted" *there*; and it is diversified from the Dasein of medieval Christendom simply by the diverse gathering-into-unity which "was granted" *there* (i.e., in another *Da des Seins*). That is why too "all refutation in the field of foundational thinking is absurd."[18]

In the absence of distinct recognition of intellect, sense and affection the "beings" "defined" relative to a given historical Dasein hold affective attitudinal sway over that Dasein, forming as it were a Home relative to it. For example, medieval Dasein was at Home in its "world" of Papacy and Empire, crusades, serfs, and sainthood. Hence these affective "beings" are beings only in totality, that is, only respecting their gathering-into-unity (*logos*) in a particular historical Dasein for whom they form a Home. Such a given historically conditioned and fashioned totality of beings we can call: World – therefore Being! And Being as the totality of this range of significance is a totality of *meaning*. Therefore (once again) the historically determined plurality of Daseins and the history constituting plurality of Being-mittences to diverse cultural epochs are mutually defining and irreducible among themselves. "The epochs never permit themselves to be derived from one another and still less reduced to the sequence of a consecutive process."[19] The Being-process, the continual and constantly renewed coming of Being to beings as the Presence within the present, is the *Singulare Tantum*. The single factor common to diverse totalities of beings in Being is the power of historical determinism which constitutes them as different, i.e., the power of the *Differenz*. This common Difference as that-which-differs can be called non-Being since it first differentiates the various Being-systems with their corresponding gatherings, their corresponding Daseins. In this sense historical determinism as prior to the truth of Being constitutes the non-truth from which Being in any given age must derive: "it does not run between the epochs, like a cord connecting them. Rather, the tradition comes each time out of the concealment of a mittence [*Logos, Geschick, Ereignis, Geschickliche*], just as different rills arise from a [single] Source [and] feed a stream that is everywhere

---

[17] Richardson, H:TPT, p. 627.
[18] "Alles Widerlegen im Felde des wesentlichen Denkens ist töricht." (HB, p. 82/285). See Richardson, H:TPT, pp. 546-7.
[19] "Die Epochen lassen sich nie auseinander ableiten und gar auf die Bahn eines durch-laufenden Prozesses schlagen." – M. Heidegger, *Der Satz vom Grund* (Pfüllingen: Neske, 1957), p. 154. Hereafter referred to as SG.

and nowhere."[20] In this sense "[the process of] presenc-ing (Being) is inherent in the lighting-up of self-concealment (Time)." And conversely, the "lighting-up of self-concealment (Time) brings forth the process of presenc-ing (Being)."[21]

Thus by merely freeing ourselves from the traditional philosophic structures founded on act and potency compositionism, and in particular by stepping back from the *Ich Denke* as the potential subject of actual experiences, we have thought ourselves into the philosophy of the later Heidegger independently of any systematic textual study of the later writings. Like Heidegger in *Identität und Differenz*, we see that the "essential nature" of man – not, to be sure, the *rationalitas* of the *homo animalis* but much rather the *humanitas* of *homo humanus* – is the same as Being,[22] and that the only thing common to diverse historical epochs is the power of the Difference.[23] Dasein, for us as for the later Heidegger, can no longer be ontic-ontological (we shall say more on this) but simply ecstatic-existential, *Ek-sistenz*, the "existential nature of man," freed from all subjectivity and counterdistinguished intentionality.[24] For us as for Heidegger, causes, substances, and subjectivity have been confined to particular historical Being-systems.[25] The "Beings" can only appear, for us as for Heidegger, as collated with a given historical mittence of Being, a given Being-system as determined by historical determinism, by "the power of the Difference."[26] All psychological faculties

---

[20] ". . . sie verläuft nicht zwischen den Epochen wie ein Band, das sie verknüpft, sondern die Überlieferung kommt jedesmal aus dem Verborgenen des Geschickes, so wie aus einem Quell verschiedene Rinnsale entspringen, die einen Strom nähren, der überall ist und nirgends." (SG, p. 154).

[21] "Anwesen (Sein) gehört in die Lichtung des Sichverbergens (Zeit). Lichtung des Sichverbergens (Zeit) erbringt Anwesen (Sein)." (Heidegger's "Vorwort" to H:TPT, p. XXI.)

[22] ". . . Zuspruch des Wesens der Identität von Mensch und Sein. . ." (ID, p. 34/32).

[23] "Was so heisst, verweist unser Denken in den Bereich, den zu sagen die Leitworte der Metaphysik, Sein und Seiendes, Grund-Gegründetes, nicht mehr genügen. Denn was diese Worte nennen, was die von ihnen geleitete Denkweise vorstellt, stammt als das Differente aus der Differenz. Deren Herkunft lässt sich nicht mehr im Gesichtskreis der Metaphysik denken." (ID, pp. 69-70/64).

[24] WM:In, pp. 15-16/214-5.

[25] ID, p. 64/58-9; G, pp. 56-7/77-8.

[26] Cf. Heidegger's well-known *Geschick des Seins* – e.g.: "Das Denken bringt nämlich in seinem Sagen nur das ungesprochene Wort des Seins zur Sprache.

"Die hier gebrauchte Wendung 'zur Sprache bringen' ist jetzt wörtlich zu nehmen. Das Sein kommt, sich lichtend, zur Sprache. Es ist stets unterwegs zu ihr. Dieses Ankommende bringt das ek-sistierende Denken seinerseits in seinem Sagen zur Sprache. Diese wird so selbst in die Lichtung des Seins gehoben. Erst so *ist* die Sprache in jener geheimnisvollen und uns doch stets durchwaltenden Weise. Indem die also voll ins Wesen gebrachte Sprache geschichtlich ist, ist das Sein in das Andenken verwahrt." (HB, p. 116/300).

". . . Das Denken ist in seinem Wesen als Denken des Seins von diesem in den Anspruch

have disappeared for us as for Heidegger.[27]

Moreover, in *Sein und Zeit*, Heidegger expressly takes up a position half-way between realism and idealism.[28] Here we recall one of the first observations made in the opening chapter of our study: to circumscribe and methodologically adequate the ambit of Intentional Life would be in effect "to set a third term between realism and idealism, between yes and no." Realism is wrong, from Heidegger's perspectives, in explaining reality as causal connections between beings, though it is right in saying that the "exterior" world is at hand; Idealism is wrong in reducing all beings to a subject, but right in maintaining that Being cannot be explained through beings (and for this reason, "as compared with realism, *idealism*, no matter how countrary and untenable it may be in its results, has an advantage in principle, provided that it does not misunderstand itself as 'psychological' idealism"[29]). And this position amounts to removing the distinction between *ens naturale* (the beings) and *ens intentionale* (Being), though a removal achieved obviously from the latter side of the dichotomy (the *Da des Seins* where "things" can be only as in Being). Consequently in *Das Ding*, Heidegger can list as the four components that integrate a "thing" earth, sky, mortals, and the divine – the "Quadrate" (*Geviert*) of Being. How could such factors integrate a single thing in any *ens naturale* sense? An inspection of examples illustrating what is meant by the four components confirms that they could not. Sky includes twilight and starlight, the divine is the "blinking messengers of the divinity," whose essence "withdraws Him from any similitude with the presencing": plainly the sky and divine dimensions of "things" contain what act-potency analysis would discern as intentional aspects. On the other hand, the earth dimension in act-potency accounting would be put down to entitative aspects: waters, rocks, plants, animals. Yet in the phenomenological thought of Being, these dimensions fuse in one "thing" – clearly a fusion of *esse naturale* and *esse intentionale*, justifiable philosophically thanks only to a methodological conception which precludes assessment of beings save precisely as participating Intentional Life, *sicut*

---

genommen. Das Denken ist auf das Sein als das Ankommende (l'avenant) bezogen. Das Denken ist als Denken in die Ankunft des Seins, in das Sein als die Ankunft gebunden. Das Sein hat sich dem Denken schon zugeschickt. Das Sein *ist* als das Geschick des Denkens. Das Geschick aber ist in sich geschichtlich. Seine Geschichte ist schon im Sagen der Denker zur Sprache gekommen." (HB, p. 117/301).

[27] Such, we have already noted, is the outcome of the KM analyses.

[28] See SZ, pp. 207-8.

[29] "Gegenüber dem Realismus hat der *Idealismus*, mag er im Resultat noch so entgegengesetzt und unhaltbar sein, einen grundsätzlichen Vorrang, falls er nicht als 'psychologischer' Idealismus sich selbst missversteht." (SZ, p. 207).

habens esse intentionale, a methodological conception able in principle to assess Being only as it enters into the comprehensibility of Dasein.

Thus just as the early Heidegger raised the question of Being in such a way that his methodology separated his direct concern from that of Aristotle and Aquinas even as the conditions or mode of thought are separated from the conditions or mode of the (primary) subjects of existence, so the later Heidegger pursues the phenomenological Being-question with increasingly inflexible fidelity to the hermeneutic situation in which phenomenological inquiry is confined by its proper research-principle, until the methodological difference at last began to manifest unmistakably that it defined an inquiry not at all into the ground-question of Metaphysics, but into the origins of thought prior to the fundamental metaphysical analytical categories of *actus et potentia* through a step back from the entire problematic which the metaphysical question of being establishes in the first place. When the full way of phenomenological thought of Being has been traversed (*saltem virtualiter*), the later Heidegger makes the reluctant concession: "Metaphysics remains the basis of philosophy"; and even his immediate qualification, "however, the basis of thinking it does not reach,"[30] begins to ring hollow.

The thinking of the reversal *is* a change in my thought. But this change is not a consequence of altering the standpoint, much less of abandoning the fundamental issue, of *Sein und Zeit*. The thinking of the reversal results from the fact that I stayed with the matter-for-thought [of] "Being and Time," sc. by inquiring into that perspective which already in *Sein und Zeit* (p. 39) was designated as "Time and Being."[31]

Thus "the interpretation of Dasein in terms of temporality" led eventually and literally away from the metaphysically presuppositioned ontic-ontological *Seinsverfassung* to historicity and the "existential nature of man," and the difference in the two expressions measures the difference between Heidegger I and Heidegger II.

Heidegger I presents authentic Dasein as an ontological possibility *grounded* in an ontic possibility. But Heidegger II repudiates thought in terms of ground and grounded.[32] And we know now why, for we have already seen in

---

[30] "Die Metaphysik bleibt das Erste der Philosophie. Das Erste des Denkens erreicht sie nicht. Die Metaphysik ist im Denken an die Wahrheit des Seins überwunden." (WM:In, p. 9/209).

[31] "Das Denken der Kehre *ist* eine Wendung in meinem Denken. Aber diese Wendung erfolgt nicht auf grund einer Änderung des Standpunktes oder gar der Preisgabe der Fragestellung in 'Sein und Zeit'. Das Denken der Kehre ergibt sich daraus, dass ich bei der zu denkenden Sache 'Sein und Zeit' geblieben bin, d. h. nach der Hinsicht gefragt habe, die schon in 'Sein und Zeit' (S. 39) unter dem Titel 'Zeit und Sein' angezeigt wurde." (Heidegger's "Vorwort" to H:TPT, p. XVII).

[32] ID, pp. 69-70/64. (As cited in fn. 23 of this Chapter.)

chapter VIII that such thinking for Heidegger rests in the end on the tradi-tional metaphysical distinction between the possible and the actual, between potency and act. Once the later Heidegger had stepped below that distinc-tion, it was inevitable that he eventually remove from his consideration the distinction between the ontological and the ontic as well, since it is itself, as an attenuated form of the *entitativum-intentionale* distinction, an applica-tion of the correlativity of the possible and the actual.

What remains then of the idea of man in his Dasein? Man the historical being. The "Letter on Humanism" contains a long passage in which Hei-degger steps back from the distinction between the possible and the actual because, he says, such a distinction derives (obviously) from the distinction of act and potency: he describes the undifferentiated reality thus uncovered as historical destiny.[33]

Once Heidegger is forced to abandon the ontic-ontological (act-potency) structure of Dasein, authentic Dasein only exists as cast (*Wurf*) of *Sein* which as Father Richardson says is the thinker. But that thinker can only think the various fated meanings of *Sein*. So also *Sein* according to its various incompatible meanings – Spiritualism, Materialism, etc. (*Was ist Metaphysik*, "Einleitung," p. 7) – is but a *Geschick* of the *Differenz*. *Existenz* is thus "freed" from any root outside historical meaning. For a *Seiendes* is but that to which the evolving world meaning draws near. Thus, the *Differenz*, out of which all *Geschicke des Seins* hide more than they reveal of the meaning of *Seienden*, remains the inscrutable mystery underlying historical *Existenz*, *Seiendes*, and *Sein*.[34]

Heidegger's thought must be seen in short not only as other than metaphys-ical thinking (the early Heidegger); it must be seen as the contrary opposite of such thinking (the later Heidegger). If "the claim that Metaphysics poses the [phenomenological] question of Being lands us in utter error,"[35] the idea that Phenomenology lays the foundations for Metaphysics by adjudicating its ground question lands us in error equally utter. To illustrate this con-trariety, let us consider once again Heidegger's phenomenological analysis

---

[33] See HB, pp. 56-8/272-3.

[34] Powell, "The Late Heidegger's Omission of the Ontic-Ontological Structure of Dasein," p. 22. The text continues: "Moreover, our modern Western conception of man as *animal rationale* or person, and consequently our Western ethics built on rational principles implying as it does *veritas* as *conformitas*, in sum the whole root meaning of the world to modern Western man, *all this* the late Heidegger reduces to a *Geschick* of the inscrutable *Differenz* out of which emerged the fundamental act-potency meaning that lends its color to the *Existenz* of modern Western man (HB, p. 73/280). In brief, the whole meaning of modern Western *Existenz* is exposed as rooted in a historical fate emerging from the un-knowable mystery of the *Differenz*." (Cf. p. 136 of printed version).

[35] "... gelangt das Vorstellen auf den Gipfel der Verwirrung, wenn man behauptet, die Metaphysik stelle die Seinsfrage." (WM:In, p. 12/211).

of a thing (*res*), only this time in order to contrast it with the metaphysical conception of a thing.

In the essay *Das Ding*, a "thing" is explained as the drawing near (*Nähern*) of four meaning-factors: earth, sky, the divine, and mortal man.[36] The "thing" gathers the meaning-factors and lets them tarry (*verweilen*). The meaning-factors occur in varying (*frei*) proportions in a "thing." But the meaning-factors constitute a simple total world-meaning: they play into one another, but their play just happens (*ereignen*), and requires no cause. The simple total world-meaning is the World, and the World can have no cause: *die Welt weltet*. The "thing" lets the total simple world-meaning tarry as what-is-currently (*ein je Weiliges*) in the worlding of the World (*aus der weltenden Welt*). The term *Welt*[37] here signifies *Sein* which for Heidegger is the historical *meaning* of *Seienden*; and *Sein* is essentially involved in human nature,[38] from which it is not even correlatively distinct.[39] In contrast, the act-potency philosophy of a "thing" explains it merely from distinct dimensions intrinsic to the thing itself and takes no account of the tarrying of the current phase of the evolving world meaning involved in human nature. Hence Heidegger can take the doctrine of the distinction of essence from existence as a sign of the forgottenness of Sein.[40]

Thus by rejecting the act-potency roots of the initial ontic-ontological approach to the *Da des Seins*, Heidegger freed himself from an understanding of Dasein precisely as non-historical. Non-human things have no history: not animals, not plants, not minerals, not even God.[41] Any analysis seeking

---

[36] "Das Ding" in *Vorträge und Aufsatze* (Pfüllingen. Neske, 1954), pp. 176-9. Hereafter referred to as VA. See also pp. 153-4 and 158-9. And Demske, *art. cit.*

[37] *Welt* in this text is the meaning of *Das Ding* as integrated out of the world's four meaning factors. Usually, *Welt* is *das Seiende im Ganzen* whereas *Sein* is its meaning (*Sinn*). Cf. Max Müller, *Existenzphilosophie* (Heidelberg: Kerle, 1964), pp. 137-8. (Powell's note.)

[38] WM:In, pp. 13-14/212-13.

[39] "In Wahrheit können wir dann nicht einmal mehr sagen, 'das Sein' und 'der Mensch' 'seien' das Selbe in dem Sinne dass *sie* zusammengehören; denn *so* sagend, lassen wir immer noch beide für sich sein." (SF, p. 76).

[40] In HB, p. 73/280. The entire passage cited is taken from Powell, "The Late Heidegger's Omission of the Ontic-Ontological Structure of Dasein," p. 4. (Cf. pp. 119-120 of printed version).

[41] "Sind wir überhaupt auf dem rechten Wege zum Wesen des Menschen, wenn wir den Menschen und so lange wir den Menschen als ein Lebewesen unter anderen gegen Pflanze, Tier und Gott abgrenzen? Man kann so vorgehen, man kann in solcher Weise den Menschen innerhalb des Seienden als ein Seiendes unter anderen ansetzen. Man wird dabei stets Richtiges über den Menschen aussagen können. Aber man muss sich auch darüber klar sein, dass der Mensch dadurch endgültig in den Wesensbereich der Animalitas verstossen bleibt, auch dann, wenn man ihn nicht dem Tier gleichsetzt, sondern ihm eine spezifische Differenz zuspricht. Man denkt im Prinzip stets den homo animalis, selbst wenn anima als animus sive mens und diese später als Subjekt, als Person, als Geist gesetzt werden. Solches Setzen ist die Art der Metaphysik. Aber dadurch wird das Wesen des Menschen zu gering geachtet und nicht in seiner Herkunft gedacht, welche Wesensherkunft für das geschichtliche Menschentum stets die Wesenszukunft bleibt. Die Metaphysik denkt den Menschen von der animalitas her und denkt nicht zu seiner humanitas hin." (HB, p.

to explain the human world in terms of *man's* essential, i.e., irreducibly unique, nature accordingly must remain faithful to the incomparability of the historical being to non-human beings; and this incomparability demands that the understanding of historical man qua historical, of the *humanitas* of *homo humanus*,[42] be derived exclusively from his particular Being-system and the non-Being or Untruth of historical determinism behind it – not at all from "beings" existing "independently". For such derivation from beings would imply that Being could also be derived from and explained in terms of beings (inasmuch as Being and Dasein are "locally" one), while the attempt to derive either Dasein or Being from the beings would necessitate conceiving of these beings as independent entities – a conception taken from the *naturalia* side of the *intentionale-entitativum* distinction: and that is something which pure Phenomenology cannot allow. So Heidegger is led to declare in *Gelassenheit* that neither the relation of Being to Dasein nor the relation of Being to beings can be thought of either as ontic or even as ontological.[43]

And yet, the basic question of *Sein und Zeit* is not in any sense abandoned by reason of the reversal. . . Contrary [to what is generally supposed], the question of *Sein und Zeit* is decisively whol-ified in the thinking of the reversal. He alone can whol-ify who has a view of the whole. This "wholification" or fulfillment likewise furnishes for the first time an adequate characterization of Dasein, sc. of the essence of man [as] thought in terms of the truth of Being as such.[44]

That is why "it is quite essential to the thinking in *Sein und Zeit* that the historicity of Dasein be grasped."[45] That is why "the thought that thinks the truth of Being thinks historically," and why for *Denken des Seins* à la Hei-

66/277). It is remarkable that Heidegger admits here that an analysis other than his own is capable of speaking rightly concerning man – one that co-divides man against other living beings: plant, animal, mineral, God. But such an analysis (he is quick to add) seems to bypass the origin of what is unique to man – that, for historical man, is his essential future. This I understand to mean: what is unique to historical man is his historically determined future. (Cf. Powell's "Heidegger's Retreat from a Transcultural Structure of Dasein," fn. 21.)

[42] Cf. HB, pp. 11-12/298; 90-91/288-9.

[43] G, pp. 55-6/76-7.

[44] "Dadurch wird jedoch die Fragestellung in 'Sein und Zeit' keineswegs preisgegeben . . . Dagegen wird im Denken der Kehre die Fragestellung von 'Sein und Zeit' auf eine entscheidende Weise er-gänzt. Ergänzen kann nur, wer das Ganze erblickt. Diese Ergänzung erbringt auch erst die zureichende Bestimmung des Da-seins, d. h. des von der Wahrheit des Seins als solchen her gedachten Wesens des Menschen (vgl. 'Sein und Zeit', par. 66)." (Heidegger's "Vorwort" to H:TPT, pp. XIX-XXI).

[45] "Weil es gilt, die Ek-sistenz des Da-seins zu denken, deshalb liegt dem Denken in 'S. u. Z.' so wesentlich daran, dass die Geschichtlichkeit des Daseins erfahren wird." (HB, p. 82/285).

degger "there is not 'systematic' thought accompanied by an illustrative history of past opinions."[46] All refutation in the realm of "foundational" thinking is absurd, because the proper seat of man's historicity lies prior to any act-potency analysis, half-way between realism and idealism.

I understand Heidegger's work as a prolonged study of the origins of thought prior to the categories of act and potency, and thus understood, his work is continuous with the tradition of the Thomists, Scotists, and Hegel. For Heidegger moved into *Ek-sistenz* by stepping back out of act-potency Metaphysics. Concerning a return back step out of Heidegger's *Existenz* into an act-potency philosophy or *any philosophy having roots outside of historical meaning*, Heidegger has nothing to say except that one can say something "richtig" outside his experience of "Wahrheit." Those who accept Heidegger's back step out of act-potency but who are not willing to remain in a purely historical meaning to man and his world bear the whole burden of the return back step.[47]

For the consequences of the reversal are virtual to the phenomenological question of Being as such: "neither did I invent it," says Heidegger, "nor does it affect merely *my* thought. The reversal is in play within the matter itself."[48] And even considered merely insofar as the phenomenological exigencies of the reversal affect Heidegger's thought, "the thought of Heidegger I becomes possible only if it is contained in Heidegger II."[49] Those who seek an understanding of the central question of philosophy by way of Phenomenology simply trap themselves, wittingly or not, into considering the purely historical and timebound dimension of philosophy, i.e., philosophy as it appears and develops with man's Intentional Life and necessarily resides therein ("never escapes its ground"[50]). But the central question of philosophy in its proper concern and nature will forever lie beyond their reach and adjudication, for "philosophy does not concentrate on its ground; it always leaves its ground – leaves it by means of Metaphysics"[51] – and for that very special, strictly circumscribed, negative (therefore non-represen-

[46] "Darum ist das Denken, das in die Wahrheit des Seins denkt, als Denken geschichtlich. Es gibt nicht ein 'systematisches' Denken und daneben zur Illustration eine Historie der vergangenen Meinungen. . . Das Geschehen der Geschichte west als das Geschick der Wahrheit des Seins aus diesem (vgl. den Vortrag über Hölderlins Hymne 'Wie wenn am Feiertage. . .', 1941-S. 31)." (HB, p. 81/284).
[47] Powell, "The Late Heidegger's Omission of the Ontic-Ontological Structure of Dasein," p. 22. (Cf. p. 137 of printed version).
[48] "Die Kehre spielt im Sachverhalt selbst. Sie ist weder von mir erfunden, noch betrifft sie nur mein Denken." (Heidegger's "Vorwort" to H:TPT, p. XIX).
[49] "Aber I wird nur möglich, wenn es in II enthalten ist." (*Ibid.*, p. XXIII).
[50] ". . . sie engeht ihm gleichwohl nie." (WM:In, p. 8/208).
[51] "Die Philosophie versammelt sich nicht auf ihren Grund. Sie verlässt ihn stets, und zwar durch die Metaphysik." (*Ibid.*)

tational in essence) but nonetheless real transcendence of the temporality and historicity of Dasein there is no need that thought "escape its ground" in *Ek-sistenz*.[52]

[52] See John N. Deely, "Finitude, Negativity, and Transcendence: The Problematic of Metaphysical Knowledge," in *Philosophy Today*, XI (Fall, 1967), pp. 184-206.

CHAPTER XI

CONCLUSION. THE DENOUEMENT OF OUR RE-TRIEVE

"La critique de la connaissance ou l'épistémologie n'existe pas en tant que discipline distincte de la métaphysique. Lui donner une existence à part, c'est poser un troisième terme entre le réalisme et l'idéalisme, entre le oui et le non, ce qui est toute la prétention des modernes avec leur... notion de pur 'phénomène, qui vide de l'être [i.e., de l'*esse entitativum seu ens ut subjectum exercens existentiam*] le concept même de l'être..."
Jacques Maritain, *Les degres du savoir*, pp. 154-5/80.

Our re-trieve of the original Heideggerean problematic has achieved its finality. We have touched in sequence on the need for such a re-trieve (Chs. I & II); the experience of the forgottenness of Being which such an effort must begin by re-calling (Ch. III); the difficulty of formalizing this experience in a definite question serving to guide further inquiry (Ch. IV); the double set of considerations necessary to analytically adequate the ontic-ontological structure of Dasein presented in *Sein und Zeit* (Chs. V & VI) – pointing out with some care (Ch. VII) that the contribution of Heideggerean thought to the progress of philosophy stems principally from thematizing the dimension of Dasein which gives the notion its "objectively scientific priority"; the priority of the phenomenological *Seinsfrage* as a presuppositioned priority, inasmuch as it is essentially involved with the *Da des Seins*, to that extent dependent on a consideration of whatever the notion of Dasein itself can be shown to structurally presuppose, – or, more exactly, *structurally imply* (Ch. VIII); the discovery of Phenomenology as the philosophical attitude alone proportioned preclusively to the thought of Being (Ch. IX); a means of testing philosophically the integrity of our understanding of the inner élan of Heidegger's thought (Ch. X); and finally, we were able through this programmatic development to locate within the perspectives of Thomistic thought the proper sense of Heidegger's reinterpretation of the question of Being.

This disclosure itself of the "place" of *Sein* tells us at once why *Denken des Seins* catches more easily the spirit of a Maréchal than a Maritain; for Heidegger is not at all concerned (thematically) with that *esse* or being which can only be thought "en le pensant distinct du connaître";[1] rather is he concerned with something a good deal closer to what Maréchalian thought attempts to thematize as "l'idée d'être virtuellement présente dans notre pouvoir cognitif."[2] Yet it has been thanks principally to Maritain that we have been able to unmistakably mark the junction of Heidegger's way with Thomism, and in the very placing of ourselves at that juncture is disclosed to us the profound reason why Heidegger's way of philosophizing thrives best in the scholastic atmosphere engendered by Maréchal in bringing Thomism before the Kantian style of transcendental critique. Yet too a juncture defines a parting more than a meeting of ways, even though it is at junctures that one best gets one's bearings: when all proper perspectivizing has been achieved, the necessity of widening and deepening the scholastic problematic of *esse intentionale* is not rendered any the less demanding.

The insistence that the basic reality is "primary substance," that whatever exists depends on primary substance, that basic existence has essential unity that can only be achieved by form, and that the life of the mind modifies accidentally the soul of the knower – all these propositions have worked together to (needlessly) blind traditional philosophy to the decisively intersubjective, formally constitutive features of cultural, social, and personal realities which are the preoccupation of contemporary reflection. What traditional philosophizing has failed to take sufficient account of, and what Heidegger demonstrates the need for considering thematically, is the possibility of understanding the irreducibility of the order of *esse intentionale* strictly and consistently as the sphere and level wherein man's historical existence is worked out and his "self-identity" in the properly human sense consequently maintains itself. Heidegger is certainly right in distinguishing his *existentialia* from the *praedicamenta* categories of Metaphysics in view of the fact that the realm of *esse intentionale* always transcends in what is proper to it categorial interpretation and grasp, "constitutes unto itself alone a whole metaphysical order apart, wherein meet in common both the distinction between essential form and existence in the line of being and the distinction between operative form and the operation in the line of

---

[1] DS, p. 448/226.

[2] "Les données sensibles à chaque moment de notre existence, ne pourraient nous amener à la connaissance d'une réalité existante si elles n'étaient valorisées en fonction de l'idée d'être virtuellement présente dans notre pouvoir cognitif." G. Verbeke, "Le Développement de la connaissance humaine d'après St. Thomas," *Revue Philosophique de Louvain*, XLVII (1949), 442.

action – now transposed on to one and the same line, the line of knowing."[3] Heidegger is right therefore in considering that "every philosophy which revolves around an indirect or direct conception of 'transcendence' [including then Heidegger's own] remains of necessity essentially an ontology, whether it achieves a new foundation of ontology" – the hope of the early Heidegger – "or whether it assures us that it repudiates ontology as a conceptual freezing of experience" – the suspicion of the later Heidegger.[4]

But on this account Heidegger is simply mistaken in contending that "the nature of truth always appears to Metaphysics in the derivative form of the truth of knowledge."[5] "If, when speaking of the mental word and its distinction from the thing, St. Thomas ordinarily cites definition and ennunciation rather than the simple concept," i.e., the concept simply considered as a *modus specialis* of *esse intentionale*, "it is precisely because in these cases there is something that is entirely our own (the mental composition), and this makes the distinction clearer than would the mere difference of state or *esse* between concept," i.e., the kind of existence that supervenes upon things in order that they be known, "and the object" or rather, "transobjective subject," i.e., the thing itself possessing and exercising an existence such that it is maintained within the world of nature.[6]

But that "mere difference of state or *esse* between" is precisely what Heidegger has devoted a lifetime of philosophical reflection to:

Beings, nature in the widest sense, could in nowise be manifest if they did not find an *occasion* to enter into a World. We speak hence of the possible and occasional

---

[3] ". . . la connaissance . . . constitue à elle seule tout un ordre métaphysique à part où viennent se rejoindre, transposées dans une même ligne qui est celle du connaître, à la fois la distinction de la forme essentielle et de l'existence dans la ligne de l'être, et celle de la forme opérative et de l'opération dans la ligne de l'action." (DS, p. 227/117).

[4] "Dagegen bleibt jede Philosophie, die sich im mittelbaren oder unmittelbaren Vorstellen der 'Transzendenz' bewegt, notwendig Ontologie im wesentlichen Sinn, mag sie eine Grundlegung der Ontologie bewerkstelligen oder mag sie die Ontologie der Versicherung nach als begriffliche Erstarrung des Erlebens zurückweisen." (WM:In, p. 21/219).

[5] "Das Wesen der Wahrheit erscheint der Metaphysik immer nur in der schon abkünftigen Gestalt der Wahrheit der Erkenntnis und der Aussage dieser." (WM:In, pp. 10-11/210).

[6] "Si saint Thomas, lorsqu'il parle du verbe mental et de sa distinction d'avec la chose, met ordinairement en cause la définition et l'énonciation plutôt que le simple concept, c'est justement qu'ici il y a quelque chose qui nous appartient tout à fait en propre, – la composition mentale, – qui rend cette distinction plus manifeste que ne le fait la simple différence d'état ou d'*esse* entre concept et objet." (DS, p. 787/395-6). Cf. *De veritate*, q. 3, art. 2: "Species (sc. impressa) qua intellectus informatur ut intelligat actu, est *primum quo* intelligitur; ex hoc autem quod est effectus in actu per talem formam operari jam potest formando quidditates rerum et componendo et dividendo; unde ipsa quidditas formata in intellectu, vel etiam compositio et divisio, est quoddam *operatum* ipsius, per quod tamen intellectus venit in cognitionem rei exterioris; et sic est quasi *secundum quo* intelligitur."

entry into a World of beings. Entry into a world is not a process of the entering being, but something that "happens to"[7] the being. And this happening is the existing of Dasein, which as existing transcends. Only when in the wholeness of being the being is "beingly" in the mode of the temporalizing of Dasein, is there the hour and the day of the entry of beings into World. And only when this primordial history, the transcendence, takes place, that is, when a being of the character of Being-in-the-World sets in among beings, is there the possibility of beings manifesting themselves.[8]

Yet it must be said that for all its rigor, Heidegger's *Denken des Seins* went astray from the very outset because reflexivity, though clearly recognized as such, was used as though it were primary (see Appendix II). "Only by way of what Heidegger I has thought does one gain access to what is to-be-thought by Heidegger II,"[9] because the phenomenological conception of method and the nature of phenomenological research are set forth only in the early writings; later ones presuppose the phenomenological stance, and work out more and more consistently the ineluctable consequences of such a stance integrally maintained. Thus it is in Phenomenology that the continuity of Heidegger's way is found, in denial of the adequacy of entitative analysis to comprehend the Being of knowledge and awareness-possibility generally – "das Sein des Bewusstseins und des Selbstbewusstseins." The difference between the early and the later writings arises principally from the gradual elimination or suppression of distinctions and structures which had to presuppose act-potency analysis in a direct sense.

Sein und Zeit allowed the idea of an entitative order to provide a context (setting and structure) for exploring *Sein*, the order of *esse intentionale*, in its own terms. By basing his problematic on this particular way of distinguishing rather than the accustomed route of the substance-accident application of the act-potency categories, he set himself free from all questions of subjectivity at a single stroke; for *esse intentionale is* intersubjectivity: it is not a

---

   [7] "Mit ... geschieht" – "happens to" or "happens together with": the first possible translation is the more genial in the context of the early Heidegger; the second accords more that of Heidegger II.

   [8] "Seiendes, etwa die Natur im weitesten Sinne, könnte in keiner Weise offenbar werden, wenn es nicht *Gelegenheit* fände, in eine Welt einzugehen. Wir sprechen daher vom möglichen und gelegentlichen *Welteingang* des Seienden. Welteingang ist kein Vorgang am eingehenden Seienden, sondern etwas, das 'mit' dem Seienden 'geschieht'. Und dieses Geschehen ist das Existieren von Dasein, das als existierendes transzendiert. Nur wenn in der Allheit von Seiendem das Seiende 'seiender' wird in der Weise der Zeitigung von Dasein, ist Stunde und Tag des Welteingangs von Seiendem. Und nur wenn diese Urgeschichte, die Transzendenz, geschieht, d. h. wenn Seiendes vom Charakter des In-der-Welt-seins in das Seiende einbricht, besteht die Möglichkeit, dass Seiendes sich offenbart." (WG, p. 39).

   [9] "Nur von dem unter I Gedachten her wird zunächst das unter II zu Denkende zugänglich." (Heidegger's "Vorwort" to H:TPT, p. XXIII).

relation which isolated subjects ("substances") "enter into," but much rather an ontological state or condition equiprimordial with the entitative state or conditions constituting subjectivity. That is why Heidegger can say with literal intent: when we think of the Heidelberg bridge, we stand through the distance to the bridge.[10] Since the principle of identity is the fundamental structural principle of the entitative order as such, and since research directed into entitative structures as such must be guided immediately by the logical translation of that principle, namely, the principle of contradiction, Heidegger, based as he was on the *entitativum-intentionale* (ontic-ontological) distinction only in order to inquire directly into *intentionale* structures as such (existentialia), could at once declare himself "against logic"[11] and announce that no matter how extensively and intensively research into the entitative order is pursued, science will never find Being.[12]

The difficulty that eventually had to be accounted for (and for that simple acknowledgement is not a substitute) lay in the fact that the two orders are somehow necessarily linked in order for each to be itself: Being cannot *be* except in and for beings, so that if an analysis of beings as such cannot supply for an analysis of Being, no more can an analysis of Being as such supply for an adequate consideration of the beings. Any methodological conception, in short, preclusively proportioned to either the one or the other order (which is not quite the same as to be initially concerned more directly with, say, the entitative conditions of things) would eventually prove inadequate to the task of First Philosophy.

---

[10] "Wenn wir jetzt – wir alle – von hier aus an die alte Brücke in Heidelberg denken, dann ist das Hindenken zu jenem Ort kein blosses Erlebnis in den hier anwesenden Personen, vielmehr gehört es zum Wesen unseres Denkens *an* die genannte Brücke, dass dieses Denken *in sich* die Ferne zu diesem Ort *durchsteht*. Wir sind von hier aus bei der Brücke dort und nicht etwa bei einem Vorstellungsinhalt in unserem Bewusstsein. Wir können sogar von hier aus jener Brücke und dem, was sie einräumt, weit näher sein als jemand, der sie alltäglich als gleichgültigen Flussübergang benützt." (VA, p. 157).

[11] "Die Vorlesung entscheidet sich gegen die 'Logik'." (WM:Ep, p. 45/352). "Heidegger's criticism rests basically on the fact that 'logic' is necessarily concerned only with beings, '. . . for thinking is essentially thinking about something. . .' (WM, p. 28: 'Denn das Denken, das wesenhaft immer Denken von etwas ist,. . .'). Since Non-being is not a being, it cannot be encompassed by 'logic.' To wish to consider it by purely 'logical' thought processes is to doom oneself from the first moment to contradiction, for it is to make Non-being a being, sc. an object of 'logical' thought. . . Thus we are to conclude that 'logic' does not have the last word in metaphysics, which must, when all is said and done, be grounded in an experience which is pre-, or at least praeter-, 'logical' (see WM, pp. 30, 36-7)." (Richardson, H:TPT, pp. 204-5). "All that Heidegger insists upon is that prior to the laws of logic (or, for that matter, of ethics) there is a law of Being which first intimates to man the pattern of arrangement that subsequently can be transformed into the laws of human thought and activity." (H:TPT, p. 549). See also pp. 176, 178, 250, 284, 386.

[12] WM: Ep, p. 45/353. Cf. preceding footnote.

Heidegger has stepped out of act-potency metaphysics to which belong man as *animal rationale* and *veritas* as *conformitas*. But he does not deny that something *Richtiges* can be said about *animal rationale*[13] or that the declarations of Physics be *richtig*;[14] and this *richtig* is plainly *veritas* as *conformitas*.[15] And Heidegger sees the all but insurpassable "*Groteske*" in the view that his efforts seek to destroy Metaphysics.[16] Thus it seems that his thought should not be interpreted as an encompassing account of well-founded thought. Types of thought [including obviously the Metaphysics tied up with the notion of "rational animal"] remain that Heidegger's way of thinking does not explain.[17]

And the problem which Heideggerean philosophy (or, alternatively, integral Phenomenology) proves incapable of solving is not at all, as Sartre thought, one of passing from the ontological to the ontic level in Dasein – since, as Richardson and Biemel point out, and as we have seen for ourselves, it is impossible to disjoin them in the first place; the problem is to *maintain their distinction* within the "unity" or wholeness of Dasein. Phenomenology fails in this precisely because the discernment of distinct dimensions that are identical is a prerogative of Metaphysics, that is, of an avowedly *actus et potentia, capacitas et perfectio* analysis, and not at all of properly phenomenological considerations, inasmuch as the recognition of a whole with really distinct dimensions, that is, of an *unum per se*, is the central conclusion, pivotal reference and guiding insight of act-potency analysis. Defaulting this discernment by reason of its principled constrainment to the *intentionale* side of the *entitativum-intentionale* distinction – a constrainment which full fidelity to the phenomenological research-principle must in the end render absolute in the sense that by virtue of it what is most formal and proper to the entitative order is ruled out of consideration, literally lies below the horizon of the phenomenological problematic – Phenomenology must abandon its claim to adequate the aboriginal questioning of Being with which philosophy began, or fall into a kind of reverse inauthenticity since it can not of itself consistently recognize let alone render account of the ontic features as such of Dasein (according to which it has the secondary fundamental features of particularity and mineness) as distinct from the ontological features. Thus:

[13] HB, p. 66/277.
[14] VA, p. 168.
[15] WW, p. 8.
[16] "Das Groteske ist kaum mehr zu überbieten, dass man meine Denkversuche als Zertrümmerung der Metaphysik ausruft und sich gleichzeitig mit Hilfe jener Versuche auf Denkwegen und in Vorstellungen aufhält, die man jener angeblichen Zertrümmerung entnommen – ich sage nicht, zu verdanken – hat. Es braucht hier keinen Dank, aber eine Besinnung." (SF, p. 92).
[17] Powell, "The Late Heidegger's Omission of the Ontic-Ontological Structure of Dasein," p. 11. (Cf. p. 125 of printed version).

When Heidegger says *Dasein* is not a subject he does not thereby foreclose all study of subjects. On the contrary, Heidegger's fundamental experience finds various subjects, and each one differs in a unique way. Subjects differ by *falling out of the light of Being*: "Plants and animals are never in the light of Being."[18] "They hang worldless in their environment."[19] World, of course, is Being-meaning. But man, in so far as he is a rational animal and is still fundamentally an animal,[20] also hangs "worldless" in his environment and never enters into the light of Being. This simply means that *subjects as subjects are independent of the fate of Being-meaning*.[21]

No one who has successfully held fast the lines of our analysis can dispute the conclusions of Ralph Powell: "Given Heidegger's criteria, metaphysics seems to have withstood its attempted destruction,"[22] and "those who accept Heidegger's back step out of act-potency, but who are not willing to remain in a purely historical meaning to man and his world, bear the whole burden of the return back step"[23] (i.e., bear the whole burden of indicating an alternative method for discerning transcultural elements in human thought and commitment).

[18] HB, p. 70/279.

[19] *Ibid.* Note how these statements of the later Heidegger contrast strikingly with the texts from the early Heidegger cited in Ch. VI (cf. esp. p. 85, fn. 20). For the latter, "it remains a problem in itself to define ontologically. . . how and where the Being of animals, for instance, is constituted by some kind of 'time'." (SZ, p. 346; cf. pp. 55, 97). For the former, the matter has become simpler, and for reasons which are no longer obscure: if the entitative and intentional are indeed two distinct and mutually irreducible orders or kinds of existence, one could only be surprised if preclusive consideration of either at the expense of the other did not lead to a corresponding simplification. That this particular simplification intrinsically implicates distortion as well is of course exactly the problem.

[20] *Ibid.*, p. 66/277.

[21] Powell, "Has Heidegger Destroyed Metaphysics?", p. 59. See remarks in fn. 19 above.

[22] *Ibid.*

[23] Powell, "The Late Heidegger's Omission of the Ontic-Ontological Structure of Dasein," p. 22 (Cf. p. 137 of printed version).

POSTSCRIPT

A NOTE ON THE GENESIS AND IMPLICATIONS OF THIS STUDY

Perhaps the best "Preface" to this study could have been taken from the substance of a letter dated September 20, 1966, which Heidegger addressed to Dr. Schrynemakers as Chairman of the Heidegger Symposium sponsored by the Philosophy Department of Duquesne University in Pittsburgh, October 15-16, 1966. In that letter Heidegger submitted, among others, the following questions which, as a matter of fact, have formed the central considerations of the preceding study:

1. Has the question posed in *Sein und Zeit* about the "meaning of Being" (as Being) been at all treated as a question?
2. If so, in what way and by reference to what has this question been discussed?
3. Have the critics ever asked whether the question posed is possible or impossible?
4. What do the answers to the above questions contribute to the characterization of the relationship in which Heidegger's thinking stands to the tradition of Western philosophy?
5. Where are the bounds of the questioning in *Sein und Zeit*?[1]

These last two questions particularly express the central thrust in the preceding analyses – and so much so indeed that we may say it has been our main intention to determine the bounds of the questioning in *Sein und Zeit* precisely by characterizing carefully and unmistakably the authentic relation which obtains between Heidegger's thinking and the tradition of scholastic philosophy which, extending as it does from Aristotle via the Arab Commentators through Boethius, Aquinas, Descartes, Kant, and Hegel into our own day, most nearly adequates the necessarily imprecise notion of "traditional

---

[1] "Ist überhaupt die in 'Sein und Zeit' gestellte Frage nach dem 'Sinn von Sein' (als Sein) als Frage aufgenommen? Wenn ja, in welcher Weise wurde die Frage und nach welchen Hinsichten erörtert? Hat die Kritik jemals gefragt, ob die gestellte Frage möglich oder unmöglich ist? Was ergibt sich aus der Beantwortung der jetzt genannten Fragen für die Kennzeichnung des Verhältnisses, in dem Heidegger's Denken zur Überlieferung der abendländischen Philosophie steht?

"Wo liegen die Grenzen der Fragestellung in 'Sein und Zeit'?"

Western philosophy". This may seem a pretentious claim to stake regarding a thought as complex and "unique" as Heidegger's is generally taken to be. The reader must decide on this for himself, of course: but we may at least expect him to postpone his judgment until he has mastered the pages which have been presented as bearing this claim out.

Within the great scholastic mainstream I have (for reasons documented, so far as the notion of *esse intentionale* is concerned, elsewhere[2]) navigated principally according to the flow of the Thomistic current. In fact, a reader acquainted with only this final version of my manuscript might well be disposed to consider that my work took its principal inspiration from the writings of Jacques Maritain. Such an impression, while understandable, would be altogether mistaken. The core and original direction of my Interpretation of the Heideggerean *corpus* were set, to tell the truth, in a lengthy seminar paper dated March 15, 1966, at which time not one of the major Maritain texts cited so frequently in this study had yet been read. Already in that seminar study the conviction had been reached *that* "esse intentionale" indicated the area in which the Heideggerean movement of thought intersects with the traditional (Thomistic) one. But *what* this "esse intentionale" (and therewith "Sein") meant, what the term signified and the reality in itself therefore was – for this decisive understanding I gladly acknowledge my full debt to the contemporary master, perhaps the greatest of living philosophers, Jacques Maritain.

However, at that seminar stage of the writing, I was anxious to secure an authoritative criticism of my understanding of Heidegger from beyond the small seminar circle within which it had first taken a definite form. Such a critique was most graciously provided by no less a Heidegger scholar than William J. Richardson.

In critiquing that original seminar paper which provided the core for the present analysis, Fr. Richardson wrote me as follows:

My chief difficulty. . . consists in my inability to see the cogency of your argument that Heidegger's Being is nothing more than the *esse* (pp. 11, 27) or *ens* (Appendix) of *esse intentionale*. To begin with, I am not at all sure what you mean by this, for a wave of the hand away from Husserl and toward Maritain is not quite enough to supply apodictic evidence to a jaded old mind like my own.

Furthermore, even if I do understand what you mean, I would be more willing to concede that 'Being-as-it-is-in-the-intellect' is probably the closest approximation in Thomistic terms to what Heidegger is talking about than I would that the two problematics are one.

[2] John N. Deely, "The Immateriality of the Intentional as Such", *The New Scholasticism*, XLII (Spring, 1968), pp. 243-306.

(Here Fr. Richardson is referring to a lengthy textual citation from a book by
Ralph Powell which was one of the central concluding observations of the
seminar paper but which in the present study has been retained only as a
footnote on the text, specifically, fn. 64 of Chapter VII.)

One could develop the point at length, but in a word, let me say that I think this
conception fails to take account of the 'mittent' Character of Being as it emerges in
Heidegger II, hence neglects both its temporal and historical character. In a Heideggerean perspective, this is a serious matter.

   Correspondingly, it seems to me that you intellectualize *Dasein* especially by
giving too much weight to the Macquarrie-Robinson translation of *Verstehen* as
'understanding' (hence *Verständigkeit* as 'intelligibility').[3]

In a general way, the entire recasting of the lines of original argument and
extensive study of Maritain's major texts which this present investigation represents is a coming to terms with Fr. Richardson's "chief difficulty" and its
corollary; but in particular two points may be made with reference to the
detailed study that has just been completed.

   First of all, as regards the temporal character of *ens quod est intra animam*
(which, it should have become plain, is not the simple equivalent of Powell's
intellectualized "Being-as-it-is-in-our-intellect"), the reader is referred back
to Chapter X above, esp. pp. 160-61.[4] Secondly, as regards the historical r
"mittent" character of such "Being of beings" "as it emerges in Heidegger
II," it is undeniable that so far as Thomistic thought is concerned, Heidegger is caught in a profound confusion as to what is meant by saying
that "Being provides the Problem Area of possible investigation for Metaphysics." It is on this second point that some indications must be given over
and above anything that has been suggested in the preceding study.

   Much of the confusion over the subject of Metaphysics among contemporary philosophers, it has been observed,[5] stems from a tendency to equi-
valate our primordial and *semper concomitans* awareness of "Being" with
the notion of being which provides a proper subject for formally metaphysical inquiry. In numerous passages, and in particular with his thematization
of the "preontological comprehension of Being",[6] Heidegger contributes to

   [3] Personal letter of August 1, 1966.
   [4] See also fn. 11 of Chapter VIII above.
   [5] See Anthony Schillaci, *Separation: Starting Point of Metaphysics* (Rome: International Pontifical Athenaeum "Angelicum", unpublished doctoral dissertation, 1961), pp.
451-4. A compressed expression of this important but relatively inaccessible work is
available in the article by John N. Deely, "Finitude, Negativity, and Transcendence: The
Problematic of Metaphysical Knowledge," *Philosophy Today*, XI (Fall, 1967), pp. 184-206.
The observation is also made in the course of Jacques Maritain's *A Preface to Metaphysics*
(New York: Mentor-Omega, 1962).
   [6] SZ, p. 15.

the confusion over this point. For *ens ut primum cognitum stricte consider-atum* is not even quite *ens quod est intra* as contradistinguished from *ens quod est extra animam*, but the *vita intentionalis* (as lived prior to any possible opposition of *esse entitativum* to *esse intentionale*) wherein man "on the way" to reflexive awareness and conscious selfhood (*sui-apprehensio in actu signato*) from the outset dwells. Yet it is certainly something very much like this (indistinguishable from it, in fact) which Heidegger conceives to be the ground of Metaphysics *as such*; and it is doubtless this that Heidegger takes to be the "being" which Metaphysics ought (a structural ought, that is) to be directly and immediately concerned with as with its proper and proximate ground:

Going beyond beings pertains to the essence of Dasein. But this "going beyond" is Metaphysics itself. That is why Metaphysics belongs to human nature. It is neither a department of scholastic philosophy nor a field of chance ideas. Metaphysics is the fundamental happening, the "ground phenomenon," of Dasein. It is Dasien itself... We cannot at all transfer ourselves into Metaphysics because insofar as we exist we already stand within it.[7]

Small wonder that Heidegger in later writings comes to regard the "grounding" of Metaphysics, as he sought from the first to accomplish it, as being after all a "passing out of" and "leaving behind of" Metaphysics! In fact, that is exactly the case; but for reasons very different than those which Heidegger himself seems inclined to assign. For Heidegger does indeed emerge from the current (and long-standing) confusion as to the "being" of Metaphysics in which he began – but he does not emerge on the shore of St. Thomas' carefully precised *ens commune* which, as the subject of Metaphysics, is explicitly equivalated with *ens inquantum ens, ens finitum, ens ut sic*; and is as carefully distinguished against *ens transcendentale* at one end of the scale as it is against *ens primum cognitum* at the other.[8] Rather does Heidegger emerge on the side of *ens primum cognitum stricte consideratum*, – and this by virtue of intrinsic methodological necessity (see Chapter IX above).[9]

[7] "Das Hinausgehen über das Seiende geschieht im Wesen des Daseins. Dieses Hinausgehen aber ist die Metaphysik selbst. Darin liegt: Die Metaphysik gehört zur 'Natur des Menschen'. Sie ist weder ein Fach der Schulphilosophie, noch ein Feld willkürlicher Einfälle. Die Metaphysik ist das Grundgeschehen im Dasein. Sie ist das Dasein selbst.
"...Wir können uns gar nicht in sie versetzen, weil wir – sofern wir existieren – schon immer in ihr stehen." (WM, p. 41/348). To mention an observation Maritain once made: "You can see how dangerous it would be to confuse these two phases, these two states, and to imagine... that... the metaphysical habitus is specified by being as it is primarily attained by our intellect." (*A Preface to Metaphysics*, p. 26).
[8] See John N. Deely, "Finitude, Negativity, and Transcendence," esp. pp. 194-5, 202-4. Schillaci, *op. cit.*, pp. 454-9, also p. 436. St. Thomas, *In Met.*, IV, lect. 1, n. 534; XI, lect. 3, nn. 2194 and 2203; lect. 7, n. 2259; *Summa contra gentiles*, I, ch. 26, n. 5.
[9] Also Richardson, H:TPT, pp. 14-15, 273 fn. 38, 623.

On this score, Heidegger's laborious analyses develop seminal insights which to tell the truth were hinted by Aristotle[10] and mentioned too by Aquinas after him;[11] and the maturation of these insights thanks to Heidegger makes no small (even though *per accidens*) contribution in its effective establishment, or, better, *exemplification*, of the impossibility of founding ontological inquiry critically conceived on the *primum cognitum* as such.[12] But certainly nothing is determined thereby either for or against the possibility of a Metaphysics in the authentic Thomistic sense.

We can say moreover that Heidegger's claim that "present-ative" or "representational" thinking is "a type of thinking that is intrinsic to metaphysics as such"[13] is an inevitable consequence of any clarification of this initial confusion over the nature of Metaphysics achieved by keeping strictly, i.e., methodologically or "in principle", to the *primum cognitum* which (Maréchalian thinkers notwithstanding[14]) is not a facultied access to the "intelligibility" of the sensible world opening unto an infinite or "transcendental" horizon. In short, the "being" of Metaphysics is not at all to be found in any radicalization of the comprehension of Being that underlies everydayness (that would lead in the end not to *das Sein des Seienden* under its proper aspect but to the *anima intellectiva seu spiritualis radicaliter sumpta*, i.e., to that *intellectus agens* which is not at all the faculty of reason, *Vernunft*, in the classical sense[15]), but must be sought in an entirely different direction, "an entirely different phase in the process of human intellection."[16]

[10] See *Metaphysica*, IV, ch. 10, 1005a30-1005b; XII, ch. 7, 1072a18-20; ch. 10, 1075b25-6.
[11] See esp. *In IV Met.*, lect. 5, n. 593.
[12] Cf. Richardson, H:TPT, pp. 15, 205, 382, 534, *et alibi*. Also John N. Deely, "Finitude, Negativity, and Transcendence."
[13] Richardson, H:TPT, p. 18 fn. 46. To the contrary, see Deely, "Finitude, Negativity, and Transcendence," esp. pp. 186, fn. 6 p. 199, fn. 26 pp. 202-3; and see particularly Jacques Maritain, *An Introduction to Philosophy*, trans. E. I. Watkin (newly designed ed.; New York: Sheed & Ward, 1962), Part II, Chs. II and III, pp. 107-9 and 120-5, respec.
[14] Cf. fn. 70 of Chapter IV above.
[15] See Chapter IV above, esp. 57-61, and Chapter VII, pp. 95-97. Also Maritain, CI, p. 4: "I use the words intellect and reason as synonymous, in so far as they designate a single power or faculty in the human soul. But I want to emphasize, from the start, that the very words reason or intellect... must be understood in a much deeper and larger sense than is usual. The intellect, as well as the imagination, is at the core of poetry. But reason, or the intellect, is not merely logical reason; it involves an exceedingly more profound – and more obscure – life, which is revealed to us in proportion as we endeavor to penetrate the hidden recesses of poetic activity. In other words, poetry [as also history and culture] obliges us to consider the intellect both in its secret wellsprings inside the human soul and as functioning in a nonrational (I do not say antirational) or nonlogical way." (On this last point, cf. Deely, "Finitude, Negativity, and Transcendence," fn. 26 p. 202.)
[16] Maritain, *A Preface to Metaphysics*, p. 26.

The real contribution of Heidegger to the progress of philosophy, in short, is not to be found in the area of Metaphysics' foundations so much as in having brought into view the inescapable consequences of any integrally maintained phenomenological ontology. The "bounds of the questioning" in *Sein und Zeit* are the limits of Phenomenology itself, and the way from the early to the later Heidegger is the way to the realization of those limits as virtual to the phenomenological research-principle, "zu den Sachen selbst," faithfully applied. "Let it suffice to say that in disengaging the sense of foundational thought, we delineate Heidegger's conception of philosophy as well."[17]

Such in broad strokes are the decisive contentions emerging from our study. We must include among them the crucial realization to which Heidegger forces philosophy, namely, the realization that the order or level of *esse intentionale* constitutes unto itself a sphere apart, in the sense of being formally, if not materially, irreducible to any treatment of being in terms of substance-accident; for, by securing this realization in a thematic way, Heidegger opens the way for a properly philosophical, that is, ontological, consideration of the decisive formalities of historical, cultural, social, and personal data which are primarily intentional, that is *inter*subjective, and only derivatively or "secondarily" subjective, that is, entitative.[18] "Foundational thought. . . therefore is a profoundly historical thought."[19]

[17] Richardson, H:TPT, p. 24.

[18] See esp. Chapters V and VI above. Thus even as thorough a study as Krempel's massive *La doctrine de la relation chez saint Thomas* (Paris: Vrin, 1952) seems never to have come to terms with what is formally constitutive in the notion of *esse intentionale* – e.g., see p. 617.

[19] Richardson, H:TPT, p. 21.

THE THOUGHT OF BEING AND THEOLOGY

> "Heidegger indeed says that philosophy can be no sub-
> stitute for theology, but he also maintains that if theology
> is to attain to conceptual clarity, it must have regard to
> those existential structures which are exhibited in *Sein und
> Zeit*. For in so far as theology has to do with man in his
> temporal and historical existence, it treats of themes which
> must be studied existentially. In particular, Heidegger be-
> lieves that the existential analytic provides for the in-
> vestigation of history in a way which directs attention not
> to the reconstruction of past facts but to the elucidation of
> repeatable possibilities of authentic existence; and . . . it
> is this approach which Bultmann, in his demythologiz-
> ing project, applies to the historical element in Christian-
> ity."
> John Macquarrie, *Twentieth Century Religious Thought*,
> pp. 355-356.

But what in all that has been said in these pages bears any possible direct
import for theology? Precisely, as Professor Macquarrie's comments suggest,
the central notion of Dasein, the Intentional Life of Man. We have already
had occasion to cite and agree with the young Heidegger's observation that
"Dasein's ontico-ontological priority was seen quite early, though Dasein itself was not grasped in its genuine ontological structure, and did not even become a problem in which this structure was sought."[1] Now it seems to us
that herein perhaps the root of the dilemma of contemporary theology over
the question of "original sin" (and therewith the larger and simply funda-

---

[1] See in this study Chapter VII, p. 88 ad fn. 1. In fact, it is this want of any thematic
consideration of the "non sunt idem" in St. Thomas' "intelligere et esse non sunt idem
apud nos" that gives the truest sense to Dondeyne's observation: "Si on peut parler ici
d'oubli (*Seinsvergessenheit*), c'est en ce sens seulement que dans la métaphysique tradi-
tionelle la différence ontologique n'a pas été suffisamment thématisée, prise pour thème
explicite des méditations, ce qui, au dire de Heidegger, a conduit à la confusion de l'être et
de l'étant. . ." (*Art. cit.*, p. 49). Need we state again that "l'être et l'étant" cannot be read
legitimately as "esse et essentia"??

mental problematic of the "life of grace") waits to be uncovered. To begin with, Heidegger himself gives explicit indications along this line:

Through the ontological interpretation of Dasein as Being-in-the-World, nothing is decided either positively or negatively about a possible Being-towards-God. But indeed through the elucidation of Transcendence, an *adequate concept* of *Dasein* was attained for the first time, with respect to which being it can now be *asked* how the God-relation of Dasein is ontologically constituted. [2]

But quite apart from this direct reference, we do not wish to bring our own study to completion without remarking a most remarkable point, the significance of which we are not prepared to even attempt to estimate. For, to tell the truth, the analysis at this point demands a skill and technical training well beyond the competence of a straightforward philosopher.

True as Heidegger's claim to problematic originality is, so far as Thomistic thought is for the most part concerned, the *ens* of *esse intentionale* was made the key consideration for not only one quite limited phase of Critica (i.e., in philosophy), but in at least one area of Thomistic theology as well, namely, the problem of the sense in which grace may be said to make us gods by participation, *consortes divinae naturae* (II Peter, 1, 4). The answer of scholastic theology on this question is perhaps more pregnant with significance for understanding and explaining the nature of Sacred Scripture (revelation, inspiration, etc.) and the relation of nature to grace, the distinction between the natural and supernatural orders which is at the very heart of the Christian faith – more pregnant with theological implication and intelligibility, in short, than has to now been realized. How can man receive a communication of what properly belongs to God alone? How, that is to say, can a finite subject of existence formally, i.e., physically and literally, participate in the nature of the infinite *Ipsum Esse Subsistens*?

Thomists give the answer: the soul is thus rendered infinite in the order of its *relation to the object*. A formal participation in Deity, which would be impossible were it a question of having Deity for its essence (for it is a pure absurdity that that which is not God should receive as its essence the very essence of God), is possible if it is a matter of having Deity as object. [3]

[2] "Durch die ontologische Interpretation des Daseins als In-der-Welt-sein ist weder positiv noch negativ über ein mögliches Sein zu Gott entschieden. Wohl aber wird durch die Erhellung der Transzendenz allererst ein *zureichender Begriff* des *Daseins* gewonnen, mit Rücksicht auf welches Seiende nunmehr *gefragt* werden kann, wie es mit dem Gottesverhältnis des Daseins ontologisch bestellt ist." (WG, p. 39 fn. 56).

[3] "Les thomistes répondent: C'est dans l'ordre de la *relation à l'objet* que l'âme est ainsi infinitisée. Une participation formelle de la déité qui serait impossible s'il s'agissait d'avoir la déité pour essence (que ce qui n'est pas Dieu reçoive pour essence l'essence même de Dieu, c'est absurdité pure), est possible s'il s'agit d'avoir la déité pour objet." (DS, p. 504/254).

Without slightest shadow of pantheism (and this precisely because the whole character of *intentionale* is specified by existence in other than the entitative mode), "by vision, the creature becomes the true God Himself, *not in the order of substance, but in the order of that immaterial union which constitutes the intellectual act*"[4] – not in the order that is to say, of the entitative, but in the order alone of *esse intentionale*. "That is how grace, while leaving us infinitely distant from pure Act (in the order of [entitative] being), is still (in the order of spiritual operation and relation to its object [therefore intentional being]) a formal participation in the Divine Nature."[5] Moreover, "there is nothing metaphorical in this, nothing merely moral: it is a 'physical' reality, as the theologians say, that is, an ontological reality, all that is most positive and effective, the most solid of all realities."[6] On this difficult topic, the following texts are classical: John of St. Thomas, *Cursus Theol.*, I-II, q. 72, disp. 17, a. 3, n. 28; q. 110, disp. 22, a. 1 (Vivès, t. VI, pp. 564 and 790ff., respectively; I P., q. 58, disp. 22, a. 3 (Vives, t. IV); St. Thomas Aquinas, *In I Sent.*, dist. 14, qq. 1 and 2; *Summa theol.*, I, q. 43. Consult also the remarkable work, classical for the modern context, by Francis L. B. Cunningham, *The Indwelling of the Trinity*, e.g., p. 323: "A purely assimilative union on the ontological plane (as distinguished from the intentional) cannot explain this new presence which specifies the mystery, since on that level man is not united to God Himself but only to a similitude of Him."

We are not trying to push a point too far. There is no question here of attempting to introduce a slightest confusion between the intellectuality we have by nature and that which we have by grace, for we are not blurring the formal objects which distinctively specify each in its own order. What seems to us needful of consideration anew in this area is simply the mode of *esse intentionale* which, according to what is proper to it, establishes that irreducible order or mode of things through which God makes it possible for man to come to Him. And we ask too about the possibility of applying a concept which theology has found so useful in securing an understanding of our supernatural destiny to a problem concerning which theology still seeks to secure an understanding and which precisely is crucial to the nature

---

[4] "...par la vision la créature devient le vrai Dieu lui-même, mais dans l'ordre de l'immatérielle union qui fait l'acte intellectuel, non dans l'ordre de la substance." (DS, p. 504/255).

[5] "Voilà comment la grâce, tout en nous laissant, – dans l'ordre de l'être, – infiniment distants de l'Acte pur, est dans l'ordre des opérations spirituelles et de la relation à l'objet une participation formelle de la nature divine." (DS, pp. 506-7/255).

[6] "Rien de métaphorique ici, rien de simplement moral: une réalité 'physique' comme disent les théologiens, c'est-à-dire ontologique, tout ce qu'il y a de plus positive et efficiente, la plus solide des réalités." (DS, p. 506/255).

of our supernatural origin, so to say, namely, the problem of grace and "original justice" or "sin".

Perhaps such an attempt calls for nothing less than a thorough rethinking of the nature of grace itself and the manner and modes according to which it is at work in the human spirit. The initial perspective would displace emphasis on any concern with grace as an entitative habit inhering statically in the essence of the soul (since accidental modification of a subject is but a condition for the entitative order *implied by* – therefore secondary with respect to – all finite awareness), focussing rather on what is directly primary, namely on grace as a *relation* to divine realities, and in the pure line of awareness-possibility (*intentionale*), in which respect it would not be in the soul as in a subject in the entitative sense of the word "in".[7] And we show intrinsic methodological cause for suggesting this displacement of emphasis.

Undoubtedly, the sharing in the intimate and proper life of God enjoyed by the graced soul involves a problem of relationship between God and the intellectual (taken here in the root sense) creature.

From this aspect, since predicamental relations are specified by their fundament considered in relation to their terms (as John of St. Thomas has explained[8]), the problem would consist first of all in the proper determination of the *term* implied by this new presence [of God in and to the graced soul] (. . .) and only after this in the specification of the fundament [in this case, the entitative consequences of this presence through grace] – even though in this fundament the formal reason of the new relation would be found.[9]

It is the localization of the term, in short, which properly specifies and determines the problematic in question. "Once the term in question is specified, however, the true formal explanation remains to be found"[10] – and that may be better achieved through existentialistic rather than categorial analysis.

In any event, we suggest, it is here that Heideggerean thought may be of service to theology, and not in hopelessly clouded efforts to link up the *Sein* of Heidegger with the *esse naturae* of Thomas, and still less in the effort to somehow identify *Sein* with *Esse Per Se Subsistens*, or (à la Löwith), to link its import with the "Christian revelation of God who too is not a being" (i.e., *Seiende*).[11]

[7] Cf. DS, p. 165 fn. 1/85 fn. 2.

[8] *Cursus Phil.*, Logica, II, q. 17, art. 6 (ed. Reiser, I, pp. 602-3).

[9] Francis L. B. Cunningham, *The Indwelling of the Trinity* (Dubuque: The Priory Press, 1955), p. 10. See Leo von Rudloff, "Des heiligen Thomas Lehre von der Formalursache der Einwohnung Gottes in der Seele der Gerechten," *Divus Thomas* (Fr.), 1930, pp. 181-2.

[10] *Ibid.*

[11] According to Löwith in his book, *Heidegger. Denker in dürftiger Zeit* (2nd ed.; Göttingen: Vandenhoeck und Ruprecht, 1960), p. 20, no one can honestly claim to under-

stand what Heidegger means by "Being" (*Sein*), but "those who will come nearest to understanding it are believers, who think they find in Heidegger's ontological talk of 'revelation' and 'unveiling' an access to the Christian revelation of a God who too is not a being – believers who as such do not pretend to comprehend with the reason the God of revelation." It was such statements as this by theologians that I had expressly in mind when I mentioned the discussions of *The Later Heidegger and Theology* in Chapter 1 of the present book. (J. M. Robinson, co-editor of *The Later Heidegger and Theology*, cites the above view of Löwith with apparent approbation on p. 13, fn. 37.)

APPENDIX II

METAPHYSICS AND THE THOUGHT OF
M. HEIDEGGER

[Si on songe] à dresser en un corps de doctrine spécial la
partie réflexive et critique de la méthaphysique, [on laisse]
ainsi comme en friche de vastes régions du savoir. ///
C'est pourquoi . . . nous pensons . . . que ce qu'il y a à
retenir – après décantation – de la phénoménologie et des
"decouvertes" dont elle se fait gloire ressortit seulement à
la partie réflexive et critique de la philosophie.
Jacques Maritain, *Les degrés du savoir*, pp. 161/83 and
196 fn. 2/101 fn. 3.

One would think that in assessing the thought of Martin Heidegger relative
to the problem of a critically departured or "founded" Metaphysics, care
would be taken to understand first of all just how Heidegger conceives the
structure of Metaphysics, since only then will one be able to decide what the
"phenomenological destruction of Western ontology" in fact could overcome. Again, it is a matter of the "limits of the questioning" in *Sein und Zeit*.

As Heidegger conceived them, "ontology and phenomenology are not two
distinct philosophical disciplines among others. These terms characterize
philosophy itself with regard to its object and its way of treating that object.
Philosophy," in short, by its proper name (for Heidegger), "is universal
phenomenological ontology";[1] and Phenomenology begins only with a
certain "reflective turn of sight" carefully characterized and understood.

It strikes us as odd to say the least that such texts have not been permitted
to achieve what their sense plainly requires: here, in the very *status quaestionis*
of Heidegger's major writing, the "Thought of Being" is identified with
what we have called with Maritain "the mind's second movement."[2] But

---

[1] "Philosophie ist universale phänomenologische Ontologie, ausgehend von der Hermeneutik des Daseins, die als Analytik der *Existenz* das Ende des Leitfadens alles philosophischen Fragens dort festgemacht hat, woraus es *entspringt* und wohin es zurückschlägt."
(SZ, p. 38). See also p. 61.

[2] DS, pp. 147-9/76-7. That is why the following remark made by Maritain with an eye
to E. Husserl's work applies with only incidental qualifications to M. Heidegger's work

this identification precisely dissociates Heidegger from the ground question
of Metaphysics as Aquinas conceived it since, for Aquinas, it was "the
mind's first movement" which provides "the starting point for philosophy as
a whole" including – and indeed principally-Metaphysics:[3] what is at stake is
a recognition of the primacy of nature over reflection. All that we remark
here would have to be returned to in a proper study and treated in depth if
possible objections were to be adequately accounted for. For the present
context however it is sufficient to establish on the basis of all that has been
said to now liminal observations, though it must be made absolutely clear in
this regard that while it must be recognized that the whole weight of Heidegger's philosophizing rests on the mind's second movement (and every
word in Heidegger's exposition of the notion of Phenomenology proclaims
this point) which in Thomism has properly been the starting point of *Critica*
and never of Metaphysics proper, it would be a gross error to locate Heidegger's Being within the perspective of what has to now been the preoccupation of epistemology relative to Metaphysics.[4] This is equally true of the
critical problem as Idealism has posed it ("How does one pass from *percipi*
to *esse*?"), and as Realism has posed it "(On the different levels of elabor-
ating knowledge, what value must be assigned to *percipere* and what to
judicare?"). For Heidegger (we have seen), the knowledge "validity" question conceptualizes Dasein in terms of a derivative and therefore deficient
or incommensurate modalization.[5] Not to see this is to miss entirely the
chasm which separates Heidegger from the artificially reinforced (by means

also: ". . .souci. . . de construire [read this verb now in the English sense of "to construe,"
i.e., to interpret or give a sense to] au sein d'un processus réflexif. . . c'est pourquoi la
phénoménologie est regardée par lui comme la philosophie elle-même, et comme rempla-
çant l'ancienne métaphysique et l' 'ontologie naïve'." (DS, p. 196 n. 2/101 n. 3).
[3] The point is made by Aquinas in forthright terms: "Postquam Philosophus removit a
principali consideratione huius scientiae ens per accidens et ens secundum quod significat
verum, hic incipit determinare de ente per se, *quod est extra animam*, de quo *est principalis
consideratio huius scientiae*." (*In VII Met.*, lect. 1, n. 1245). Even Lonergan, who himself
prefers to philosophize in the Marechalian style, recognizes this absolute primacy of
nature over reflection in the thought of St. Thomas: as a general rule, he writes, "in the
writings of St. Thomas, cognitional theory is expressed in metaphysical terms and established by metaphysical principles." – "Insight: Preface to a Discussion," in *Proceedings of
the American Catholic Philosophical Association*, Vol. XXXII (1958), p. 71. The accurate
conception of a critical starting point for Metaphysics in continuity with St. Thomas' larger
teaching on the nature of philosophical science has in my research nowhere been set forth
with anything like the clarity, (textual) comprehensiveness, and internal consistency
achieved by Anthony Schillaci in his study, *Separation: Starting Point of Metaphysics*
(Rome, 1961). It is an academic tragedy that this study has not appeared in print in a
complete form.
[4] E.g., cf. DS, pp. 170-75/88-9 and 246-8/127-8.
[5] Cf. SZ, pp. 61-2. Richardson, H:TPT, pp. 98, 178-9, 370, 420, *inter alia*.

of "brackets") philosophical position of Husserl. As far as this question of knowledge is considered in its historical perspective, we must say with Dondeyne that "la philosophie heideggerienne, comme remontée aux fondements et recherche de l'être, se situe dans le prolongement de la pensée *transcendentale* que Kant instaura."[6] But if we take this question of "knowledge" in philosophical perspective as a problem-area for ever deepening reflection and consider Heidegger in terms of his proper concerns as well as historical continuities, we must say rather: "C'est dans le prolongement de cette problématique *transcendentale*, inaugurée par Kant, que se situe, *à la manière d'une "Wiederholung"*, la noétique heideggerienne. Heidegger. . . approfondit et élargit cette problématique tout en la transposant dans une perspective nouvelle, qui est celle de la phénoménologie, entendue comme philosophie de la rencontre."[7]

How does Heidegger "deepen and enlarge" this noetic problematic? We have seen this in detail: "Heidegger shifts the emphasis from an investigation of man's reason (Kant) to an investigation of man in his totality,"[8] in view of the fact that "metaphysics thinks of man as arising from *animalitas* and does not think of him as pointing toward *humanitas*,"[9] i.e., historical ex-sistence.

Man in his totality, then: keeping in mind all the reservations that have been brought forward on this question of the relation between Dasein and man and Dasein and Being, let us precise the phrase. It means the focus of (problematic) emphasis as shifted by Heidegger away from pure reason (*Vernunft*) to its common origin with sense. "The decisive factor in Heidegger's Kant-interpretation is his analysis of the transcendental imagination. The acceptance or rejection of his reading depends on this and this

---

[6] Dondeyne, p. 269.

[7] *Ibid.*, p. 277.

[8] Richardson, H:TPT, p. 31. Cf. Churchill's "Introduction" to his translation of KM, p. xvii.

[9] "Die Metaphysik denkt den Menschen von der animalitas her und denkt nicht zu seiner humanitas hin." (HB, p. 66/277). "Das Wesen des Menschen besteht aber darin, dass er mehr ist als der blosse Mensch, insofern dieser als das vernünftige Lebewesen vorgestellt wird. 'Mehr' darf hier nicht additiv verstanden werden, als sollte die überlieferte Definition des Menschen zwar die Grundbestimmung bleiben, um dann nur durch einen Zusatz des Existenziellen eine Erweiterung zu erfahren. Das 'mehr' bedeutet: ursprünglicher und darum im Wesen wesentlicher. Aber hier zeigt sich das Rätselhafte: der Mensch ist in der Geworfenheit. Das sagt: der Mensch ist als der ek-sistierende Gegenwurf des Seins insofern mehr denn das animal rationale, als er gerade weniger ist im Verhältnis zum Menschen, der sich aus der Subjektivität begreift. Der Mensch ist nicht der Herr des Seienden. Der Mensch ist der Hirt des Seins." (HB, pp. 89-90/288). Cf. fn. 56 of Chapter IX in this study.

alone."[10] That is to say, "the transcendental imagination is the center of the entire man," and – here is the decisive point – "is equivalent to There-being," to Dasein.[11]

Heidegger changes the problem of (explicit and "conceptual") knowledge to the problem of awareness in its full complexity, though still with the emphasis on the a-priori. In this shifted emphasis,

It is capital to note that consciousness (therefore subjectivity) is, ontologically speaking, subsequent to the orientation (therefore transcendence) of the self which consciousness makes manifest. What is primary is the self, not as subject but as transcendence. That is why consciousness, ontologically subsequent, must be explained by something which is ontologically prior, sc. the Being of the self which consciousness manifests. To reverse the procedure – and here we may detect an undeniable, if unexpressed, polemic against the idealist – is to distort the whole problematic.[12]

Fr. Richardson insists that "any comparison between Heidegger and the idealists (Hegel in particular) must take full cognizance of the perspective suggested here."[13] Granting that, we must say three things.

First of all, Heidegger "transcends" realism and idealism only in the sense that he never reaches that stage of analysis where a decision between the two ways becomes inescapable and where alone, for St. Thomas, a critically departured Metaphysics becomes a possibility to be considered. In that sense, it is more accurate to say that he *subscends* rather than *transcends* the problem.[14] The *Denken des Seins* is more properly said to lie *before* (in a simple de facto rather than de jure sense) rather than *beyond* the rightly specified metaphysical problematic. It does not go *above* metaphysical thinking so much as lie *below* it, and *even below that negative-existential judgment which, as the foundation of Metaphysics, makes such thinking in the first* (adequate) *place possible.*[15] If there is a valid sense in which it may be said that Heidegger's thought marks a third way between realism and idealism, it is that sense suggested at the beginning of our study, specifically, Heidegger seeks to secure methodologically a precise circumscription in its totality of man's Intentional Life, and to that extent isolate the *full* noetic problematic as such, or, as we phrased it, "in its integrity and at its source."

---

[10] Richardson, H:TPT, pp. 121-2.

[11] *Ibid.*, pp. 153-4.

[12] *Ibid.*, p. 157.

[13] *Ibid.*, p. 122 fn. 48.

[14] A similar conclusion is reached by Ralph Powell: cf. "Has Heidegger Destroyed Metaphysics?", p. 59.

[15] See John N. Deely, "Finitude, Negativity, and Transcendence: The Problematic of Metaphysical Knowledge," *Philosophy Today*, XI (Fall, 1967).

Secondly, what Maritain wrote concerning Husserl must, when all enlargement and deepening (to say nothing of rectification) of perspectives is accounted for, be said of Heidegger as well: "What is to be retained of Phenomenology (after decanting it), and of the 'discoveries' in which it glories, belongs only to the reflexive and critical part of philosophy."[16] Though here it is to be noted at once that Heidegger has managed to achieve for philosophy something analogous to what Freud did for science, namely, render the unconscious and preconscious as well as the conscious levels of man's intentional life (including therefore social, cultural and – what in a certain way includes the others – historical existence) problematic and integral to any consideration of the human condition, particularly to any consideration of man as a "meta-physical" questioner. For the first time, philosophy can confront the out-standing task of taking systematic account of historical, social, cultural, and psychological determinisms as they affect all awareness.

And finally, while Heidegger himself remains so faithful to the inner restraints of his first intuition and subsequent methodological conception as to remain throughout his philosophizing anterior to the necessity of setting out upon one of the two (historically) possible metaphysical ways (realism/ idealism), it must be said that if idealism has as its common denominator "to mix a preoccupation for constructiveness with what is an affair of pure reflexivity (even though this preoccupation be not admitted and even be hidden beneath the appearances of methodical rigorousness); a preoccupation, at least, with making the setting up of philosophy depend on that reflexive enterprise as on its preamble, if not with making philosophy itself consist in that very step";[17] if this be allowed, then it must be said that Heidegger's deepest philosophical sympathies lie with Idealism.[18]

---

[16] "...ce qu'il y a à retenir – après décantation – de la phénoménologie et des 'découvertes' dont elle se fait gloire ressortit seulement à la partie réflexive et critique de la philosophie." (DS, pp. 196-7 fn. 2/101 fn. 3).

[17] "Il est essentiel en effet à tout idéalisme de mêler à une démarche de pure réflexivité un souci constructif, (si inavoué qu'il soit, si dissimulé sous des apparences de simple rigeur méthodique), – au moins le souci de faire dépendre de cette démarche comme préalable la constitution de la philosophie, sinon de faire consister la philosophie dans cette démarche elle-même." (DS, p. 145/75).

[18] E.g., SZ, p. 207: "Gegenüber dem Realismus hat der *Idealismus*, mag er im Resultat noch so entgegengesetzt und unhaltbar sein, einen grundsätzlichen Vorrang..."

SELECTED
BIBLIOGRAPHY

BOOKS

Adler, Mortimer J. *The Difference of Man and the Difference it Makes*. New York: Holt, Rinehart & Winston, 1967.

Aristotle. *The Basic Works of Aristotle*. Ed. Richard McKeon. New York: Random House, 1941.

Aquinas, Thomas. *In Librum Boetii de Trinitate Commentarium*. Ed. M. Calcaterra. Rome: Marietti (Opuscula Theologica II), 1954.

— *In Aristotelis Octos Libros Physicorum Expositio*. Ed. P. M. Maggiolo. Rome: Marietti, 1954.

— *In Aristotelis Tertios Libros de Anima Expositio*. Ed. A. M. Pirotta. Rome: Marietti, 1959.

— *In Aristotelis Duodecim Libros Metaphysicorum Expositio*. Ed. M.-R. Cathala and R. Spiazzi. Rome: Marietti, 1950.

— *Quaestiones Disputatae: De Veritate*. Ed. R. Spiazzi. Rome: Marietti, 1950.

— *Quaestiones Quodlibetales*. Ed. R. Spiazzi. Rome: Marietti, 1956.

— *Summa Contra Gentiles*. Ed. Leonina Manualis. Rome: Marietti, 1952.

— *Summa Theologica*. (Textus Leoninus) Rome: Marietti, 1952.

Bergson, Henri. *The Creative Mind*. Trans. by Mabelle L. Andison. New York: The Philosophical Library, 1946.

Biemel, Walter. *Le Concept de Monde Chez Heidegger*. Paris: Vrin, 1950.

Cajetan, Thomas de Vio. *Commentaria in summam theologicam* (textus Leoninus). Rome: Marietti, 1962.

Cobb, John B. and Robinson, James M., eds. *The Later Heidegger and Theology*. New York: Harper and Row, 1963.

Cunningham, Francis L. B. *The Indwelling of the Trinity*. Dubuque: The Priory Press, 1955.

Dilthey, Wilhelm. *The Essence of Philosophy*. Trans. by Stephen A. Emery and William T. Emery. Chapel Hill: University of North Carolina Press, 1954.

— *Pattern and Meaning in History*. Ed. H. P. Rickman. New York: Harper, 1961.

Gilson, Etienne. *L'Etre et l'essence*. Deuxieme ed.; Paris: Vrin, 1962.

— *The Philosopher and Theology*. Trans. by Cecile Gilson. New York: Random House, 1962.

Grene, Marjorie. *Martin Heidegger*. London: Bowes & Bowes, 1957.

Heidegger, Martin. "Brief über den Humanismus," in *Platons Lehre von der Wahrheit*. Bern: Francke Verlag, 1947.

— "Letter on Humanism." Trans. by Edgar Lohner in *Philosophy in the Twentieth Century*. Ed. by William Barrett and Henry D. Aiken. New York: Random House, 1962. Vol. III.

— *Die Kategorien- und Bedeutungslehre des Duns Scotus*. Doctoral dissertation of 1916.

— *Einführung in die Metaphysik*. Tübingen: Max Niemeyer Verlag, 1966.

— *An Introduction to Metaphysics*. Trans. by Ralph Manheim. New Haven, Conn.: Yale University Press, 1959.
— "Einleitung" to *Was ist Metaphysik*? 5th ed.; Frankfurt: Klostermann, 1949.
— "The Way Back into the Ground of Metaphysics," in *Existentialism from Dostoevsky to Sartre*. Trans. and ed. by Walter Kaufmann. New York: Meridian Books, 1956, pp. 206-221.
— *Gelassenheit*. Pfüllingen: Neske, 1959.
— *Discourse on Thinking*. Trans. by John M. Anderson and E. Hans Freund. New York: Harper and Row, 1966.
— *Holzwege*. Frankfurt: Klostermann, 1950.
— *Identität und Differenz*. Pfüllingen: Neske, 1957.
— *Essays in Metaphysics*. Trans. by Kurt F. Leidecker. New York: The Philosophical Library, 1960.
— *Kants These über das Sein*. Frankfurt: Klostermann, 1963.
— *Kant und das Problem der Metaphysik*. Frankfurt: Klostermann, 1951.
— *Kant and the Problem of Metaphysics*. Trans. by James S. Churchill. Bloomington: Indiana University Press, 1962.
— "Nachwort" to *Was ist Metaphysik*?
— "What is Metaphysics: Postscript." Trans. by R. F. C. Hull and Alan Crick in *Existence and Being*. Ed. Werner Brock. Chicago: Gateway, 1949, pp. 449-361.
— *Der Satz vom Grund*. Pfüllingen: Neske, 1957.
— *Sein und Zeit*. 8th ed.; Tübingen: Max Niemeyer Verlag, 1963.
— *Being and Time*. Trans. by John Macquarrie and Edward Robinson. New York: Harper and Row, 1962.
— *Unterwegs zur Sprache*. Pfüllingen: Neske, 1959.
— *Vom Wesen der Wahrheit*. Frankfurt: Klostermann, 1954.
— "On the Essence of Truth." Trans. by R. F. C. Hull and Alan Crick in *Existence and Being*, pp. 292-324.
— *Vom Wesen des Grundes*. Frankfurt: Klostermann, 1955.
— *Vorträge und Aufsätze*. Pfüllingen: Neske, 1954.
— *Was Heisst Denken*. Tübingen: Niemayer, 1954.
— *Was ist das – die Philosophie*? Pfüllingen: Neske Verlag, 1956.
— *What is Philosophy*? Bi-lingual ed. presented by Jean T. Wilde and William Kluback. New Haven, Conn.: College and University Press, 1956.
— *Was ist Metaphysik*? 5th ed.; Frankfurt: Klostermann, 1949.
— "What is Metaphysics?" Trans. by R. F. C. Hull and Alan Crick in *Existence and Being*, pp. 325-349.
— *Zur Seinsfrage*. Frankfurt. Klostermann, 1956.
— *The Question of Being*. Bi-lingual ed. presented by Jean T. Wilde and William Kluback. New Haven, Conn.: College and University Press, 1958.
Henry, Michel. *L'essence de la manifestation*. Paris: Presses Universitaires de France, 1964.
Husserl, Edmund. *The Phenomenology of Internal Time Consciousness*. Ed. by Martin Heidegger. Trans. by James S. Churchill. Bloomington: Indiana University Press, 1964.
John of St. Thomas. *Cursus Philosophicus Thomisticus*. Ed. B. Reiser. 3 Vols. Turin: Marietti, 1930.
— *Cursus Theologicus*. Paris: Tournai, 1931.

Kant, Immanuel. *Prolegomena to Any Future Metaphysics*. Ed. Lewis White Beck. New York: The Liberal Arts Press, 1950.

King, Magda. *Heidegger's Philosophy*. New York: Macmillan, 1964.

Klubertanz, George P. *Philosophy of Being*. New York: Appleton-Century-Crofts, 1955.

Lachance, L. *L'Etre et ses propriétés*. Montreal: Lévrier, 1950.

Langan, Thomas. *The Meaning of Heidegger*. New York: Columbia University Press, 1961.

Macquarrie, John. *An Existentialist Theology*. London: SCM Press, 1955.

— *Twentieth Century Religious Thought*. New York: Harper and Row, 1963.

Maritain, Jacques. *Creative Intuition in Art and Poetry*. New York: Pantheon Books, 1953.

— *Distinguer pour unir ou les degrés du savoir*. 7th ed.; Paris: Desclée de Brouwer, 1963.

— *The Degrees of Knowledge*. Trans. from the 4th French edition under the supervision of Gerald B. Phelan. New York: Charles Scribner's Sons, 1959.

— "Freudianism and Psychoanalysis," in *Scholasticism and Politics*. Trans. by Mortimer J. Adler. New York: Image Books, 1960, pp. 139-161.

— *A Preface to Metaphysics*. New York: Mentor-Omega, 1962.

— *The Range of Reason*. New York: Charles Scribner's Sons, 1952.

— *Réflexions sur l'intelligence*. Paris: Desclée de Brouwer, 1924.

— "Sign and Symbol," in *Redeeming the Time*. Trans. by Harry L. Binsse. London: The Centenary Press, 1943, pp. 191-224.

— *Theonas*. Trans. F. J. Sheed. New York: Sheed & Ward, 1933.

Menninger, Karl. *The Human Mind*. New York: Knopf, 1964.

Müller, Max. *Existenzphilosophie*. Heidelberg: Kerle, 1964.

Novalis. *Schriften*. Ed. by Kluckhohn. Leipzig: Bibliographisches Institut, n. d. Vol. III.

Peifer, John. *The Mystery of Knowledge*. New York: Magi Books, 1952.

Pöggeler, Otto. *Der Denkweg Martin Heideggers*. Pfüllingen: Neske, 1963.

Powell, Ralph Austin. *Truth or Absolute Nothing*. River Forest, Ill.: The Aquinas Library, 1952.

Ranly, Ernst W. *Scheler's Phenomenology of Community*. The Hague: Martinus Nijhoff, 1966.

Regis, L. M. *Epistemology*. Trans. by Imelda Choquette Byrne. New York: Mac-Millan, 1959.

Richardson, William J. *Heidegger: Through Phenomenology to Thought*. The Hague: Martinus Nijhoff, 1963.

Robinson, James M. and Cobb, John B., eds. *The Later Heidegger and Theology*. New York: Harper and Row, 1963.

Rover, Thomas D. *The Poetics of Maritain*. Washington: The Thomist Press, 1965.

Sartre, Jean-Paul. *Being and Nothingness*. Trans. by Hazel E. Barnes. New York: The Philosophical Library, 1956.

Simon, Yves. *Introduction à l'ontologie du connaître*. Paris: Desclée de Brouwer, 1934.

Simonsen, Vagn Lundgaard. *L'Esthétique de Jacques Maritain*. Munksgaard, Copenhague: Presses Universitaires de France, 1953.

Sorokin, Pitirim A. *Social and Cultural Dynamics*. New York: Bedminster Press, 1937. Four Volumes.

Spiegelberg, Herbert. *The Phenomenological Movement*. 2 Vols. 2nd ed.; The Hague: Martinus Nijhoff, 1965.

Thévenaz, Pierre. *What is Phenomenology?* Ed. by James M. Edie. Trans. by James M. Edie, Charles Courtney, and Paul Brockelman. Chicago: Quadrangle Books, 1962.

Van Riet, Georges. *Thomistic Epistemology*. Trans. by Gabriel Franks. St. Louis: B. Herder Book Co., 1963. 2 Vols.

Versenyi, Laszlo. *Heidegger, Being, and Truth*. New Haven, Conn.: Yale University Press, 1965.

Vycinas, Vincent. *Earth and Gods*. The Hague: Martinus Nijhoff, 1961.

Weinberg, Julius R. *Abstraction, Relation, and Induction*. Madison: University of Wisconsin Press, 1965.

Withok, Philipp, ed. *Deutsches Leben der Gegenwart*. Berlin: Wegweiser Verlag, 1922.

ARTICLES

Borgmann, Albert. "Philosophy and the Concern for Man," *Philosophy Today*, X (Winter, 1966), pp. 236-246.

Dalbiez, Roland. "Les sources scolastiques de la théorie cartésienne de l'être objectif," *Revue d'Histoire de la Philosophie* (Octobre-Decembre, 1929).

Deely, John N. "Finitude, Negativity, and Transcendence: The Problematic of Metaphysical Knowledge," *Philosophy Today*, XI (Fall, 1967), pp. 184-206.

— "The Immateriality of the Intentional As Such. Apropos of a Recent Book." *The New Scholasticism*, XLII (Spring, 1968), pp. 293-306.

— "The Situation of Heidegger in the Tradition of Christian Philosophy," *The Thomist*, XXXI (April, 1967), pp. 159-244.

Demske, James M. "Heidegger's Quadrate and Revelation of Being," *Philosophy Today*, VII (Winter, 1963), 245-257.

De Petter, D. M. "De oorsprong van de zijnskennis volgens de H. Thomas van Aquino," in *Tijdschrift voor Philosophie* (Juin, 1955).

De Waelhens, Alphonse. "Reflections on Heidegger's Development: Apropos of a Recent Book," *International Philosophical quarterly*, V, (September, 1965), 475-502.

— "Réflexions sur une problematique Husserlienne de l'inconscient, Husserl et Hegel," in *Edmund Husserl*, 1859-1959. The Hague, Martinus Nijhoff, 1959.

Donceel, Joseph. "Philosophy in the Catholic University," *America*, 115 (September, 1966).

Dondeyne, Albert. "La différence ontologique chez Heidegger," *Revue Philosophique de Louvain*, LVI (1958), Part I pp. 35-62, Part II pp. 251-293.

Heidegger, Martin. "Versuch Einer Zweiten Bearbeitung. Einleitung. Die Idee der Phänomenologie und der Rückgang auf das Bewusstsein," in *Husserliana*, Band IX, Phänomenologische Psychologie. Den Haag: Martinus Nijhoff, 1962.

Herausgegeben von Walter Biemel; Ergänzender Text von Martin Heidegger, pp. 256-263.

Laporte, Jean-Marc. "The Evidence for the Negative Judgment of Separation," *The Modern Schoolman*, XLI (November, 1963), 17-43.

Lonergan, Bernard. "*Insight*: Preface to a Discussion," *Proceedings of the American Catholic Philosophical Association*," XXXII (1958), pp. 71-81.

— "Metaphysics as Horizon," *Cross Currents* (Fall, 1966), 481-494.

Lotz, Johannes B. "Being and Existence in Scholasticism and in Existence-Philosophy," trans. by Robert E. Wood, *Philosophy Today*, VIII (Spring, 1964), 3-45.

Powell, Ralph Austin. "Has Heidegger Destroyed Metaphysics?" *Listening*, vol. 2 (Winter, 1967), 52-59.

— "The Late Heidegger's Omission of the Ontic-Ontological Structure of Dasein," in *Heidegger and the Path of Thinking*, edited by John Sallis (Pittsburgh: Duquesne University Press, 1970), pp. 116-137.

Richardson, William J. "Heidegger and God – and Professor Jonas," *Thought*, XL (Spring, 1965), 13-40.

— "Heidegger and Theology," *Theological Studies*, 26 (March, 1965).

— "Heidegger and the Quest of Freedom," *Theological Studies*, 28 (June, 1967), 286-307.

— "The Place of the Unconscious in Heidegger," *Review of Existential Psychology and Psychiatry*, V (Fall, 1965), 265-290.

Ricoeur, Paul. "Philosophie de la volonté et de l'action," in Proceedings of *Second Lexington Conference on the Phenomenology of Will and Action*. Pittsburgh: in preparation for publication by Duquesne University Press.

Rimbaud. "Lettre du Voyant" to Paul Demeny, first published by Paterne Berrichon in *La Nouvelle Revue Française* (October, 1912).

Rukavina, Thomas F. "Heidegger's Theory of Being," *The New Scholasticism*, XL (October, 1966), 423-446.

Simonin, M. D. "La notion d'*intentio*," *Revue des Sciences Philosophiques et Théologiques* (juillet, 1930), 445-463.

Verbeke, G. "Le développement de la connaissance humaine d'àpres St. Thomas," *Revue Philosophique de Louvain*, XLVII (1949), 437-457.

Von Rudloff, Leo. "Des heiligen Thomas Lehre von der Formalursache der Einwohnung Gottes in der Seele der Gerechten," *Divus Thomas* (Fr.), 1930, 175-191.

UNPUBLISHED MATERIAL

Powell, Ralph A. "Heidegger's Retreat from a Transcultural Structure of Dasein." Paper resulting from a faculty seminar conducted at St. Xavier College, Chicago, Illinois, Summer of 1966.

— "The Late Heidegger's Omission of the Ontic-Ontological Structure of Dasein." Paper based on seminar and course work prepared through the first semester of 1966-67 academic year.

Richardson, William J. Personal Letter to Author. Bronx, New York: Fordham University, August 1, 1966

INDEX OF PROPER NAMES